A Life in Urdu

A Life in Urdu

*Personal Encounters and Selected Essays on
Urdu Literature by Ralph Russell*

Edited and with a Foreword by
MARION MOLTENO

OXFORD
UNIVERSITY PRESS

Oxford University Press is a department of the University of Oxford.
It furthers the University's objective of excellence in research, scholarship,
and education by publishing worldwide. Oxford is a registered trade mark of
Oxford University Press in the UK and in certain other countries

Published in India by
Oxford University Press
22 Workspace, 2nd Floor, 1/22 Asaf Ali Road, New Delhi 110002, India

© Oxford University Press India 2023
© Marion Molteno 2023 for the Introduction

The moral rights of the author have been asserted

First Edition published in 2023

All rights reserved. No part of this publication may be reproduced, stored in
a retrieval system, or transmitted, in any form or by any means, without the
prior permission in writing of Oxford University Press, or as expressly permitted
by law, by licence or under terms agreed with the appropriate reprographics
rights organization. Enquiries concerning reproduction outside the scope of the
above should be sent to the Rights Department, Oxford University Press, at the
address above

You must not circulate this work in any other form
and you must impose this same condition on any acquirer

ISBN–13 (print edition): 978–9–39–105094–8
ISBN–10 (print edition): 9–39–105094–8

ISBN–13 (eBook): 978–9–35–497434–2
ISBN–10 (eBook): 9–35–497434–1

ISBN–13 (OSO): 978–9–35–497439–7
ISBN–10 (OSO): 9–35–497439–2

DOI: 10.1093/oso/9789391050948.001.0001

Typeset in Minion Pro 10/13
by Newgen Knowledge Works Pvt. Ltd.
Printed in India by Rakmo Press Pvt. Ltd.

Foreword

This is a book for anyone who is interested in Urdu literature or the society that has produced it. It is a collection of Ralph Russell's writing, spanning the experience of over sixty years and reflecting the breadth of his engagement, both as a scholar and as a human being.

He came to India for the first time in 1942, aged twenty-three, and for the rest of his long and fruitful life, he devoted himself to the study of Urdu and its literature. He never stopped learning, from everyone he met, and everything he read. His deep knowledge came from immersing himself in the thoughts and outlooks of the writers he translated, yet he retained the fresh perspective of someone who could see their world also from the outside. This unusual combination, his sensitivity to the literature, and his skill as a translator and interpreter, made his contribution unique, and gave him a special standing in the eyes of those who love Urdu literature.

He first became known through two books written in collaboration with Khurshidul Islam, first published in 1968 and 1969 and which continue to be widely read: *Three Mughal Poets: Mir, Sauda and Mir Hasan*, and *Ghalib: Life and Letters*. From the next forty years, he continued to write and publish, and brought an appreciation of Urdu poetry to thousands of readers, including many of Urdu-speaking background who could not easily read it in the original.

He was intensely interested in everything about Urdu-speaking society, from large political issues to the details of daily life, and his writing on political and historical themes has illuminated aspects that people within that society instantly recognize, but may not previously have thought about in that way. He also had the gift—rare among scholars—of being able to write in a way that could be easily understood by anyone with a general interest in the subject. Even in articles published in specialist journals, he used no academic jargon, which he thought was often an excuse for sloppy thinking or a form of pretension. He was never

vi FOREWORD

afraid of controversy, and expressed himself with vigour, which makes for engaging reading.

His influence was most directly felt by those who knew him personally. For over thirty years—1950 to 1981—he headed the Urdu section of the School of Oriental and African Studies, University of London. He spent three separate years and many shorter periods in India and Pakistan, and formed close relationships with Urdu scholars both there and in the United States. From his mid-fifties onwards, he responded to the fact that there were now sizeable Indian and Pakistani communities in cities across the United Kingdom by teaching spoken Urdu to English speakers. Thousands benefitted from his courses, and he was still teaching at home—free—until a month before his death. The effect on those he taught was inspirational, for this was not simply language teaching—he believed profoundly in the value of real communication between people of different backgrounds. Teaching Urdu was not just his pleasure, it was his form of political commitment—the contribution he felt able to make towards building a positive and inclusive society.

* * *

As Ralph's literary executor, it is my privilege to work with publishers to keep his books in print. My involvement with his writing goes back to 1982, when I started studying with him. I wanted simply to learn basic conversational Urdu, but in the course of our lessons, Ralph would refer to some aspect of the literature, making it sound so interesting that I would ask if he could suggest something I could read. He would say, 'Actually, I've written an article about that,' and go to his filing cabinet and pull out some duplicated pages, or a copy of an out-of-print journal. I knew there would be other people who would find them interesting, but who was going to know they were there? I persuaded him they ought to be in book form, and gradually the books began to appear—a history, an anthology, and collected essays. For each, we discussed what should be included and how the material should be arranged, and later I worked with him to put together and edit his autobiography. As a result, there is no part of his writing, published or unpublished, which we did not discuss in detail.

The starting point for this book was a collection of essays published in 1999 when he was 80 years old, entitled *How Not to Write the History of Urdu Literature, and Other Essays on Urdu and Islam.* It brought together articles written over the previous twenty-five years and published in a range of academic journals. This edition, coming out more than a decade after his death, has been substantially revised to draw on things written since, and to pay tribute to the breadth of his contribution to Urdu studies. Chapters that would have been of interest mainly to scholars have been replaced by others with broader appeal, and more than half the chapters are new.

Part I: Personal Encounters starts with extracts from his autobiographical writing, mostly written late in life but with an immediacy that comes not just from an excellent memory but from detailed notes made at the time. The later pieces reflect his lively interest in learning about the way of life of Muslim South Asians, and engaging with them.

Part II: On Urdu and Its Literature gives tasters of his writing on Urdu literature, across three centuries and a range of genres. For his major studies on eighteenth- and nineteenth-century writers, you would need to read his other books, but I have included a brief essay on the anti-fundamentalist outlook of *ghazal* poetry—still the genre most universally loved by Urdu speakers—and an outline of the principles that have guided him in translating the greatest ghazal poet, Ghalib.

Part III: On Language and Literary History includes three essays on aspects of literary history, followed by *How Not to Write the History of Urdu Literature*—the title essay of the 1999 volume—as an example of his vigorous polemic style. These were all addressed to other Urdu scholars and are therefore likely to be of interest primarily to readers who know a good deal about Urdu literature, but even if you don't, you'll find they are written in a way to make them easily understandable.

Within Parts II and III, I have given the dates when the major part of that chapter was written. I hope this will enable you to read the more topical pieces in the context of their own time, but also to get an idea of the development of his thought—and consistency of his passionate engagement—over a life in Urdu of more than sixty years.

In the *Afterword*, through the voices of a few of those who knew him, you will get a sense of the extent of his influence.

Including in one volume articles of such different kinds—personal, historical, and literary—follows Ralph's intention from the 1999 volume. In the Preface to that, he wrote: 'I hope to make clear the spirit in which

viii FOREWORD

I have approached my life's work. From the days of my first encounter with Urdu, it has been my constant desire to communicate as fully as possible with the people whose language and literature it is. I do not believe there is any other satisfactory basis for fruitful study, and those pieces which give some picture of my interaction with the people who speak and write Urdu are intended to provide the background to the more formal articles.'

I hope this new selection fulfils that hope even more fully. And if it tempts you to read more, there is a list of his major books at the end.

At the time he was writing each of these pieces, he had no thought that they might one day be part of single book, yet alongside the great variety of topics, there are common threads that give the whole a surprising unity of thought. They all reflect his lively interest in anything that Urdu literature and Urdu speaking society could teach him, and the enthusiasm to share what he had learnt with those who could not read Urdu for themselves. They are all personal in tone—whether describing a conversation with a villager or arguing with a fellow scholar, his own voice, his way of looking at life, is always there. There are echoes and links across all the separate chapters—because for him everything connects. Literature reflects changing values in society; politics, language, and religious identity influence each other; engaging with individuals gives insight into broader issues. He often said that he had found things in Urdu literature which accorded with his deepest personal values, particularly the tolerant humanism of Sufi-inspired poetry. In the increasingly troubled times of the late twentieth century, he took every opportunity he could find to highlight this anti-fundamentalist strand of Islam.

To people who knew him in only one context, it was sometimes a puzzle how the different parts of his life fitted together. For him, there was no separation between them—the politically committed communist, the meticulous scholar, the challenging critic, the generous colleague, the lively teacher, the enthusiastic friend—they were all just him, a man who loved people, enjoyed the simple things in life, and grew with each new experience. We are lucky that he put so much of what he felt and thought into writing—some of it gathered here now, for us to dip into, be inspired by his enthusiasms, and challenged by his definite opinions.

Marion Molteno

Contents

PART I: PERSONAL ENCOUNTERS

1. Learning Urdu in Wartime India: 1942–1945 — 3

2. Early Encounters with Urdu Literature: 1946–1950 — 19

3. Experiencing Village Life: 1950 and 1976 — 41

4. An Infidel among Believers: 1999 — 60

PART II: ON URDU AND ITS LITERATURE

5. An Eighteenth-Century Satirist: 1959 — 73

6. Rusva and Premchand: Stories of Courtesans: 1970 and 2003 — 80

7. Popular Literature: 1973 — 91

8. Remarkable Women—Two Memoirs: 2002–2006 — 97

9. Urdu Poetry Versus the Fundamentalists: 2001 — 104

10. On Translating Ghalib: 1969 — 111

PART III: ON LANGUAGE AND LITERARY HISTORY

11. Leadership in the Progressive Writers' Movement, 1935–1947: 1977 — 129

12. Aziz Ahmad and Urdu Sources on South Asian History: 1983 — 150

13. Hindi and Urdu, Languages and Scripts: 1996 — 159

14. How Not to Write the History of Urdu Literature: 1987 — 175

X CONTENTS

Afterword: Ralph Russell—As Others Saw Him 187
Books by Ralph Russell 205
Editor's Note 207
Sources and References 211
Index 219

PART I
PERSONAL ENCOUNTERS

1

Learning Urdu in Wartime India

1942–1945

My launching into the world of Urdu, like so much else in life, was a matter of chance. Until 1942, I don't think I had ever even heard of Urdu, but in January of that year, I found myself—aged twenty-three—on a troopship bound for India. The Indian Army was being rapidly expanded to meet the threat of the Japanese, who had advanced with lightning rapidity to India's eastern borders. I was part of a large draft of British infantry officers who had been conscripted into the army, done their basic training, and were now being sent on attachment to the Indian Army.

I knew a bit more about India than many of the others on that ship, for since the age of sixteen, I had been a communist and committed to the cause of Indian independence. I knew I would need to become fluent in an Indian language, for there would be no other way to communicate with ordinary people around me. I was going to be in command of a unit of Indian soldiers, and I wanted to be able to talk to them about what was happening in India, and make it clear that I supported those who were struggling to end British rule. Urdu was then the language used in the Indian Army—for army purposes, it was written in a Roman script, i.e. using the English alphabet, with some of the letters adapted. All who joined the army were required to learn it, including those Indian soldiers who came from regions where Urdu was not spoken.

At school, I had greatly enjoyed studying both Latin and Greek, but this time I hoped to have the opportunity to learn a new language by using it as I acquired it, to talk, over however limited a range, with people who knew no English. I soon discovered that isolated as we in the army were from civilian life, it was going to be difficult to create the opportunity for this. But as I write this over fifty years later, I still have vivid memories of some of these early encounters, and the people who helped me learn the

A Life in Urdu. Edited and with a Foreword by Marion Molteno. Oxford University Press. © Oxford University Press India 2023. DOI: 10.1093/oso/9789391050948.003.0001

4 A LIFE IN URDU

language, and through whom I gained my first experiences of life in a society and culture that were new to me.

The Camp in Kakul

For our training, we were based in Kakul, about two miles north of Abbotabad, a beautiful area in the Hazara District of the North-West Frontier Province. The Indian Army in those days employed Urdu speakers whom they called *munshis*—the term really means a rather superior grade of clerk, but it was the term used in the Indian Army for civilian employees who had the thankless task of teaching Urdu to unenthusiastic British officers, most of whom hadn't wanted to go to India, and didn't see why they should waste time and effort on this inferior language. I and one or two others were exceptions, free of the imperialist prejudices of most of our colleagues. Even within that small group, I seemed to be about the only one who took learning Urdu seriously. One of my treasured memories is of the munshi who was doing his best to get Urdu into the thick heads of his reluctant class, surveying us all and saying, 'All you gentlemen are good' [though they most certainly weren't], 'but this gentleman [indicating me] is appreciable'.

One of the few of my fellow officers who had a positive approach to being in India was a young man called Rufus, and on a couple of weekends, he and I went with the chief munshi, a Hindu, up the lower slopes of the hills behind the camp. We took our lunches with us and climbed quite a long way up the hills. There was a marvellous view from the top. The rocks jutted through the thin soil and the grass was coarser than any I had ever come across in England. High up on the mountainsides, there were isolated peasant huts, each with its little terraced fields, goats and cattle feeding on the grass, and people mowing it for hay. We were never alone, however, far we climbed, and the children especially swarmed around us and seized our haversacks, hoping to act as our guides and make themselves useful in other ways, and so earn a little *bakshish*—this was the first Urdu word I had learnt, on the train journey up from Bombay. We shared our lunches with them, and while the others were talking, I tried to converse with them, taking my turn in their game of throwing stones at things and seeing who would be first to hit the mark, running races, and so on. After dinner, at my request, they sang songs to us in Punjabi, and the munshi translated them for us. They were traditional folk songs, love songs chiefly, and very good too, though very different from ours. Then they demanded that I should sing in return, so I sang them the Irish song 'Kevin Barry'. Though they didn't understand a word of it— as I had understood none of theirs—they seemed very pleased. They were very nice-looking children with strong white teeth, jet black hair, and gleaming brown eyes. There were five of them and all but two were barefoot. The rocks are very sharp in many places, and the soles of their feet must have been like leather, because they ran and leapt about along the mountain paths without turning a hair. I ultimately returned down the mountainside with one small child on either side, firmly clasping my hand and chattering away in great spirits. All this much to the astonishment of the villagers, who according to the munshi were not likely to have ever seen an English sahib doing such things.

* * *

The only Indian I saw daily was my 'bearer', a civilian servant allocated to each officer, trained in Raj styles of subservience that made me extremely uncomfortable. My bearer was a Kashmiri called Sabaz Ali Khan. I am short—the army recorded my height as five feet four and three quarter inches—but Sabaz Ali came only up to my shoulder. He had a grave and rather shy air about him. He had long moustaches and dressed in a turban, the standard *qamis* and *shalvar* of the people in that area, a long brightly coloured jacket, and sandals. I soon learned the way an English officer sahib was expected to behave. I could never do anything for myself. He would lay out my clothes, choosing the appropriate ones himself, send my things to the laundry whenever he thought fit (i.e. after about two hours' wearing), hold my mirror up for me to do my hair, go down on the floor to take off my shoes, even hold my trouser legs off the floor while I was putting them on. I couldn't even peel an orange without him standing at my right hand ready to take the peel from me and carry it across to the waste-paper basket. I began to make him let me do a few things for myself, like insisting on taking my own shoes off. It took him a while to get over his initial astonishment and reconcile himself to the fact that sahibs were now not the pukka sahibs they used to be. We got to the point where he stopped pestering me about what I ought to and ought not to do, but we didn't ever get onto a relaxed footing personally. He had been a bearer for more than twenty years, too long for him to be able to change, or feel comfortable with the idea of a relationship other than subservience. But on one point, we did understand each other. When he saw that I really wanted to learn to speak Urdu, he willingly agreed to only use Urdu when speaking to me, and from then on, he took a benevolent interest in my progress. He would sometimes talk with me for quite a long time into the evening, about the war, about the ways of British officers, about various people in the camp—which were 'rogues' and which 'good men'. I gradually learnt a little about his family—he had a wife and two children in Kashmir, whom he saw only on a brief annual leave. All the rest of the year, he was working in the plains—a pattern that was almost certainly typical of most servants of his kind.

* * *

Apart from the camp servants, almost the only Indians we saw were hawkers of various commodities who used to come around our tents. Most of them combined a fawning servility with a roguery that had to be experienced to be believed. The reason was both obvious and understandable, but that did not make it any easier to get past that to a more natural way of interacting with them. But one day, a young hawker came to my tent selling books, and it was almost immediately obvious that he was different from the others. He was a lad of about sixteen, wearing the standard *qameez shalvar* and a red fez with a black tassel, and he had self-confidence, cheerfulness, and independence almost unique amongst Indians of that class who had any dealings with the British. My Urdu was still very limited but enough to find out that his name was Qabul Shah, that he worked for a bookshop in Abbotabad and lived in one of the nearby villages. We took to each other from the start. He often used to stay for up to two hours, talking to me and Rufus, sometimes bringing with him a friend, Muhammad Akbar. The conversations were both pleasant and very good for our Urdu. Qabul Shah's own language was Punjabi, or maybe Hindko, but his Urdu was good, and like many others around Abbotabad, he could read and write it. Rufus tried to persuade him to be his bearer, but he would not agree, as that would have involved travelling with us when our unit was sent elsewhere. He told us that his father had died when he was about three, and he lived at home with his mother. She would never allow him to go away as she would always be worrying if he was OK.

Sometimes on a Saturday night, we would all four go to the cinema in Abbotabad. Rufus and I had heard that the language of popular films was actually very good Urdu, and thought it would be good for our own progress to listen to this kind of everyday colloquial speech. The whole event was very entertaining. We sat upstairs in a balcony for first-class ticket holders (one rupee four annas)—in armchairs, far more comfortable than cinema seats in England. The balcony was split in two by a great board partition, and on the other side sat the first-class ladies. Down below was a sort of bear-pit where the second and third class sat. A lofty wooden fence of stout palings across this space ensured that no third-class person could sneak into a second-class seat, and I wondered how people could see through it to the screen. Down there, the sexes didn't seem to be segregated. It was a vocal and appreciative audience. The first time we went, the film was showing a woman calling the roll at a women's adult education class, and the spectators were calling out all kinds of names of their own in addition, amidst great peals of laughter. When the soundtrack failed for thirty seconds or so, you'd have thought all hell had been let loose—a great whistling and chanting—altogether creating a very enjoyable atmosphere.

Some of the films had some good songs. I remember particularly one called *Doctor* which had a song I still sing. It sadly recalls the days when his wife was still alive—

guzar gaya voh zamana, kaisa, kaisa.

The film I enjoyed most was called *Bombay-vali*. The heroine was an English actress. It had plenty of villains and crooks, plenty of fisticuffs, and a dog-like Rin-Tin-Tin, the dog-hero of films I had seen in childhood. The chief villain was a large landlord who was ultimately prevented from swindling all his poor tenants and neighbours by the astuteness of the Bombay-vali, ably assisted by her dog. The enthusiasm of the audience was terrific. I had a marvellous time, and as for Qabul Shah, I'd never seen him so engrossed. He always slipped off his sandals and put his feet

8   A LIFE IN URDU

up on the seat, and so sat squatting with one knee level with each ear throughout the performance.

* * *

One of the munshis, Aurangzeb Khan, a young man about my age, was a Muslim from the Frontier Province who had taken his degree at Punjab University. He spoke fluent but inaccurate English, had read all of Shakespeare and would quote reams from him, and he knew a great deal of English literature that I didn't. He was a fervent supporter of Jinnah and the idea of Pakistan, and an equally bitter opponent of anything Hindu. He took a poor view of my taste for popular Indian films and of my association with such low company as Qabul Shah.

His father was a landlord who owned about 3,000 acres near Manshera, not far from Abbotabad. Aurangzeb Khan explained to us that the relationship between landlord and tenants was 'just like the feudal system'. The poorest tenants, who had practically nothing of their own, were provided with seed and the loan of oxen and plough, and in return, paid the old man seventy-five per cent of their crop in rent. There were extra dues to pay when the landlord's eldest son was married and on all sorts of other occasions. Rufus and I once got the opportunity to glimpse this lifestyle when Aurangzeb Khan invited us and two others to his home. Manshera was an interesting little town, showing no trace of European influence. Like most of the North West Frontier Province, its population was almost entirely Muslim, but Aurangzeb Khan pointed out to us a narrow alley that he said was the Hindu quarter. In his father's house, we were given a colossal meal—Indian food was a novel experience for us, for the food in the officers' mess was conventionally British. We ate with our fingers and washed our hands before and after in a stream of running water poured from a jug by one small boy into a basin held by another. Some of the sweets were covered in a film of silver paper, which we were told one eats. It was all delicious, but I couldn't help wondering what the tenants were eating.

Aurangzeb Khan was usually an arrogant man, but in the presence of the august old man, he was meek and mild. He waited on all the guests, remained standing the whole time, and ate his own meal only after everyone else had finished. After lunch, we all sat under a sort of verandah while two more small boys got a hookah going and then carried it around for the guests to puff at in turn. We saw no women, and the men of the family I found rather trying. They had served the British for over fifty years. They had organized the hottest possible reception for Congress leaders visiting the district, and now felt injured because they had not got what they regarded as their just reward from the British in the way of government contracts and something more than a lieutenancy in the army for Aurangzeb Kahn, who had no military experience of any kind.

* * *

By June 1942, our (very inadequate) training was said to be complete, and we were to be transferred to Allahabad in the north Indian plains. Before leaving, we were to have ten days leave in Murree, a 'hill station' in the foothills of the Himalayas to which British civil and military top brass would go on leave in the hottest weather to escape the heat of the plains. Just before we left Qabul Shah suddenly announced that he was willing to become a bearer after all, and would like to come with me. I jumped at the chance, and dismissed Sabaz Ali—probably quite unfairly. I gave Qabul Shah an intensive course in his new duties as a bearer. He'd never before cleaned a pair of shoes, polished a Sam Browne belt, made a bed, or had anything to do with European clothes. But he learnt these skills quickly. We got on very well together and he seemed to have lost his doubts about coming away from home. Rufus hired Qabul Shah's friend, Muhammad Akbar, so the four of us and Sullivan, another officer friend, set off together for Murree.

It was only about forty miles away but the journey took us two days. An army truck took us back down the steep road to Havelian, where we waited for a train. At the station, a few of us got talking to some children and persuaded them to sing to us. I thought them extraordinarily pretty, and found their Urdu clear and easy to understand—which maybe had something to do with my own competence now being greater. The train took us to Rawalpindi—sweltering by day and with mosquitos swarming all night—and the last stretch we did by taxi, rising dramatically up to about 7,000 feet, and into a complete change of climate, beautifully cool. We were surrounded by magnificent scenery—great pine-clad hills, with little terraced fields, the earth a deep purple colour, and in the distance, the snowy peaks of the Himalayas.

10   A LIFE IN URDU

My most pleasant memory of those days is of Rufus and me taking Qabul Shah and Muhammed Akbar to see the Walt Disney cartoon film *Pinocchio*. In Abbotabad, the cinema audience had been almost entirely Indian, but here the audience was almost entirely British, and *Pinocchio* was not dubbed and had no subtitles. We had considerable difficulty in convincing the astonished person in the box office that we really meant what we said in asking for the same price tickets for our bearers as for ourselves, but we ultimately got inside. Qabul Shah, to my great pleasure, behaved quite normally, squatted on his seat, and stared quite unconcernedly at the scores of majors and their ladies on all sides. I don't think he understood much of what was happening in the film. Muhammad Akbar knew quite a lot of English and got the whole story and enjoyed it, despite his disappointment when, after the first ten minutes or so, he said gravely that he thought the actors were not real people but only drawings, and Rufus confirmed his opinion.

* * *

In Transit

No one had told us what we would be doing in Allahabad. When we got there, it transpired that the answer was nothing. We were in transit, to somewhere as yet unidentified. After five days, Sullivan and I were posted to Lucknow, while Rufus was posted elsewhere and passed out of my life. For another twelve days, we hung around, and then I was posted to a unit in Delhi, once again separated from the people I knew.

The unit to which I was now attached was one of many being raised in response to the need to reinforce the Burma/India border, and the sepoys, as Indian soldiers were called, were all new recruits. The officers' time was spent looking after practical arrangements for this sudden new intake, working long hours through the fiercest heat of the day. We were living under a thatched roof supported by a pole at each corner and open to the air on all four sides. I sweated profusely and ceaselessly, and valued cold water to an extent I would never have believed possible, but I managed to maintain my usual energy. One of the more pleasant aspects of life was the presence of small boys who worked the punkah all day and were very pleasant to talk to. Finally, to everyone's relief, the rains settled in.

Occasionally in my time off, I got out on a bicycle to explore Delhi and its bookshops, and once to the nearby Jumna River that had broken its banks in the rains. Whole villages were underwater—the villagers were coming into relief camps, and some of our men were put onto rescue work. But it was even more difficult here than it had been in Kakul to get the chance to talk to Indians. The army was cut off from the rest of the city and no British person ever went into the Indian part. I was very glad of Qabul Shah's company. Though the things we could talk about were inevitably limited—both by my limited Urdu vocabulary, and by his youth and lack of experience of life—he was a cheerful and high-spirited youngster, and he was also responsible for my education in more senses than helping my Urdu. I discovered that his mother had made provisional arrangements for his marriage and he thought he had worked out who it was who had been chosen as his wife. It had never occurred to him that he might have any say in the matter. He didn't seem very interested when I explained this system to him but he later informed me that he would see to his own marriage and choose his own wife. I don't suppose he ever did. All of this now seems very naive to me. Only years later, when my contacts with Indians were much broader, did I begin to understand that the issue of arranged versus free choice marriage is a much more complex one than I had thought.

He was frankly curious to find out why I was disposed to talk to everyone without assuming the dignity of my lofty rank (second lieutenant!) I told him that society depended for its life on the people who worked and produced—workers and peasants—and that rich people owed everything to them and could do nothing without them: that people like myself who realized this respected working people, including sweepers, cooks, and other menials alike, and that I hoped the day would come when that attitude would be adopted by everyone, and the rich people, now so universally respected, would be made to work. He accepted that so far as it affected relationships between the rich and himself, but to swallow it in so far as it affected his own attitude to sweepers and others whom he had from childhood regarded as his inferiors was a bit difficult. After all, a sweeper was a sweeper.

* * *

12   A LIFE IN URDU

While we sat in army camps waiting to be given a job of work to do, the political situation around us was becoming ever more tense. Once Congress had declared the 'Quit India' movement, there were 'disturbances', as British officialdom described them, all over India. Stuck out in Kingsway Camp, we saw nothing of the rioting in Delhi, but I might easily have been one of those sent to quell them, and I felt very fortunate that I was not.

I remember vividly a conversation with one of the Indian NCOs—non-commissioned officers. He was about twenty-one, an Andhra from one of the coastal districts of what was then Madras Presidency. In civilian life, he had been a tailor, and in his childhood had, like many Andhras of his home district, been in Burma. I therefore assumed that he might have a greater knowledge of world affairs than most, and I started asking him questions to find out exactly what he did and didn't know, to understand how he saw the world. He knew about the Italians because there was a large prison camp full of them near the army training centre in Bangalore; and he had heard that the Japanese were in Burma, but knew nothing about the Germans, nor did he know which nations were fighting on our side. I was pretty shaken, and it was not until much later that I came to see that I had no reason to expect that he would know these things. Why should he? Like most of the great numbers of war-time recruits, he had joined the army to 'fill his belly', and wasn't in the least concerned with whatever it was the army had recruited him to do.

Even on matters nearer home, a similar situation applied. I looked for ways to let him and others see that I was opposed to the fierce repression that the government was practising, and that I sympathized with Congress's aspirations, but I soon discovered that I might as well have saved my breath. None of them liked British rule but they didn't see that there was anything they could do about it and so they took little interest in current developments. If Gandhi, who had the education and the spiritual strength, chose to do something, *he* perhaps could achieve something. Reverence for Gandhi was general, but names like Nehru and Azad meant nothing to them.

On the Burma Border

By November 1942, I was finally given a posting to a Company that was heading for the Burma border, where we remained till almost the end of the war. Qabul Shah and I now had to part company, for civilians were not permitted to accompany units on active service. We had been each other's daily companions for months, and were both regretful, but we had known all along that this would happen.

Ours was a transport company, responsible for building roads and driving the trucks that brought in supplies. We were based a little beyond Dimapur in Assam, the nearest point on the railway for supplies to the main concentration of front-line troops. One other lieutenant and I were in charge of a unit, much of the time detached from the others, with the task of keeping the railhead clear.

For the months when our unit was detached, I had an unusual degree of freedom to get to know the men in my unit without being observed. They were essentially all simply villagers in uniform, in their late teens and early twenties, mostly from peasant families, and almost all from South India—'Madrassis', as they were called. It wasn't difficult to find common ground with them. For a start, I liked Indian food, and I enjoyed the more popular type of Indian music, like film songs and folk songs. One song I learnt at this time was

zindagi hai pyar se, pyar men milae ja
husn ke huzur men apna sar jhukae ja, apna dil uthae ja
Life comes from love, immerse yourself in love
In the presence of beauty bow your head, lift up your heart

It came from a still popular film of some years earlier called *Sikandar* (the Persian and Urdu equivalent of Alexander the Great), which portrays the invasion of India. I never saw it but I was told that the cavalry are portrayed riding into battle singing this song—which is quite striking, giving its meaning. Only years later, I came to understand that the sentiment of the song is central to most Urdu poetry, and there is almost no context in which it would seem out of place to Indian listeners.

The main thing that made communication easy between us was that they sensed my real interest in them as people. I talked to them about my experience of village life in Yorkshire, and they knew I was interested in their experience of life in Indian villages. I knew that these men, young as they were, had experienced more than their share of the hardships of life. I thought I could help them to begin to understand, and eventually to find

14 A LIFE IN URDU

the confidence to claim, the rights to which they and all working people were entitled, and as part of this, to support the struggle for Indian independence. But I knew if I expressed what the British government deemed 'pro-Indian' sentiments to them, they might well suspect that this was a ploy to draw them out and then haul them up before the authorities, and that only time and patience would serve to create the trust I hoped for. So I worked with them and talked about everything that interested them, and gradually we got to know each other.

If I ever tried to get a discussion going on a serious topic, it became obvious that I was up against something more fundamental than lack of general knowledge or political caution. It was difficult to get a straightforward answer to even the most ordinary question. They would either give the answer they thought I wanted, or if they couldn't guess what that might be, they would say, 'How can I say, Sahib?' or 'Just as *you* wish, Sahib'. I began only gradually to understand that this derived from the kind of society they had grown up in. They had no historical or personal experience of the ideas and practices of democracy which I, like many English people, took for granted. The idea that everyone has the right to hold their own opinion, and at any rate, in everyday affairs to express it, was unknown. To disagree with higher authority by expressing a different opinion was unthinkable, even on quite minor matters. If I asked any of my men why they had joined the army, they would say, 'To help the British government'—though it was obvious to us both that this could not be true. Eventually, a stage was reached where most of them would speak honestly enough to tell me the real reason—and in almost every case, it was as the result of some family quarrel or economic necessity. I only ever met two who had joined with their parents' knowledge, and not one who didn't regret having joined and wanted more than anything else his discharge from service.

* * *

My fellow lieutenant in the unit was an Urdu speaker, a Pathan named Muhammad Nawaz Khan. He was about my age, capable without being fussy, and rather proud and reserved. He held himself aloof from the men and said he did not like them as much as Northern Indians, but he always treated them reasonably, and though he was not popular, they respected him.

LEARNING URDU IN WARTIME INDIA   15

He and I shared a small tent but it took a while to get to know him well as our times overlapping were limited. The work went on continuously, day and night, and as the only two officers there, we each took a twelve-hour duty, midnight to midday and then midday to midnight. He was a devout Muslim. Before I got to know his regular prayer times, I came into our tent in the evening to find him standing there barefooted, dressed in white baggy trousers and shirt and red fez, with his hands clasped and eyes closed in prayer. He took no notice of my interruption, and I retired until his orderly—a Muslim sepoy—told me that he had finished his prayers. He was not a demonstrative man and I never ventured to ask much about his personal life but came to know that he had studied constitutional law, English, and Persian at Punjab and Aligarh universities. He was the son of a landlord, a family which had long been in British government service. He had joined the army as an officer cadet just a year earlier. Long afterwards, he told me that I was the only British officer in the company who treated him without showing any trace of racial prejudice. Before he had been commissioned, he had not had the slightest idea that such discrimination existed in the army, whereas he had come to see that it was universal. His first reaction was naturally a feeling of bitterness at the petty humiliations, turning gradually to a secret contempt, rarely expressed even to me. He saw more and more that none of the officers except us two was doing a hand's turn of work in the company; and he was amazed that none of the other British officers had bothered to learn a minimum of Urdu without which they could neither understand their men nor be understood by them. He also objected to the somewhat uproarious drunkenness that from time to time occurred in the offices' mess. He said it was beyond his comprehension that any intelligent man could sit down for the evening with the object of getting drunk.

After we moved back to join the rest of the company, we had a bigger tent where we each had our own partitioned room. He would come into my room after his evening prayer and talk about his religion, explaining its doctrine and ritual. He also spoke a lot about his personal affairs, especially about his wife, of whom he was very fond. His marriage had taken place in the usual way—he had not known his wife until after the marriage ceremony was over, though he had seen her once or twice before. He thought himself very fortunate that (as he told me with great emphasis) he 'liked her in every way' and became more fond of her by the day. I asked him about purdah and he said that he was opposed to it, but that in his own home area, it was quite impracticable to act upon his convictions. His wife kept strict purdah there, but when she was with him in his first posting in Karachi, and later in Delhi, she did not. He would sometimes ask a bit about England—my village, and about student life at English universities. His sincerity and the quiet but confident way in which he followed his own convictions without regard to others' opinions of him appealed to me.

As time went on, his willingness to discuss politics grew. He had by now learned that I was a communist and said that everyone was entitled to their own views. He was interested in the communist attitude to religion and said that communism would make a great appeal to Pathans were it not for its irreligiousness. His interest in constitutional law led us to discussions of the 1935 Government of India Act. He was interested in social questions, particularly as they affected the peasantry. He asked me once whether if he became a communist that would oblige him to give all his lands to his tenants. I said I didn't think so, but that he ought to encourage them to speak up for themselves and that he should reduce their rents and obligations to what, in present circumstances, they thought, and the All-India Kisan Sabha (Peasant League) thought, were fair. He was clearly serious about trying to work out a principled way of living, but I knew that he would have to be willing to encounter immense opposition from his family if he ever tried to put them into practice.

When he next went home on leave, he told me on his return that he had acted on the principles he had come to accept during our conversations. Against the opposition of his family, he had reduced the rents and obligations of the peasants on his land.

* * *

We met almost no one outside the men of our own company. But there was one exception, a little boy called Hadis Muhammad. I had first seen him soon after we got to Dimapur, at a time when our section was alone working on the railhead. He appeared one morning in our cook-house, a small boy with an even smaller boy in tow. 'What are you doing here?' I asked. He cheerfully replied that he was begging for food. I was struck by the complete absence of that hear-breaking servility which in India one finds even in the smallest children, and I took to him at once. He told me his name and that he came from Bhagalpur, Bihar, about three days' train journey from Dimapur. He was about eight years old, as far as he could remember—most Indian villagers I met didn't know their exact age—and his brother Hafiz was about five. Their father was dead and their big brother could not earn enough to support both his mother and them, so he had told them they must fend for themselves.

I arranged for the boys to stay and help the cooks, and said that I would feed and clothe them in return. I often used to sit talking with them—it was an excellent practice in colloquial Urdu. They were remarkable children, clean, cheerful, and above all, perfectly self-possessed. I came to like them very much. Khan was an amused but sympathetic observer of how fond we were of each other. Sometimes he would say to Hadis, 'Give the sahib a kiss', and we would all laugh.

When my section moved to join the rest of the Company at Milestone Four, the Major told me I must get rid of the boys. I was very sorry to have to do so, and I tried to explain to them as best I could, fearing they would be upset. But they accepted it without a murmur and went off quite cheerfully. I think they were almost as familiar with the hundreds of miles of Eastern India's rail and river lines as they were with their own hometown.

I never expected to see them again. But I did encounter Hadis again, months later and some three hundred and fifty miles from Dimapur. I had been away on some duty or other, and was due to stay at an army rest camp on my way back. I got off the train at the nearest station, but from the station to the rest camp was a good two miles, and as the train pulled out, I looked about hopefully for waiting transport. There was none. I set off to walk down the dusty road, carrying my kit and sweating uncomfortably in the hot sunshine. One or two trucks passed me, but none of them heeded my appealing signals and I was still walking when a convoy of three-tonners began to pass. 'No good expecting any of these to stop', I thought, and walked on. Even as I was thinking so, I heard one slow down, and turned to see the driver, a broad Madrassi grin on his black face, beckoning me to get in. I thought, 'He's supposed to be driving in convoy—he shouldn't have stopped'—and for a moment, I wondered whether, in the interests of convoy discipline, I should tell him so. But his friendly manner and my own gratitude combined to dismiss so pedantic an idea. I got in and sat down beside him in the front seat. 'Can you catch up with the convoy again?' I asked. 'Doesn't matter', he replied, 'I know where I have to go'.

A little way ahead a small boy was walking along the road. There seemed to be something familiar about his carefree gait, and as we drew nearer, I saw that it was Hadis Muhammad. 'Hadis!' I shouted. He turned around, and recognizing me at once, laughed and waved, obviously as happy and unperturbed as ever. We had passed him now. I leaned out of the cab. 'Where's Hafiz?' I shouted. He shouted something back, but I could not hear him. The driver began to pull up. 'I can't stop him again', I thought, and told him to drive on. And that was the last I saw of Hadis.

2

Early Encounters with Urdu Literature

1946–1950

I was fluent in conversational Urdu before I read any of its literature. I had no idea what to expect, and even less idea that it would become such an enrichment in my own life.

I was twenty-eight and since finishing my university degree, I had been in the army—mostly in India, where I had learnt Urdu. Now the war was over, I had been demobilized, and I needed to think seriously about what I was going to do with my life. I wanted if at all possible to find a job that would enable me to maintain close contact with people and issues there. I learnt that scholarships were being given to study various languages at the School of Oriental and African Studies (SOAS), part of the University of London. It had recently had a reappraisal of its role; those who got the scholarships and did well enough might be offered an appointment to the staff thereafter. I applied to study for a degree in Urdu, and was accepted.

SOAS, 1946–1949

When I think back now to the expectations I had when I entered SOAS, it makes me laugh. I thought that my studies could hardly take all my time, and that would leave me plenty of time for political activities. I had been studying languages and literature since the age of eleven, and had always been good at it. I loved the literature of the English, Latin and (still more) Greek writers I had read, and of European classics available in translation, and I looked forward to making the acquaintance of Urdu literature too. I had to choose a second language as a subsidiary subject, and chose Sanskrit, thinking that too would be relatively easy as it was a sister language to Latin and Greek. With both Urdu and Sanskrit, I thought,

A Life in Urdu. Edited and with a Foreword by Marion Molteno, Oxford University Press. © Oxford University Press India 2023. DOI: 10.1093/oso/9789391050948.003.0002

20 A LIFE IN URDU

I would easily be able to learn a number of other Indian languages and so equip myself to work effectively in India.

It didn't take me long to discover that I had been singularly optimistic. Sanskrit demanded much more time and effort than I had expected, but the real shock was how difficult I found the work in Urdu. Though I had been speaking it daily for three years, and in the last year or so had also begun to read it with the help of a dictionary, my reading material had been confined to the Urdu edition of the army newspaper, the prescribed text for the army's higher exam in Urdu (*Khvab-o-Khayal,* an autobiography of a man who started life as a sepoy)—and translations of Marxist-Leninist classics into Urdu by the recently legalized Communist Party of India. But the vocabulary of *Foundations of Leninism* was, shall we say, of very little help when it came to reading literature and poetry.

I remember vividly the impact on me of the first book in our syllabus, Nazir Ahmad's *Taubat un Nasuh* (The Repentance of Nasuh)—the story of a man's attempts to make his family true Muslims following his own miraculous recovery from an attack of cholera. For those who don't know Urdu, I should explain that Nazir Ahmad was a nineteenth-century writer who had been thoroughly educated in Arabic and Persian, from which Urdu draws much of its literary vocabulary—so it is not surprising that to my dismay, there was hardly a sentence I could understand. I was also absurdly disconcerted when I saw that the author set out the dialogue in a way I had previously met only in the printed text of a play. Not:

Nasuh said, 'I don't know'

but:

Nasuh: I don't know.

Why this should have bothered me is hard to say, but it's an example of how a small matter of form can be an obstacle to people appreciating literature from another culture, with its own set of literary conventions.

I had an equally disconcerting introduction to Urdu poetry. My teacher began reading with me a type of poem called a ghazal—a form that derived from Persian literature and had for centuries been popular.

EARLY ENCOUNTERS WITH URDU LITERATURE   21

All I knew about ghazals was that they were love poems, and I vaguely knew from things I had heard in India that Urdu was famous for its love poetry. I like love poetry and had come to the class with pleasurable anticipation. I came out a sadder, but not, I am afraid, a very much wiser man—there was almost nothing about the ghazal we had read that I understood or liked.

Within a very short time, I had to acknowledge that I found studying Urdu much more difficult than I had expected, and—to my considerable disappointment—that the literature I was being exposed to had not much in it that I found immediately enjoyable. My disappointment, and the sense of shock at the task that lay before me, was extreme.

* * *

There was a group of seven students in the India department, all studying Sanskrit, and a camaraderie quickly developed between us. We were all men in our late twenties who had spent anything up to the last six years in the armed forces, and most were there on government scholarships because by being called up into the army, they had missed the chance to go to a university. But I was the only one studying Urdu—in fact I discovered I was the first person ever to study for an Urdu degree in a British university, for until now, there had been no clear structure for offering first degrees. With no precedent as to which literary texts or how many to include in the syllabus, my teachers had erred on the side of including almost everything they thought important. I could see no way I was going to get through it in the available time.

The standard pattern of classes was that I sat with my teacher and we read the text together, and he explained whatever I couldn't understand. There was no other possibility, because there were no aids to an independent study that had been available when I had studied Latin or Greek, and that existed in some degree for Sanskrit—no annotated books which could help me read independently, no English translations. There was at least an Urdu–English dictionary, compiled by John T Platts, a civil servant in India in the nineteenth century (doubtless drawing on the knowledge of many Indians whom he didn't acknowledge), and published by Oxford University Press in 1884. It is an excellent dictionary and I came to rely on it greatly.

22   A LIFE IN URDU

I know from the histories of that time that the winter in which I was beginning to come to terms with Urdu literature was the worst that century in Britain. Snow fell continuously from the end of January to the middle of March 1947, often accompanied by gale-force winds. The Thames froze. Fuel could not get through. Power to industries was cut, the streets were dark, household electricity consumption severely rationed, houses barely heated. Yet I have no memory of any of that. What I remember is sitting up in my room in lodgings in the evenings, writing up what I had learnt during the day. I used a system I had first developed at school—I had got a copy of one of our Greek texts bound with interleaved blank pages, where I could write the meanings and other notes. Before coming to SOAS, as soon as I had seen the list of prescribed Urdu texts, I had asked a friend who was going back to India to buy them and send them to me. When they arrived, I had taken them to a bookbinder and asked him to rebind them with interleaved black pages. Of course, he didn't know that in Urdu, you begin reading from what in English would be the back of a book, so I had to renumber all the pages in pencil for his guidance. Now with a flood of new words and grammatical nuances coming at me every day, the interleaved texts were invaluable.

The long hours at my desk didn't bother me. After all the years in the army, when so much time was spent hanging about, it was enjoyable to be taking on a new intellectual challenge. And though the syllabus was grossly overloaded, the requirement to read widely was actually a welcome one.

There were three teachers of Urdu at SOAS at that time—and as I was their first-degree student, I had no idea what they were doing before I came. They were very different from the others, but they all went out of their way to help me learn. A.H. Harley had charge of both Urdu and Hindi teaching. He had been quite high up in the Indian Education Service, and had once been head of the Calcutta *madrasa*. (I have never bothered to find out what this was, but it presumably specialized in Islamic-related subjects.) He was already past retiring age when he came to SOAS. He was one of the nicest kind of old-style liberal imperialists, and along with that, the stereotypical absent-minded professor. A student would appear at his door at the appointed time and be greeted with a surprised 'You're not with me now!'—after which he would look at the timetable on his desk and find that the student was indeed 'with him now'. He

EARLY ENCOUNTERS WITH URDU LITERATURE 23

was unfailingly helpful to me, and would always give me time and attention well beyond the call of duty, inviting me to come and read with him during the university vacations as well as in term-time.

Hamid Hasan Bilgrami was a native speaker of Urdu, who had been recruited for a post termed 'overseas lecturer'. He had been a teacher in the Doon School, Dehra Dun, and his only publication was a small book that exercised students in precis writing. As far as I know, he had not before taught at the university level, and I don't know either how extensive his reading in Urdu literature was. I remember his attributing to Sauda a poem which I later learnt was in fact one of Jurat's, and he referred to Faiz as 'Faiz Muhammad Faiz' when even I knew it should be 'Faiz Ahmad Faiz'. (Faiz was already a popular poet, having published his first book *Naqsh-e-Faryadi* in 1941. The simplest literal translation of the title might be 'Marks on Paper', but the phrase is a well-known quotation from Ghalib.) But as a teacher and a man, Bilgrami was both conscientious and kind, and I owe him a lot. When I went on my first study leave in 1949, he provided me with letters of introduction to such luminaries as (among others) Zakir Husain, then Vice-Chancellor of Aligarh University, the literary critic Ihtisham Husain, and the eminent scholar Abdul Haq.

Of my three teachers, by far the most remarkable was Captain A.R. Judd, and my debt to him is immense. His command of Urdu was astounding. He not only spoke it with complete facility and accuracy, and with a fluency which I have never encountered in any other speaker of English-as-a-mother-tongue, he also wrote it in an elegant flowing hand—a skill I have never acquired. Having himself learnt Urdu as a foreign language, he understood better than a native speaker the difficulties that confront an English learner and knew how to explain them.

The story of how he acquired this expertise is particularly interesting. As a working-class boy, who spoke English with a strong regional (Norfolk) accent, he had left school at fourteen, which in his boyhood was the standard school-leaving age, and went into the army as soon as he was old enough. He was a private in a regiment that had been posted to India during or shortly after the First World War, and stayed there continuously up to the Second World War. Once there, he had soon acquired an intense interest in Urdu and had set himself to master it. As many since his day have learnt, this endeared him to Urdu speakers and he received their willing help. Impressed by his unusual progress, they introduced

24 A LIFE IN URDU

him to such famous figures as Kwaja Hasan Nizami, essayist and spiritual guide, the poet Bekhud, and the scholar Abdul Haq. When the Japanese entered the Second World War in 1941, the army establishment, untypically, recognized Judd's remarkable talent and employed him on the task of translating army manuals into Urdu. He needed a team of Urdu speakers with a good knowledge of English to work under him, and the army evidently felt that they needed to enhance his authority by promoting him to the rank of captain.

Judd's major interest was in the language, and within that, he had a particular fondness for what he called 'idiom and proverb'. The only fault in his Urdu was the inappropriate profusion with which he introduced proverbs into his conversation, producing an effect rather like that an English speaker would produce if his every sentence included something like 'Too many cooks spoil the broth'. But he had the most extraordinarily extensive vocabulary in Urdu. He could, without any previous preparation, read and explain anything in Urdu you put before him, so all I had to do was sit down beside him, open the book, and say, 'Begin here'. I never encountered any Urdu word of which he didn't know the meaning. Given his lack of formal education in English, this had the curious result that he often knew a word in Urdu without knowing it had an exact English equivalent, and would have to explain it by describing the circumstances in which it was used.

But his ignorance of Urdu literature was astounding—or perhaps not, given that he had never had the opportunity to formally study it. One example of this became clear when we were reading Sarshar's *Fasana e Azad* (The Tale of Azad). It is one of the most celebrated proto-novels of the nineteenth century, yet Judd had clearly never heard of it. Sarshar delights in exuberant language and writes in a racy colloquial style which it was a pleasure to read, and this pleased Judd no end. He exclaimed, '*This* is a good book! Who wrote this?'—picked up the book and looked at the spine, but the author's name was not given there. In any case, Sarshar's name would have meant nothing to him. He was interested in it as *language*, not as literature, and although he must have read a lot to acquire the vast vocabulary he had, he must have done so with that sole purpose in mind. So he neither knew nor cared who Sarshar was, and if *I* was interested, he left it to me to find out from the other teachers.

EARLY ENCOUNTERS WITH URDU LITERATURE   25

Fasana e Azad had no equivalent in the literature I was familiar with. It is enormously long—four volumes, averaging nearly 800 pages of nearly A4 size and two columns of print—so of course, we could read only selections. There is no characterization and only the thinnest of plots, with one episode following another right to the end, but I was beginning to be able to appreciate what I was reading on its own terms. Gradually the hours of trying to master a huge new vocabulary began to pay off, and I could enjoy the wonderfully vivid portrayals this book gives of social life in Lucknow at a time when it was, with Delhi, one of the two main centres of Urdu culture.

Another classic which I studied at this time was Muhammad Husain Azad's *Ab e Hayat*, first published in 1880, with wonderfully vivid accounts of the lives of poets, of whom I particularly remember Mir and Sauda. The title means 'The Water of Life'—by now, I was used to the fact that Urdu titles often give no indication of what the book is about. This one refers to a traditional story about a search for the water of life that would confer immortality, so Azad was probably suggesting that poetry itself (or perhaps his book) was immortal. Another was Mir Amman's *Bagh o Bahar*—the title means 'The Garden and the Spring'. Written in 1801, it had an interesting history—it was written for the Fort William College in Calcutta, intended for British officials in India to learn Urdu. It was a tale of four dervishes, actually five stories set within a single frame story, in the style made familiar to English readers in *Arabian Nights*. Lucknow critics of the time considered its style not nearly literary enough, but it subsequently became popular enough among Urdu speakers for it to be repeatedly published.

The biggest problem for me still was coming to grips with the ghazal, the love lyric universally regarded by Urdu speakers as the greatest glory of their literature. Before I ever got to grips with its content, I was baffled by aspects of its form—that the couplets within one ghazal seemed to have no link in meaning. In other poetry, I knew—not just in English—a poem is a poem, each with one theme. You have to think of the ghazal, people said, like a pearl necklace—beautiful, separate pearls held together on a single string. But it was certainly not the case that every couplet was a pearl. It seemed more like a string on which were a mixture of occasional pearls and a lot of cheap beads of coloured glass. And then, it was commonly said that ghazals were love poems but much of the time they

26 A LIFE IN URDU

didn't seem to be, and even where particular couplets were about love, I couldn't relate at all to the situations being portrayed—they seemed far, far different from those of my own experience. There seemed to be a lot of extravagant self-pity on behalf of the lover, and absurdly cruel behaviour by the beloved.

On top of all this, I had great difficulty appreciating the metres. I sought help from Harley, but the more I pressed him, the more I came to feel that, though he did not like to confess it, he too did not find much in the ghazal to appeal to him. Judd couldn't help because, as he himself always stressed, his interest was confined to 'idiom and proverb'. And though Bilgrami was able to help me come to grips with the mysteries of Urdu verse metres, neither he nor my postgraduate student comrades could help with the other problems, because they had grown up with the ghazal and couldn't see that there was a problem.

This situation made me pause to think, and think pretty hard. There was clearly something I was missing, and I realized that my inability to understand was a limitation that lay in me. Years later—once light had begun to break through—I wrote fully about this whole experience in an article called *The Pursuit of the Urdu Ghazal,* which gave the title to my book *The Pursuit of Urdu Literature,* so I won't write more about it here.

But one significant thing even at this stage was that, though I found the ghazals of Ghalib just as difficult to understand as any other, those couplets that I *could* understand I immediately liked. He was thus from the start already on his way to becoming my favourite poet, as he is the favourite poet of millions of others.

Other forms of Urdu poetry were less of a mystery. Hali's treatise on Urdu poetry, *Muqaddima e Sher o Shairi* (Poetry and Poetics), published in 1893, helped me get a context. In it, he attempts to define poetry, and in the light of his definition, then proceeds to survey the whole range of classical Urdu poetry, genre by genre, condemning what he regards as its undesirable features and making proposals for reform. I liked the vigour of his views, though in later years, I found that I didn't at all agree with his conclusions! We also studied substantial selections from a volume called *Nazm-e-Muntakhab* (Selections of Poetry). I still have my copy of this poetry collection, produced in Calcutta in 1909 as a set book for a 'Degree of Honour examination in Urdu'. Judd once said to me in a rather conspiratorial tone that it was a good selection but that no Indian

EARLY ENCOUNTERS WITH URDU LITERATURE 27

would admit this because it had been compiled for Indian Army officers. In those days, of course, I did not know enough to form a judgement, but I have now looked at it again and it seems to me to be a rather extraordinary selection. It includes no poet before Atish (1764–1846). I can't remember how much of it I was required to read but I do remember reading some quite insipid, moralizing verses from its selection of Akbar Ilahabadi. It was only in later years that I realized that the compilers had rigorously excluded all verses in which Akbar had mocked enthusiasm for the British and their ways—that is, precisely that part of his verse for which he is justly famous!

A quarter of the book was taken up with two major long poems, complete and unabridged, both of which introduced me to aspects of life for Urdu speakers of which I had no previous experience, and gave me a sense of the power of poetry in their collective consciousness. One was Anis's famous *marsiya* which begins *Jab qata ki musafat-e-shab aftabe ne ...* The *marsiya*—an extended elegy on the martyrdom of Imam Husain at the battle of Karbala—is a form of poetry for which there is no parallel in English, but unlike the ghazal, I could understand what it was about and appreciate the power of the poetry. The other was Hali's *Musaddas,* recounting the past glories of Islam to inspire Muslims to change their present deplorable condition. Its original title translates as 'The Flow and Ebb of the tide of Islam'.

There was in academia at the time a (quite unjustified) convention that you didn't include in a syllabus anything by a writer who was still living. This might have been the rationale for the most glaring gap in our syllabus—there was nothing by the only poet whose name I knew before coming to SOAS—Iqbal. When I told my Urdu-speaking friends this, they were amazed, as well they might be. When I asked Bilgrami about the omission, he said, 'Some mature minds think it is too early to write about Iqbal. I myself have not written about him'.

All three of my teachers were appreciative of the fact that I took my studying seriously. One of my fellow students once told me that Harley had told him that I spoke Urdu so well that he, Harley, had to take care not to make any mistakes when *he* spoke. As head of Urdu teaching, Harley had the old-style conviction of the absolute need to maintain a show of knowing more than Bilgrami or Judd who were subordinate to him, and this sometimes led to amusing incidents. He once appeared when I was

28 A LIFE IN URDU

having a class with Judd and, speaking in Urdu, asked me if I intended to use the coming vacation to get further in Urdu. I said I thought I could make substantial progress '*agar main musalsal kam karun*'—if I work continuously. He held up his finger and said, 'Not *musalsal - silsilevar*'. After he'd gone, Judd said, 'You were quite right, but don't tell him I said so'.

Judd, as one would have expected, had always been the undeserving victim of British class snobbishness, but his justifiable confidence of his superiority in Urdu to, for example, British officers in the Indian Army, enabled him to laugh at this. The attitude of his social 'superiors' at SOAS, including Harley, was polite but distant, and Bilgrami's attitude regrettably matched theirs. I once spoke to Bilgrami about Judd's extraordinary command of Urdu; his only response was to look as if someone had held something that had a nasty smell under his nose, and to say, 'We don't use proverbs all the time'—a valid criticism of Judd's Urdu, but no warrant for treating Judd with contempt. I later learnt to my great satisfaction that Bilgrami's attitude was not shared by others of his class, the English-speaking Urdu speakers who had worked under Judd during the war. One of these was Shanul Haq Haqqi—poet, journalist, lexicographer—who has written amusingly and appreciatively of him in his autobiography.

* * *

It was now clear to me that my main initial difficulties had mostly been language ones, and as this gradually became less of an obstacle, I could go back to earlier things I had read in a new way. I came to appreciate the power of Nazir Ahmad's prose and the excellence of his characterization. His description of the cholera epidemic in Delhi, or of Nasuh's dream of the Day of Judgement—a dream so vivid that it marks the turning point in his life—are magnificent pieces of writing and make a most powerful impact.

I began to try my hand at translating. I chose some of his best descriptive passages—and found to my surprise that it was impossible for contemporary English idiom to convey their flavour. Their power derives from a skilful use of a range of literary devices, which just wouldn't work for most contemporary English-speaking readers. I too, when I had first encountered them, thought them a bit outlandish, but by now, they appealed to me strongly, and I thought many of his descriptive passages

EARLY ENCOUNTERS WITH URDU LITERATURE 29

brilliant. The nearest parallel in English are the solemn and sonorous prose of, for example, such passages as that on faith, hope, and love in the Bible, or the General Confession in the seventeenth-century Book of Common Prayer:

> We have erred and strayed from thy ways like lost sheep; we have followed too much the devices and desires of our own hearts; we have offended against thy holy laws; we have left undone those things which we ought to have done, and we have done those things which we ought not to have done.

Strongly marked rhythms, alliteration, and the multiplication of near-synonyms (erred and strayed, devices and desires) are features of such passages, and Nazir Ahmad's prose too has many of these. But it also has many more—self-consciously poetic diction, hyperbole, play on words, rhyming passages, and successive, parallel statements of a single theme, expressed first in splendid language abounding in Arabic and Persian loan words, and then in the homely language of indigenous colloquial speech. An English-speaking reader would be disconcerted to come upon passages of this sort of style in a modern novel of family life—which is what *Taubat un Nasuh* is. But Nazir Ahmad's readers, I soon realized, were people whose first acquaintance with the written word was made through the poetical prose of the Quran, people in whom the love of poetry and an appreciation of just such literary devices was universal. His readers would have enjoyed reading such prose as much as he must have enjoyed writing it.

In a later book, he describes a scene of the uprising of 1857. The main character, accompanied by his servants and subordinates, is returning home in the evening and comes upon the corpses of Englishmen killed by the rebels. The sun is setting and the corpses are lying in the shadow of a wall. Nazir Ahmad writes,

> There was the sun wrapped in the bloodstained shroud of the sunset, ready to be lowered into its grave in the west. And here were these shroudless corpses, wrapped in the black mourning shroud of the shadow of the walls.

30 A LIFE IN URDU

On the Urdu reader, the simultaneously stressed likeness and unlikeness of the setting sun to the dead bodies, and the paradox of 'unshrouded' corpses 'shrouded' in the dark shadow would make a great impact, and would not be felt to be in the least far-fetched; and this is but one example of the way in which Nazir Ahmad used such devices in a way completely relevant to his essential purpose.

Studying Among Urdu Speakers, 1949–1950

I took my degree in 1949 and got a first, whereupon (in accordance with the terms of the scholarship) I was appointed as a lecturer in Urdu. Recently provision had been made for the grant of periodical study leave for lecturers to spend in the country of their speciality, and I pressed strongly for this to be granted to me before I started teaching. I had learnt all I could have in three years, but culturally limited by the fact of studying in London. I knew that an essential part of becoming competent to teach Urdu and its literature was that I should spend time among people for whom Urdu literature was the culture they had grown up with. Harley didn't see the need for this but consented to go along with it.

So from November 1949 to September 1950 in South Asia. For six months, I was based at Aligarh Muslim University, and after that made shorter stays in several other cities which were major centres of Urdu studies in both India and Pakistan—Delhi, Lucknow, Hyderabad (Deccan), Lahore, and Karachi—where I was able to meet and talk with numerous writers and scholars.

My introduction to Aligarh was—to me—astonishing. I was fortunate to have from Bilgrami an introduction to Zakir Husain, then the Vice-Chancellor, and had written to him before I came. On arrival, I was amazed to see he had sent a car to meet me. (Can you imagine the Vice-Chancellor of a British university treating a newly appointed lecturer from an Indian university like this?) In fact, I nearly missed the driver Zakir Sahib had sent. My wife was with me and he'd been expecting an English couple to alight from a 1st class carriage, hadn't seen one, and was walking rather anxiously up and down the platform in search of us. He hadn't found us where he expected because we had travelled third class from Delhi. In those days, there were third-class carriages with long

EARLY ENCOUNTERS WITH URDU LITERATURE 31

wooden benches running the whole length of the carriage—one along each outer wall and two back to back in the middle. I'd been practising my Urdu on the passengers, sharing peanuts with them, and having a very jolly and uproarious time.

When we arrived at Zakir Sahib's house, he learnt that as yet we had not fixed up anywhere to stay, and he at once made us his guests. We were there about a fortnight before we managed to arrange accommodation elsewhere. The more I got to know him, the better I liked him. I had known of him as one of those few prominent Muslims who had been a supporter of the Indian National Congress, and I now learnt (not primarily from him) more of his history. He was a man of wide culture who had made his name not as a scholar but as a major figure both in education and, less prominently, in politics. In the 1920s, he was associated with the Jamia Millia Islamia (University of the Muslim Community), founded originally in reaction against the pro-British policies of Aligarh. (To anticipate a little, after his term at Aligarh, he became successively Governor of Bihar, Vice-President of India, and for a short time before his death, President.)

An old friend of his was also staying with him at the time, Nurur Rahman, who quickly warmed to me—largely because on one occasion, I happened to know an Urdu word that he and Zakir Sahib were discussing, which Zakir Sahib was not familiar with. The word was *nipat,* and by sheer chance, I did know it because Judd had told me that *nipat bahra* was the idiomatic Urdu equivalent of 'stone deaf'. I don't think I've ever encountered the word again from that day to this, but Nurur Rahman was delighted, and no doubt formed a greatly exaggerated estimate of my command of Urdu.

The Urdu Department was at that time headed by Professor Rashid Ahmad Siddiqi. Coming as a guest from Zakir Husain's house, I was practically guaranteed VIP treatment. He set up a special seminar for me to meet the staff, and personally put himself out to help me. He suggested that I write something in Urdu every day and bring it to him as soon as he came to the Department every morning, and he would sit with me, correct what I had written, and explain to me where I had gone wrong. He was actually a lazy man and this arrangement soon petered out, but again, can you imagine the reverse situation—a famous writer (as he was) and head of a university department of English receiving a newly appointed Indian lecturer in English, who had just arrived in Britain, in this way?

32   A LIFE IN URDU

I think I owed the cordiality of my welcome to two things: first, the standard of hospitality for which South Asians are justly famous, but there was also a much less desirable factor, a wish to please members of the former ruling race. The proportion which each of these things occupied in people's minds varied, but I don't think there were many who were wholly free of the second attitude. Linked to this is the fact that, while a great many South Asians know English well, it was—and still is—unusual for them to meet an Englishman who has taken the trouble to learn their language well; and this meant that I was paid far more attention than I could have expected.

I had been given an open invitation to attend any of the M.A. classes I liked. On the first occasion, I attended a lecture, I noticed that there was a curtain drawn right across the breadth of the room, and learnt that this was to enable the women students to observe purdah. There was a separate entrance for them at the back of the lecture room. They would come in and sit down, and when the lecturer was ready, he would call out politely to find out if they were there. Of course, he had no means of telling whether they were *all* there.

Rashid Sahib himself lectured on Ghalib, for whom he had a particular fondness. People used to laugh and say that though he loved Urdu poetry, he could hardly ever scan a line of Urdu verse correctly, and as far as I know, he didn't deny this. On another occasion, I attended a class in the course of which Shabibul Hasan, already an accomplished Shia theologian, expressed polite but firm disagreement with Rashid Sahib's inappropriate (as he thought) use of the word *barzakh* (roughly the equivalent of purgatory).

Rashid Sahib soon deputed one of the younger lecturers, Akhtar Ansari, to take over the role of helping me, and he gladly undertook this. At first, our regular routine was that I would make translations into Urdu of passages in English literature that had appealed to me, and he would correct and discuss them with me. I remember that one was taken from Defoe's *Moll Flanders*. But we also used to talk freely about anything that interested us both. He prided himself on an exceptionally good command of English and had a cordial contempt for others whose pretensions in this respect were, he thought, unwarranted. He was delighted to learn from me of the existence of cockney rhyming slang, and thereafter regularly referred to his hat as his 'titfer'—short for 'tit for tat', the rhyming

EARLY ENCOUNTERS WITH URDU LITERATURE 33

slang for 'hat'. His distinction as an Urdu writer was as a poet whose preferred verse form was the short poem form called the *qata* (or as some pronounce it, *qita*), but he was the author of some good critical essays too, including one on what he called the Delhi school of prose writers. He was also very interested in the portrayal of children in Urdu literature. The book of his which appealed to me most was *Ek Adabi Dairi* (A Literary Diary), in which he noted his reaction to books he had read—not only those of Urdu writers but also of, for example, Tagore and Somerset Maugham—and had written on other themes—e.g. solecisms commonly found in Panjabi writers of Urdu. In the now forty-five years since I first met him, I have often thought that I too could write a book, in Urdu, on similar lines, and if I live long enough, I should still like to do so.

I also arranged for paid help from one of the M.A. students, Khalil ur Rahman Azmi. He sat with me every afternoon and read with me, SOAS style. It was with him that I read Premchand's *Gaodan*. He would tell me from time to time how fortunate I was to have his help, since he came from eastern U.P. and understood [as people from western U.P. would not have understood] the occasional 'purabi' [eastern U.P.] words and phrases that Premchand uses in this novel. After that, we went on to read articles by Mumtaz Husain, and I remember being favourably impressed by Mumtaz Husain's readiness to tackle such basic themes as 'What Is Classical Literature?'—and unfavourably impressed by the extraordinarily odd and convoluted Urdu in which he wrote about them. I also remember Khalil Sahib's great amusement once when I noticed some Urdu graffiti on a wall we were passing, and pieced it out aloud—it said 'X ghandu hai' ('X is a boy kept as a homosexual companion'. The only one-word English translation, so far as I know, is 'catamite', a word most English speakers would need to look up in a dictionary).

He talked also about his own history. It was only a couple of years since the Hindu–Muslim riots that accompanied independence; he had been attacked as he was travelling by train from Delhi to Aligarh—stabbed, thrown out of the train, and left for dead. But he recovered. In later years, he became a lecturer in the Urdu department at Aligarh, and eventually published a book on the Progressive Writers' Movement.

One thing that disconcerted me in the early days in Aligarh was the discovery that although I was now quite fluent, there were Urdu speakers of whose speech I could understand practically nothing. Rashid Sahib

34   A LIFE IN URDU

spoke so slowly and clearly that his Urdu was a joy to listen to. Masud
Husain Khan, on the other hand, was at first practically unintelligible to
me. In London, I had tried to make up for the lack of spoken practice
by arranging regular sessions with two or three Urdu-speaking friends at
which we spoke only Urdu, but I now realized that future students would
need exposure to a range of different speakers, and in later years, I took
care to vary accordingly the recordings of live conversations and interviews that I had made for my students.

The most significant encounter in my time in Aligarh—one that deeply
influenced my subsequent work in Urdu—was meeting Khurshidul
Islam. Soon after I arrived, Rashid Sahib had arranged a seminar for me
to meet members of his department and to put to them any questions
which I wanted to discuss about Urdu and its literature. The seminar
closed with a young lecturer, Khurshidul Islam, giving a very impressive,
compendious reply to all my questions. I learnt that he was a junior staff
member who had so far published little but was already held in some es-
teem as a thoughtful critic of Urdu literature.

Some days after the seminar, I was asking one of his fellow lecturers some questions, and he suggested I take them to Khurshid, who
would answer them more adequately than *he* could. So I went to see
him. I remember vividly how much he impressed me in this first conversation. It was about 11 o'clock on a winter's day and he was walking
up and down the small lawn in front of the department office in the
pleasant winter sunshine. I joined him. He met me on friendly, equal
terms, without any sort of formality, and also without any desire to
impress. He had made no move to go out of his way to cultivate any
acquaintance with me, having no reason to think that I wasn't a typical
Britisher, and I liked that about him, having begun to realize how unusual this was. What I had come to ask about was not on a major topic
of Urdu literature (the question was about the 'Adab i Latif' writers
of the early twentieth century)—but I liked the thoughtfulness and
coherence of the views he expressed. I determined there and then to
see much more of him; and each time I did, I found more in him to
appreciate.

Our backgrounds could scarcely have been more different. He was from
a traditional aristocratic family in U.P., and quite proud of this ancestry.
I was from a background that could best be described as lower-middle

EARLY ENCOUNTERS WITH URDU LITERATURE 35

class, and the first in my family to have a university education. But I was amazed at how much we had in common. First, he was a communist, though not at that time a party member. At that time, the Communist Party was compelled to work in a situation of virtual illegality, and it was at his home that its underground workers stayed when they came to Aligarh, and without regard to the danger in which this placed him, he cared for them in every possible way.

We had been raised in such different societies and educational system, yet our approach to literature was similar. For him, as for me, great literature was something that teaches you, moulds you, transforms you, bringing to you all the time a greater and truer awareness of yourself and of other people and of the universe in which you live. He was also the first Urdu speaker I had met who had read with this passionate, self-transforming interest, not only the literature of his own language but also that of the great world classics from the European Renaissance onwards. I have in the years since met many Urdu speakers whose understanding of Urdu and Persian literature is profound and sincere, but for whom 'literature' *means* Urdu and Persian literature—period. On the other hand, where people have had most of their education through English medium, the literature they know best is English literature and those works of European literature that are accessible through English translation. In my experience, this second group of people generally lacks the detailed appreciation and love of their own language's literature which the first group has; and sometimes their familiarity with European literature is worn as a badge of superiority. Khurshid differs very strongly from both these groups. His reading both in the classics of Urdu and Persian and in English and European literature is wide, and he brings to all of it an appreciation, understanding, and love that is rare. His knowledge of and assessment of the great Urdu writers seemed to me to reflect all this, and consequently to be in a class of its own.

It was through Khurshid that I now came to understand and appreciate the ghazal, as I had not been able to before. He subsequently became my close friend and colleague, and it was in collaboration with him that my first books on Urdu literature were written.

* * *

Meeting Urdu Writers

Since the middle 1930s, a major trend among Urdu writers had been represented by the Progressive Writers' Association (PWA). I was unusually fortunate during this year to be able to meet a number of its leading writers. Its main organizers were communists or communist sympathizers, but it had an influence far beyond that circle, and other major literary figures willingly associated themselves with it—Abdul Haq, and Premchand, the leading novelist and short-story writer of both Urdu and Hindi. As a British communist, I shared an outlook with the Progressives, and was easily accepted among them. It was an additional point in my favour that I was a member of the only significant British political party that had unequivocally supported Indian independence. All this made it easy for me to meet and talk with a great range of PWA writers and scholars on quite informal terms.

Of all the PWA writers, it was the short story writers who interested me most. Among these, Krishan Chander was the one I got to know best. We had met quite by chance in my first days in Delhi. The verandas of Connaught Circus were in those days full of pavement shops set up by refugees from what was now Pakistan, and I had become friendly with one who displayed communist literature for sale. One day in conversation, I mentioned Krishan Chander, whom I knew to be a leading member of the PWA. It turned out that my friend knew him, and immediately offered to take me to meet him. I was as pleased as I was surprised that there was no difficulty with this. Krishan Chander met me on friendly, equal terms, and we talked about the PWA. Again, at the end of my year's study leave, en route home, I stayed with him at his house in Andheri, Bombay. I was to stay with him again at the beginning of my later study leaves.

As a man, I liked him very much. His great popularity never went to his head and he never resented criticism. He wrote more than 5,000 stories, and judging by the rather small sample I have read, I would think that perhaps 80 per cent of them could be destroyed without literature suffering any great loss thereby. But the best of his stories are excellent. More than those of any of his contemporaries, they make a direct, simple, almost naïve appeal to his readers' deepest human sympathies, and stories of this kind are numerous enough to ensure him a permanent place among the

EARLY ENCOUNTERS WITH URDU LITERATURE 37

great writers of Urdu literature. One of the first stories I translated into English *Kalu Bhangi,* about a sweeper. The title is the name the character went by—*Kalu* means black and *Bhangi* is a sweeper, a member of one of the lowest untouchable castes.

In Lahore, I met Faiz, already the most famous poet of the post-1936 period, as he continued to be right up to his death in 1984. With characteristic South Asian hospitality, when he heard I was coming, he invited me to stay with him, which I did then and afterwards each time I was in Lahore, so I got to know him and his family well. Just across the road from where Faiz then lived, in Radio Pakistan, I met Shaukat Thanavi, the most famous humorous writer in Urdu since the late twenties. My constant companion and guide in Lahore was Ahmad Nadim Qasmi— short-story writer, poet, and editor of a literary magazine. At that time, he was the leading light in the Pakistan PWA, which soon afterwards ceased to function. He was unfailingly kind to me and gave me unlimited time. I subsequently translated one of his stories, *Bandagi Becharegi,* under the title *Compulsions.* Another person who took me about in Lahore was Abdullah Malik, well known as a communist journalist. One evening he took me to a meeting of the literary society, the *Halqa-e-Ahbab-e-Zauq* (literally 'a gathering of people of taste'!) where I heard a writer read a story called *Licence.* I didn't learn until afterwards that the reader was Manto—one of the most brilliant short story writers of the time. After the meeting, Abdullah Malik told me this and asked if I would like to go and see him at his home in Lakshmi Mansions. When we got there, I told him that I had heard him read his story and that I had liked it. He said, 'I don't suppose you understood it'. When I said I had, he said, 'Tell me what it was about, then'. I did, and he was very pleased. I much regret that I was never able to meet him again before he drank himself to death in 1955.

I had written, in Urdu, to Abdul Haq in Karachi. He had long before independence been secretary of the *Anjuman Taraqqi-e-Urdu* (Society for the Advancement of Urdu) and was generally known as *Baba-e-Urdu,* the Grand Old Man of Urdu. He responded at once and invited me to stay with him when I came to Karachi, which I did. I had many conversations with him. He was pleased with my Urdu, and asked who my teachers had been. When I told him, he praised Judd highly; and of Harley, he at once said with characteristic bluntness, '*Voh kuch nahin janta*'—he knows nothing.

38 A LIFE IN URDU

Most of the Progressive writers were men, but I was lucky to meet the two outstanding women writers among them. Ismat Chughtai I admired for her forthrightness, as I did Manto for his. Rashid Jahan came with friends to visit me. At the time, I knew nothing of her writing (which I now greatly admire) and our talk was mostly of politics. She attacked forthrightly my and the British Communist Party's (as she thought) very reformist brand of communism. But I liked very much the little I saw of her and in later years warmed very much to the personality revealed in Sajjad Zahir's account of her in *Raushnai,* his history of the PWA.

Others I met at a so-called 'Premchand Conference' in Hyderabad, Deccan. The name was an attempt to disguise the fact that it was actually set up by PWA, which was at that stage semi-legal because of its close links with the Communist Party of India. The government had not actually declared the CPI illegal, but had imprisoned all of its active cadre it could lay its hands on, and others were working underground. I travelled to Hyderabad in the same compartment as two poets (Firaq Gorakpuri and Majaz), one literary critic (Ihtisham Husain), and Abdul Alim, not primarily a writer but an excellent organizer, and in my view PWA's most effective propagandist. There was no formality of any kind. I remember going into the toilet to cut my nails, and Alim Sahib, seeing the scissors in my hand, asked if I was going to circumcise myself!

Majaz I liked a lot. He was already practically an alcoholic but a warmhearted man whose wit was proverbial. I once heard him recite at a mushaira one of his most popular poems, *Avara,* a poem full of striking imagery delivered in a way that well expressed his character. I also heard the 'poet of revolution', Josh Malihabadi, reciting his *rubais,* and a very impressive performance it was. I found his arrogance rather off-putting, but I liked his boldness and straightforwardness in my brief meetings with him, both there and later in Pakistan.

In Delhi, I met Khwaja Ahmad Faruqi, then head of the Department of Urdu in Delhi University, and Ibadat Brelvi, a lecturer at Delhi College. Soon afterwards, he migrated to Pakistan, where in my later visits to Pakistan, I always stayed with him. Many years later, I arranged for him to come as my colleague at SOAS for some years.

Aside from PWA writers, I also made a point to meet some of the older generation of writers. Masud Hasan Rizvi—already at this time a

EARLY ENCOUNTERS WITH URDU LITERATURE   39

venerable Lakhnavi—not only invited me to his house but also took me to meet other litterateurs of his generation. I had already seen his excellent edition of select marsiyas of Anis, and was later to study his *Razmnama e Anis*, an arrangement of passages from the marsiyas which told as a connected narrative the whole story of the events leading up to the martyrdom of the Prophet's grandson Husain at Karbala. Most of his other works also have a Lucknow background. By far the best and most interesting to me is his book *Hamari Shairi* (Our Poetry) published originally in 1927 but which I did not read till many years later. Dismissed by T. Grahame Bailey as 'sketchy essays in defence of Urdu poetry', it is in fact a very effective rejoinder to Hali's Victorian strictures on much of Urdu poetry, though in the characteristically diplomatic style of cultured Urdu speakers, its author refrains from saying this and claims simply to show an aspect of Urdu poetry which Hali did not treat of.

I made a special journey to Agra to meet Hamid Hasan Qadiri, a scholar of the older generation for whom I have a great regard. He can fairly be called old-fashioned—for example, his magnificent history of Urdu prose, *Dastan-e-Tarikh-e-Urdu* excludes fiction, presumably because he did not regard fiction as serious literature. But I valued his collections of essays on literature much more than the sophisticated criticism of his later contemporaries. For instance, the essay on the *rang* (colour—i.e. special characteristic) of each of six classical poets, with its down-to-earth discussion of detailed examples, is worth a lot more than the uninspired would-be Marxist analyses of Ihtisham Husain or the sophisticated stuff of later critics abounding in unnecessary references to whatever Western critics are fashionable at the time of writing.

* * *

The experience of that year far exceeded anything I could have hoped for, and was invaluable in preparing me for the work that lay ahead. I had been immersed in the way of life of educated Urdu speakers. I had spent hours discussing aspects of South Asian literature, society, and politics. I had extended the range of my own reading, and enlarged the scope of my spoken Urdu. The warm personal contacts made during that year would last, in some cases, for our lifetimes. All

40   A LIFE IN URDU

these enriching experiences informed much of what I would be able to do thereafter.

I could not have achieved any of this were it not for the fact that I was everywhere made welcome. And whatever the reason for that welcome, I was grateful to all who had made it possible.

3

Experiencing Village Life

1950 and 1976

As a university teacher of Urdu, most of the Urdu speakers I have met and become close to are from the *sharifzade*. For those who do not know Urdu, the word literally means 'sons of gentlemen' or even 'sons of the nobility'—people from cultured, highly educated families, usually comfortably off materially. From my first study leave in Aligarh in 1949–1950, I was conscious that I was being exposed to a very narrow slice of Indian society, and I have always taken whatever chances I could to talk to a wider range of people. It also seemed self-evident to me that I should try to spend some time in villages and learn what were the norms of life which define villagers' social world. Villages are where the majority of Indians live, and though practically all the men I was in charge of in the army had been villagers, I had known them only in the abnormal conditions of army life and had never had an opportunity to visit them in their homes.

I was soon to learn that very few educated Indians, even communists, shared my view, and most were astonished at the idea that I might voluntarily expose myself to the discomfort of village life.

A Visit to Umri

I got my first opportunity in 1950, towards the end of my first year of study leave in Aligarh, when my friend Khurshidul Islam offered to take my wife Molly and me to the village where he had been born and spent his childhood. This was Umri, in the Muradabad district of western UP. He said we would stay with a man whom he had known since childhood, a young landlord named Said (pronounced to rhyme with 'a need'). He

A Life in Urdu. Edited and with a Foreword by Marion Molteno, Oxford University Press. © Oxford University Press India 2023. DOI: 10.1093/oso/9789391050948.003.0003

42 A LIFE IN URDU

sent Said a postcard about our proposed visit, saying, I guess, little more than that he was bringing an English friend and his wife. This was just three years after the end of the British Raj and the poor fellow had no idea what kind of English people we were—how could he? He seemed to have thought we were the pukka sahib and memsahib of Indian legend, who drank, probably hated Indian food, and would want to go hunting. So he replied to Khurshid that if we wanted special food, we should bring our cook with us, and also we must bring our own drink (i.e. alcohol) and our own guns. ('Our guns have been confiscated', he said.)

Umri was in the district of Rohilkand, so-called because it had been settled centuries earlier by Rohilla Pathans from the North West Frontier. It was in a very isolated position, with no metalled roads linking it to the nearest small towns. To get there, we travelled by train to the nearest small town and from there, we continued by tonga—light horse-drawn vehicles, the rural equivalent of a taxi—on rough roads. For the final stretch, we had to be rowed across a river in a rubber dinghy, for Umri lay between two rivers, neither of which was bridged.

Khurshid's friend Said was very friendly and hospitable. He was a couple of years younger than Khurshid—twenty-four—and Khurshid told us that he used to be called Maulvi Munne until he objected. A *maulvi* is a person who is (or pretends to be) more learned than the average Muslim in Islamic lore, and *munne* is an affectionate style of address for a little child; so presumably as a child, he was considered to have a precocious knowledge of Islam. He knew English well but had not, like Khurshid, gone on to further education, staying in the village to manage the lands he had inherited. His grandfather had owned land in thirty-one villages; this had been divided between two brothers but Said still owned sizeable tracts of land.

Daily Life in Umri

Umri was very large in contrast to neighbouring villages, none of which had more than about three to four hundred inhabitants. One was a Muslim village, but the rest were overwhelmingly Hindu. Umri itself had some six thousand inhabitants, ninety percent of whom were Muslims. The legend was that it had been settled by the famous medieval Muslim saint Baba Farid ud Din Shakarganj.

EXPERIENCING VILLAGE LIFE 43

We stayed in Said's huge house. The women of the house observed purdah, which meant that they could not meet men who were not part of the family, but Molly was of course able to spend time with them. They knew no English and Molly knew no Urdu, but with Said or one of the other men in the family acting as interpreter, they could talk to each other. They did not move about outside the household, so the visit of an English woman was a cause of great excitement, and after we had gone, Said wrote to tell me how they still often talked about her and missed her. Molly told me afterwards that they had asked her, 'What do you think of us, confined like cattle?'—which did not necessarily mean that they aspire to, or approved of, any other style of life.

As a man, I was freer to move around with Said, who showed me all around the village. As Urdu was the mother tongue of the villagers, I could chat with people directly and Said answered my endless questions, from which I later made detailed notes, and so I was able to get a picture of how village society worked here. I knew very well that it was not typical but also that there was probably no such thing as a typical Indian village.

Because of its isolated position, there was little contact with the world outside, even with small-town life, and there seemed no particular sense of deprivation at not having the facilities which towns provide. Almost all the villagers owned some land, but those whose holdings were very small also worked on other people's land when (for instance, at harvest time) additional labour was needed. The poorer peasants also found work outside Umri, travelling anything from 30 to 100 miles to work in forests, carrying timber and loading and unloading trucks. Then there were people who served the whole village, like the village barber and the washermen, who were paid in kind at harvest time by those they had served. A peasant would pay the barber about ten pounds of grain. There was a small number of Hindus in the village, not more than two hundred or so—washermen, potters, gardeners, *bhurji*—people who roasted chickpeas or peanuts and went around selling them in the bazaars.

One result of Umri's isolation was that there was little interest in education. The British had established an upper primary school but the number of children attending it was no greater when I was there than it had been fifty years earlier. Fathers preferred to send their sons out into the *jangal* to cut loads of grass to feed the cattle with. (The English

44   A LIFE IN URDU

word 'jungle' comes from this word, but *jangal* means, as 'forest' once did in English, simply uncultivated land.) The traditional elementary Islamic schools were better attended. There were two in Umri, with about four hundred pupils between them. here children learnt to read the Quran in Arabic (in the traditional style, rote recitation, without understanding the meaning of what they were memorizing). Said, who saw himself as a benevolent landlord, had tried to encourage education by setting up a junior high school in the village. It had received government recognition but of its eighty students, the majority came from the neighbouring Hindu villages.

Alongside a traditional adherence to Islam, there were other strands to what people believed. Everyone believed in supernatural beings, Said told us, and there were many stories about them. It was generally believed that their feet pointed backwards. One, called Mohan, was said to be of enormous size. There were two *bas* trees in the village (Indian fig trees), about half a mile apart. When this huge creature lay down to rest, his head would be on one tree and his legs on the other. If anyone peed under these trees or did anything else he shouldn't, Mohan punished them. There was also the ghost of a barber that wandered around at night around the outskirts of Umri. In the turmoil around the great uprising of 1857, this barber was attacked and decapitated by someone who, for some reason, thought he was carrying a large sum of money. In fact, he had only two small copper coins on him. His ghost didn't speak to anyone or molest anyone; he just went around carrying a torch and his head. Many people, both old and young, said they had seen him.

Then, coexisting with the deeply respectful attitude to Islam was a down-to-earth scepticism about the conduct of religious leaders—a theme frequently echoed in the Urdu ghazal. Said summoned to meet us a poor peasant who had a fund of bawdy stories with which he regaled us. One or two were exact parallels to the stories in Bocaccio's *Decameron,* and one centred around the sexual adventures of a maulvi, who was shown as shamelessly self-seeking and two-faced. This enjoyment of bawdy stories coexisted with—and was probably a release from—the strict traditional conventions about sexual behaviour; and—as in almost all societies—a double standard applied to men with positions of power.

Meeting the Landlords

Said's landlord friends, whom I spent a lot of time talking with, gave plenty of evidence of a very objectionable male aristocratic chauvinism, typical of landlordism. They owned vast tracts of land and had always assumed their right to treat their tenants exactly as they pleased. One boasted that there was no sweeper woman in the village that his uncle had not bedded, with Khurshid providing the glass (in case I didn't understand this) that the women were 'more or less unwilling participants in this coupling. Even Khurshid, by conviction a communist but by early training a product of this society, went along with some of their assumptions. He described to me, with some pride, how in the old days, the big landlords had ruled the village and recognized no other authority. A generation ago, when a newly appointed police inspector had presumed to visit the village he had been seized and flogged and told he was never to set foot in it again. Along with these attitudes went a Muslim aristocratic chauvinism, nostalgically recalling the days when Muslims had ruled north India. One of Said's friends assured me, 'If we had the arms, we could rule this country again'.

They were all interested in the social status of my family, and Khurshid hastily replied on my behalf that my father had been a civil servant (and, he implied, a high-ranking one.) Afterwards, he told me it would have made a very bad impression if I had told them that he was merely a clerk.

Talking to some of the villagers in and around Umri, I was disappointed to be told quite frequently that life had been better under the British Raj, and that petty lawlessness was now much more prevalent than it had been then. Away from the towns, it had been the British district magistrate and his staff that had handled such things, and since they obviously had no kinship or factional links with any of the people they ruled over, they were generally able to make and enforce impartial judgements. Now the local authorities had such links and acted accordingly.

Throughout India at this time, the issue of land reform was on the agenda. Given the huge disparity of wealth between landlords and poor and landless peasants, there would be no way to create a more just society without a programme of land reform, and Congress had promised that they would tackle this problem after independence. The reforms

46 A LIFE IN URDU

had already been set out, though not yet implemented—this happened two years after our visit. But it was known what its effects would be, and Said explained them to us. People tilling the landlord's land as his tenants would become owners of it. Absentee landlords, who were numerous, were in effect to be given the option of continuing to be absentee and losing all their land, or keeping part of it, living on it, and taking part in the process of production. The family of Khurshid's wife, Masuda, chose the first option, as many did. Said chose the other option, to stay and work the land.

* * *

Introduction to Kanyal

Over twenty years later, I developed a connection with a village called Kanyal in the northern part of Pakistani Punjab. It happened this way. During the 1960s and 1970s, a large number of Indians and Pakistanis came to live in Britain. A good number of people who came into contact with them became interested in learning Urdu, so I began to run courses in several cities. In a town called Burton-on-Trent, which had a sizeable community of Pakistani origin, I got to know a woman called Rashida, and in 1973, when she heard that I was about to go to Pakistan, she invited me to visit her village and stay with her relatives. I knew this would be interesting in itself, but it also provided an opportunity for me to get a picture of the background of the Pakistani communities now settled in Britain, many of whom were originally from villages and towns in the Punjab.

My host in Lahore was my friend Professor Ibadet Barelvi, whom I had known since 1950, and had worked with at SOAS for six years. He was amazed at my plan, and tried his best to dissuade me from an experience he was sure would be most uncomfortable, but in the end, he accepted my eccentricity with good humour.

I was in Kanyal briefly on that first visit, but long enough to decide that the next time I came to Pakistan, I would stay longer. So in October 1976, I spent twelve days there.

Getting There

Kanyal was a village of about 600 people, in the Gujrat district of the Punjab, one of the least fertile areas in Pakistan. It lay some four miles from the main road from Lahore to Rawalpindi, on which long-distance buses ran at frequent intervals. I got off the bus at the point where the main road crossed the Upper Jhelum Canal, a broad, impressive, swift-running stream spanned, at the point nearest to Kanyal, by a brick bridge with ten arches. A public road ran along the bank, with such a damaged surface it could no longer be used by buses nor even by tongas. I walked along it for two and a half miles to the village of Qasba. From there, a track ran along the field boundaries—small strips of unploughed land about a foot wide, and raised a few inches above the level of the fields. If you were riding a bike, the depth of the dust would sometimes compel you to dismount. A motorbike could get through all right—I was once later taken along it riding pillion on a Yamaha.

My first sight of Kanyal was the outer walls of the houses running along one boundary, and, rising above them, the minaret of the village mosque. The houses clustered together, perhaps a hundred or so dwellings, with narrow, unpaved lanes in between. Most of the flat-roofed houses were built of brick, replacing the old (and, in the hot season, more comfortable) thick walls of sun-dried mud.

Patterns of Village Life

As a guest of Rashida's brother, Akram, I was part of his household, and our daily rhythm was similar to what happens in villages all over India and Pakistan. I slept alongside the other men on a *charpai*—a string bed—under the trees, and sat around having long chats with him and his brothers. First thing in the mornings, we sallied forth into the fields some distance away, each taking a *lota*—a small metal vessel the size and shape of a coffeepot—filled with water, with which you clean your bottom (always with the left hand). In immigrant households in Britain, I had often seen a milk bottle in the bathroom used for the same purpose. Once while in Kanyal, I stayed overnight with a friend of my host in a nearby village, and even in his recently built impressive house, there was no toilet.

48   A LIFE IN URDU

The village had one shop, not far from the mosque, and at the mosque, there was a place where we could wash. The water supply was from wells. None of the water from the Upper Jhelum Canal reached Kanyal, and the whole area depended entirely on rainfall. Sometimes we went to the canal and got a good wash there wearing *jangiya* (short loose trousers). There was no electricity, though it had come to Qasba, which also had several shops, a bank (to receive remittances from emigrants to Britain and elsewhere), and a Post Office—a room in the house of the man who carried out the duties of local postmaster.

Women and men had clearly defined roles, and passed their leisure hours separately—the women with other women, the men with other men—so naturally, my time was spent with Akram's male relatives, his friends, and other men in the village. I don't know Punjabi but when they were talking among themselves, I understood more than I expected to, and enjoyed listening to them—it seemed a very lively language, and people spoke in a very direct, informal way that appealed to me. Most of the men could speak Urdu reasonably fluently, and the few men and the very many women who could not, had no great difficulty in understanding it. The fact that I speak Urdu well always evokes a warm response, partly because very few British people have ever taken the trouble to learn it, so that those who have, make a correspondingly greater impact. It also surprised and pleased them that though I was an *angrez*—an Englishman—I wanted while I was there to live as they lived.

The womenfolk of Akram's household behaved freely towards him, and it was clear that most village women were strikingly unlike the stereotype picture which many in the West have. They played an active and important part in everyday life of the village, and if my own experience is anything to go by, they were not noticeably shy, and on far more free and equal terms with the menfolk than their counterparts who lived in the towns and/or belonged to more well-to-do families, and compared to their counterparts in the Muslim villages of Uttar Pradesh in northern India which I had visited.

Men and women alike wore the *tahmad*—a long sheet-like thing reaching from the waist to the feet. To put it on, they held it around the waist, and when extended, the two ends were each about an arm's length. They gathered these and then crossed them at the waist and tucked them in. I don't *think* there was anything worn underneath. The women had

EXPERIENCING VILLAGE LIFE 49

burqas which they put on to go to town but within the village, community purdah was not observed. When I visited the neighbouring village of Trikha, the young man taking me around said, 'The village is like a family: you don't observe purdah within a family'. In Trikha, there was a branch of the governing Peoples' Party of Pakistan, and though my guide said not many women came to the meetings, they did all vote; and two district PPP officials were women.

The literacy rate was generally higher than in the richer and more fertile parts of Punjab—perhaps partly because the poor quality of the land meant that many had to leave to find work, and those who stayed at school longer were more likely to find work. Schooling was free and compulsory up to the sixth class, and almost all the boys, and many of the girls, of school age were at school. But of the adults still in the village, almost all the women and very many of the men were illiterate or semi-literate. It did *not* follow (as so many literate people quite illogically assume) that they were ignorant. I never saw a newspaper during the days I was there, but migrants from the village wrote to them and came home from time to time on visits, so the villagers were not unaware of what went on in the country at large, or indeed of what was happening elsewhere. This was a couple of years after the war between East and West Pakistan; Bangladesh was now an independent country but not yet recognized by Pakistan, and a much-discussed issue was that men from the Pakistan army were being held prisoners of war in India.

The few transistor radios (always, as far as I could see, the property of young people) were tuned almost continuously to film music. But when we visited the larger neighbouring village of Trikha, one of the striking things was how evident the role of music was. As we arrived, two professional singers were singing, one also drumming and the other playing a sarangi. The song had clearly been recently composed—it expressed the feelings of the wives and sisters and brothers of the Pakistani soldiers being held in India—nine from this village alone. Before our meal, we listened to a group of four professional singers singing Punjabi folk (or semi-folk) poetry—*Hir Ranjha*, a popular tragic romance, *Saif ul Muluk*, a poem by Bulhe Shah, a Mughal era Punjabi Sufi poet; also one Urdu ghazal and other folk forms. All of them also played some instruments in accompaniment. There were two-stringed fiddle-like things, a drum, and a sort of pair of tongs—two flat iron strips about 2 feet long, joined by an iron ring—really a thing for getting the chapatis out of the oven, but it was used to beat the time in singing. One man came forward to take the money offered to them, and they would then sing a short poem in praise of the donor, mentioning him by name. 'Russell Sahib' was honoured three times in this way. I was told that the previous night a famous singer had come, paid 200 rupees in advance, and in a session lasting from about 10 p.m. to 3 a.m., had collected another 1,000 rupees in donations from his audience.

The songs were full of Sufi sentiment and I asked my guide afterwards how far these sentiments were expressed in the villagers' daily life. He was emphatic that they were.

Farming and Other Occupations

In the lands that lay around the village, the ground was uneven, and there seemed to have been much wind erosion. It was divided up among independent farmers, with holdings ranging in size from about 5 acres to 25 acres. When I first visited, the wheat crop was being harvested and I asked my companions how it was marketed. Did merchants come from the town to fetch it, or did they themselves take it to the town? They laughed and said, 'Neither! We eat it!'

Since the land was not (in most cases) fertile enough to support all the members of the family who owned it, there had been for generations a tradition of people leaving the village to take employment elsewhere, and the wages they earned helped to swell the income of the family as a whole. The one shop was run by a man who was one of four brothers—only one worked on the land, one was in Karachi, and the other in the army. The next-door neighbour of my host Akram tilled the land, one of his brothers was in the police, and one owned a camel—there were several in the village—and contributed to the family income the earnings he got by the carrying trade—on journeys that rarely went than about five miles from Kanyal. The majority of the Pakistan army had traditionally been recruited from these regions, and it was still a major outlet for the village's surplus manpower. About twenty to thirty Kanyal men were in the army, but in recent years industries in the cities, especially the textile mills of Karachi and Hyderabad, had attracted increasing numbers, and more

EXPERIENCING VILLAGE LIFE 51

than one person told me that people now preferred this work to military service. Thirty to forty men from Kanyal were working in Karachi and sixteen worked in Hyderabad. I met youngsters who had been employed in one or other of these two cities and I was struck by the evident youth of one of them. When I asked, I was told in the most matter-of-fact way that the mills liked 11–12 year olds because 'their fingers are more nimble'. I asked Akram whether there was no law in Pakistan against child labour, and he said that he didn't think there was. His close friend, Sharif—a more highly educated man—told me that he thought there was, but that he didn't suppose that it was enforced.

Conversations with Sharif were often very illuminating. He was something of a loner in the village. He had left the village many years ago to work in Karachi, was the only graduate in the village, and had only recently returned. He had spent five years in West Germany—his German, he said, was better than his English, which he spoke quite well, though with me, he always preferred to speak in Urdu.

A small number of people owned no land. These were the *kammis*, to use the Punjabi term, that is, those who served the village community as a whole—the village shoemaker and leather worker, the barber, the blacksmith, the water-carrier, the *musalli*—the man who kept the fires going when there was a big feast—and the *musafir*, whose job it was to look after the mosque and keep it clean and tidy. It was obvious that they were the counterparts of the village untouchables of Hindu society; and equally obvious that they enjoyed a higher status in their society than the Hindu untouchables did in theirs. They had traditionally been paid entirely in kind, particularly at harvest times, but now received a proportion of their earnings in cash.

With the growth of migrant labour to the towns, the dependence of these families upon the village community had greatly lessened. One of the shoemaker's sons worked at the tobacco factory in Jhelum and both he and his brother had served in the army. The *musafir's* son worked part-time at a brick kiln, and the *musalli* worked on piece rates at another brick kiln in a nearby village. All this had enhanced their standard of living, their status, and their relative independence.

There were obvious inequalities in the village, but compared to the great discrepancies between rich and poor in cities, the differences in economic standard of living in the villages were moderate. Not all families owned sufficient land to keep them in modest comfort, but those who did not could supplement it with income from family members with jobs elsewhere. As far as I could tell, all the villagers were able to maintain a simple standard of living that kept them strong and healthy. They had only one main meal a day, roundabout sunset. Throughout my visit, we had typical village food, yellow chapatis made of maize flour, with vegetables—often the leaves of a mustard plant—and *makkhan,* butter made from curd. We drank *lassi.* Meat and fish were expensive by their standards, so were not a regular part of their diet.

The degree of equality in personal relationships was striking. All lived much the same kind of life. Those I met spoke their minds freely and moved in and out of one another's houses, sitting together to talk and smoke the hookah and laugh and joke with—and at—one another. Akram's *kammi* neighbour too would sit with me and him, smoke his hookah, and mock him to his face, without him feeling any resentment.

Islam and Village Life

One of my aims in spending time in Kanyal was to get a more detailed picture of what Islam meant in the lives of its people. The essential thing—which I knew long before I went, but which it was interesting to see in practice—was that being a Muslim was part and parcel of village life, an identity people took for granted. It would never have entered anyone's head that religious belief and observance were things that they might accept, modify, or reject. They could no more conceive of not being Muslim than they could conceive of not being a Pakistani.

Children born in the village were growing up with religion all around them, as Christianity was to children in Europe in an earlier period of its history. They saw the reverent care with which the Quran was kept, and the way in which their elders read it. The month-long fast of Ramzan (Ramadan) involved the whole household, and even young children were encouraged to keep it for as many days as they felt able to manage, and praised for their success in doing so. The mosque was a centre of community life as much as a place of worship. The village men gathered there to wash in the morning, and to chat at the time of the sunset prayer. The *muezzin* giving the call to prayer also announced from the minaret any

EXPERIENCING VILLAGE LIFE 53

piece of news of general interest to the village, for example, that so and so had made a donation of such and such a sum to the mosque funds or to the local school.

Of course, human weakness was in evidence in the community, as it is in every human community anywhere. It was not easy for a visitor to the village to get an accurate picture of how far observance departed from ideals. It was part of the villagers' concept of courtesy to tell a visitor what they thought would please him or her, even if this meant embroidering a little upon the strict truth. At the time I was there, everyone was very busy sowing the wheat crop. People would be up at four in the morning and working hard in the fields until sundown and even after—I saw people ploughing by moonlight while I was there. Akram's brother-in-law was working in this way during these days, and I asked him whether he said his prayers at these busy times of the year, and whether he would stop work to say them in the fields when the appointed times came. He returned an unhesitating 'Yes' to both questions, but later, when I reported this to Sharif, who had known him intimately since childhood, he laughed and said that this wasn't true, and that he wasn't *at all* regular about his prayers.

It was clear that even those who were lax in religious observance had a genuine respect for those who were not. The latter were addressed as 'Sufi Sahib' and spoken of as 'Sufi so and so'. In the history of Islam, the Sufis were the mystics, those who stressed the essence of religion as love of the worshipper for God and other people, counterposing this to the mechanical, and often hypocritical, insistence on the outward rituals of prayer, fasting, pilgrimage and the like. In Kanyal, this contrast was no longer reflected, and it was those whose outward observances were most evident who received the title of Sufi. At the same time, I do not think it would have been accorded to anyone who was not also, in the villagers' judgement, a good and upright man.

I was myself impressed by the character and personality of the most universally respected of these 'Sufi sahibs', and since he represented so well the villagers' concept of a good Muslim, I should say something about him. His name was Muhammad Aslam, a tall, good-looking man, with a fine, resonant voice, a plain-spoken manner, and a remarkable flow of articulate conversation, illustrated at every point by appropriate quotations from Urdu and Punjabi verse. I had many conversations with him in which he told me, without inhibition, a lot about himself. His eight years in school, his excellent memory, his intelligence, and his fondness for preaching the message of Islam as he understood it had given him a good command of clear, lucid Urdu. He excelled in his recitation of the verses of *Saif ul Muluk,* a nineteenth-century poem of love and mysticism that belongs particularly to this area. I was struck by the absence from his conversation of any reference to the past glories of Islam in India and the chauvinist (one can only call it that) expression of superiority to the Hindus which I met so often among Pakistani townsmen, and among Muslims in India (townsman and villager alike). I asked Sharif (among others) about this and he said that Muhammad Aslam and most of his generation would not have had that much schooling, and wouldn't have known much about the history of Muslim rule in India, while he would have learnt about the early history of Islam from the Friday sermons preached in the mosque.

No doubt, the deference accorded to Muhammad Aslam springs partly from the fact that he was the largest landholder in the village, and a hard-working and efficient farmer; but I think it was his other qualities that are decisive. The force of his moral authority was very evident, and was accepted as fully by the sophisticated Sharif as it was by his more traditional fellow villagers. I asked Muhammad Aslam on one occasion whether everyone in Kanyal observed the Ramzan fast. He was emphatic that everyone did. I said, 'What would you think of one who didn't?' He said, 'We would beat him!' And I don't doubt that this is true.

This conversation took place at Sharif's house, and I continued it after Muhammad Aslam left. Sharif confirmed his picture, and said that people who violated the fast would do so secretly in their own homes and take care that no one else knew of it. On the other hand, he said that the obligation to say the five daily prayers was very generally not met, and my own observation supported the picture he gave. Sharif himself was the only one I met who ever excused himself when I was present in order to go and say his prayers; nor did I ever see anyone praying at prayer time except on the occasions I was in the mosque at the time of the evening prayer.

I had been struck by an incident that occurred on my first visit three and a half years earlier. I was accompanied on that occasion by a friend who had formerly been head of the department of Urdu in a Pakistani university. He was a devout man, though not in the least fanatical. We had arrived in the afternoon, and when the time for evening prayer came, he asked if he could be directed to the mosque so that he could say the evening prayer there. One of those present was sent to take him there, but none of the other men made any move to accompany him, nor did any of them retire to say the prayer in their own home. Sharif told me that if I went to the mosque in the evening, I would find relatively small numbers there, and that these would be mainly the older men who did not work full-time in the fields anymore, and boys of school age. This latter group, he said, was influenced by the emphasis laid upon Islam at school, and also they had the leisure, once school was over, to go to the mosque. My own observations on more than one occasion confirmed what he had told me.

One day while visiting Sharif's house, I picked up a book lying on the table and saw it was by Maududi, one of the most influential figures in Pakistan at that time. Maududi argued that Pakistan cannot legitimately claim to be an Islamic state until it is a theocratic one, governed by the Holy Law of Islam, and he had criticized accordingly the secular standards of its rulers since independence, derived from the largely irreligious and in his view immoral modern West. (All that changed when Zia ul Haq became president, when Maududi's influence was greatly extended.) His organization, the Jama'at i Islami, functioned as a political party too, and strongly influenced the urban lower middle class and university students. When Sharif saw that I knew of Maududi and his teachings, he told me that it was Maududi's writings more than any others that had revived the intensity of his religious feeling.

While we were talking about this, Akram came in. He smiled and said, 'If people here knew that you read Maududi, you would be refused water and the hookah'. This is a very strong expression, roughly equivalent to being sent to Coventry. (To refuse a request for a drink of water or for a smoke at the hookah is to deny the very minimum of hospitality that ordinary courtesy demands.) And though he spoke jokingly, there was obviously a serious meaning behind the words. When he had gone, I asked Sharif why the villagers were so hostile to Maududi. He said, 'It's just their ignorance'. I could get nothing more specific out of him, nor did I have the opportunity to question others about it.

The Role of Pirs

I subsequently discovered that the hostility to Maududi in Kanyal was due to his disapproval of those who believe in spiritual preceptors or *pirs*. People from Kanyal, like people everywhere else, tend to keep silent about such of their views and practices, which they fear would provoke opposition or ridicule. I noticed more than once that Akram, for all his genuine openness and friendliness, would introduce subjects by asking me what I thought about belief in such and such; and only when he felt sure that I would not ridicule his belief, whether I myself accepted it or not, would he then go on to speak of it. One such subject was a belief in *pirs*—and their powers. He opened up only when he was satisfied that I was familiar with the concept of the *pir* and respected those who accepted their *pir's* spiritual guidance. Even so, it was not from him that I learnt about the *pirs* of Kanyal.

Through the village ran a plateau, steep but not very high, overgrown with bushes. One evening as I walked around the village, I got talking to a boy and asked him what this plateau was. He replied that it was the *darbar*—court—of the *pirs*. I questioned him further, and he said that the tomb of the *pirs* was on top of the hill. No one knew their names, but on Thursday evenings, many villagers, including his own family, went up there to light a lamp by their graves. He also said that they could punish those who offended them. The next day I requested Akram's young cousin, Salim, to take me to the tombs. He readily agreed, and told me what the villagers' beliefs about them were, and when he saw that my reaction was a respectful one, he gradually revealed that he too shared these beliefs. As we approached the tomb, we took off our shoes. It was a long tomb, and some villagers thought it was that of a *pir* of more than human stature, while others thought that two *pirs* were buried there. He said that no one would cut firewood from the bushes on the hill for fear of punishment, though people from other villages could do so with impunity. And no one would sleep with their feet pointing towards the hill, as this would be disrespectful. He himself had seen the displeasure of the *pirs* one night when a guest from another village had stayed with him and had inadvertently slept with his feet towards the hill. He had groaned loudly in his sleep and it had been impossible to wake him until someone in the house had realized that he was sleeping with his feet towards the hill, and

EXPERIENCING VILLAGE LIFE   57

they had moved the bed, with the guest still sleeping on it, turning its foot in the opposite direction. Then he awoke and told them how he had seen the *pir*—a man of more than human stature—in a dream. Before we went down from the hill, Salim asked if he should seek the *pirs* blessing, and I said 'By all means' and stood respectfully silent as he did so.

A day or two later, I asked Sharif about it, and he confirmed all that Salim had said, adding, like Salim, that some Muslims believed it un-Islamic to seek the intercession of *pirs* in their prayers to God. He said that he was not certain about this, and therefore (to be on the safe side, though he didn't put it in those words) went along with the prevailing belief. The question of whether a *pir* was dead or still living was not important to them. When a man followed a certain ritual 'because his *pir* told him to' it was not clear until I asked, whether the *pir* was a living person or one who had died many years ago and appeared in a dream to give this instruction.

Equally striking was the way in which reverence for holy men coexisted with an entirely familiar attitude towards them. One evening as I stood chatting outside the mosque to Akram and Muhammad Aslam, a middle-aged man dressed entirely in black ('at the command of his *pir*', as I was subsequently told) approached us. Akram and Muhammad told me, in his presence, that he was a holy man, who never ate or drank during the hours of daylight and slept in the grave in which he would be buried when he died. He lived entirely on what people gave him in charity. Yet with their obvious respect for him went a sense of humour, and an occasional dig at him which he too laughed at. Later at Sharif's house, he arrived as we were going out. He spoke respectfully to Sharif, who replied that he was a sinner and unworthy of such respect. Sharif's wife gave him some food and he left with us, accompanying us for some distance along our way and, perhaps for my benefit, praising the former British rulers of India and contrasting them with the allegedly more arrogant officials who now control Pakistan's destinies. Later he appeared in the doorway of the room in Akram's house where men came and went after the day's work was done to chat and to smoke the hookah. He had food, but said he was afraid to move around the village now it was dark in case the dogs attacked him. The response was one of good-humoured mockery, both from those who accepted his bona fides, and those who subsequently told me they regarded him as a charlatan.

Attitudes to Differences of Belief

The population of Kanyal was almost entirely Muslim even before 1947; and since then, almost the whole population of Pakistan Punjab's villages has been Muslim, and mainly Sunni. So I did not know how they would react to differences of religious belief. Before coming to the village, I had considered how far it would be wise to keep quiet about my own views on religion. I had decided that I would not seek controversy, but would not evade it if it arose naturally. It *did* arise naturally. and on the first evening, I was there. The villagers are nothing if not blunt, and one man who assumed I was a Christian, cross-questioned me about Christian practices. He began by questioning, with fairly obvious scepticism, the alleged celibacy of priests and nuns, and passed on to explore the extent to which I observed the precepts of my own religion. I said I wasn't a Christian, and in fact was not a religious man at all. He was clearly taken aback, and the half-dozen others who were present (including Akram) listened very attentively as I continued. I said I sincerely respected religious people, and *all* people who lived a good life and treated others as they would wish to be treated themselves. To me, it didn't matter if such people were Muslims or Christians or Hindus or Sikhs or atheists. I said that I whole-heartedly agreed with the great Persian poet Hafiz (a revered figure for all Muslims), who said:

> Do not distress your fellow-men, and do what else you will
> For in my Holy Law there is no other sin than this.

As for religious observances, to me the important thing was that one should be a good person—not oppress others or seek his own interests at the expense of the equally legitimate interests of others. There were plenty of people who said their prayers and kept the fasts but who were liars and hypocrites, and to me, such people didn't deserve to be called Muslims at all.

Akram in particular seemed to feel that I had said things that needed saying, and on a number of occasions during the rest of my stay, expressed similar sentiments himself. But I, of course, know that the fact that they seemed to accept my differences does not mean that one of their own community would evoke the same reaction if he or she expressed them. My original questioner was clearly not receptive to what I said. What *did* impress him was my action on the morning of my departure in giving a sum of money to the mosque. He was both very surprised and very pleased. He said 'You're not a religious man?' I said. 'No'. He said, 'Then why have you given money to the mosque?' I said, 'Everyone here has treated me like a close friend. The mosque is an institution that serves the needs of all of you, and I want to show you all how much I have appreciated your friendship'.

How Representative Were My Impressions?

As an outsider, I would not have seen the total picture, and I am aware that it is likely that the hostilities and cruelties which characterize peasant societies were almost certainly there in Kanyal too. But that did not make what I experienced any the less real. Despite the traditional separation between men's and women's roles, and between peasant farmers and *kammi*, relationships between the people I was meeting were remarkably free and equal. That, and the readiness with which I myself was accepted into the same sort of relationship, made the experience not only immensely instructive but emotionally rewarding.

4

An Infidel among Believers

1999

First, the 'infidel' bit: I became an atheist in 1933, at the age of fifteen, and have remained one ever since. I could not, and still cannot, see any rational proof of the existence of God, and it seems to me that if you assert the existence of God, the burden of proof is upon you, not upon those of us who make no such assertion. I also felt, and still feel, that the common view of God held by religious people, or at any rate by Christians and Muslims, that God is both all-powerful and all-merciful is totally irrational. He could be one or the other, but not both. (In later years, a Jesuit friend of mine said that God is omnipotent, but that doesn't mean that He can do anything. For example, He can't create another God. It didn't occur to me until later, but this means that 'omnipotent' is a meaningless word.) As for His alleged all-kindness, when Milton wrote (and Christians still sing today) 'All things living He doth feed', he wrote something which he knew perfectly well was not true. And if, as the hymnist, Mrs Alexander said, God created 'All things bright and beautiful', He also created all things dark and ugly. So I abandoned my belief in God.

In becoming became an atheist, I moved to what I would later find was called humanism. This was the mid-1930s, and in the context of what was happening politically at the time, my humanist convictions led to communism, and I joined the Communist Party. In those days, intelligent people knew pretty well what you believed in if you called yourself a communist, but that, of course, has long ceased to be the case. Here it will be enough to say that I have never accepted, and do not now accept, any version of communism which is not in accord with humanism and respect for human rights.

Until I was twenty-three years old, the religious believers I came into contact with were all Christians, but in 1942, when I was a conscript in

---

A Life in Urdu. Edited and with a Foreword by Marion Molteno, Oxford University Press. © Oxford University Press India 2023. DOI: 10.1093/oso/9789391050948.003.0004

the British army, I was posted to India and stayed there for three and a half years. There, of course, I encountered people of other religious faiths. One of my fellow lieutenants was a Muslim, another was a Sikh; most of the hundred or so men under my direct command were Hindus, but there were Muslims and Christians too. I count myself fortunate that my first encounter with the religious diversity of India was in a situation where communal antagonism was almost non-existent. In the context of wartime, the British authorities, normally experts in 'divide and rule', had found it was not practicable to divide and rule their south Indian soldiers, and while in north Indian army units, there were separate kitchens for Hindus and Muslims, in ours everyone ate from the same kitchen.

For all the years after that, as a student and teacher of Urdu, it was amongst Muslims that I spent most of my time—Muslim writers, scholars, and students of Urdu literature. Since what I like most in life is relating to people, I have always talked readily with anyone who could talk Urdu with me, high and low, educated and uneducated, delighted to profit by the readiness of South Asians in general to communicate on almost any subject, to ask you questions which no English person would dream of putting to you, and to answer similar questions in return. With Hindus, other than English-educated secular-minded Hindus, for whom Hinduism is little more than a vague cultural tradition, I have had very little contact, a fact which I regret. With Sikhs, and with Muslims both in India and Pakistan, I have had much more. Personal relations with all of them have, with very, very few exceptions, always been friendly, and with some—one Hindu, one Sikh, and several Muslims—I have formed close friendships that have lasted more than forty years.

Some of these close friendships have been formed with deeply religious people. (By 'deeply religious' I emphatically do *not* mean those who shout loudest about their religion.) One, my colleague at SOAS, Khalid Hasan Qadiri, was present on one occasion when I was reading with my students a passage about Allah. In traditional style, it enumerated all the blessings Allah had conferred upon humankind. I paused and said, 'Yes, and He made plague and cholera and malarial mosquitoes, didn't He, Qadiri Sahib?' 'Yes', said Qadiri. 'Why?' I asked, '*I* don't know', he said—and quite clearly, he wasn't in the least perturbed. He believes that God *is* all-merciful, and if this cannot be proved by rational argument, that makes no difference. God is all-merciful: that, to him, is a fact. He

62   A LIFE IN URDU

believes, and I don't, and that is the end of the matter. That's no ground for any mutual hostility.

Two of my favourite nineteenth-century Urdu writers, the proto-novelist Nazir Ahmad and the poet Akbar Allahabadi, men of widely differing views, were united in their belief, which I share, that for religious people, it is necessary to recognize that rationality can take you only so far, and beyond that, it is all a matter of faith—and about faith there can be no argument. Either you have it or you don't. Nazir Ahmad has a brilliant article about God's creation of Adam and His decision to make humankind his *khalifa* (vicegerent) upon earth. Nazir Ahmad speaks of His doing both these things 'for reasons which He alone knows'. And Akbar writes: 'God is beyond the range of telescopes' and

> Why all this concentration on the problem?
> You ask What God is? God is God. What else?

Among my own contemporaries, the devout Muslim to whom I have felt closest was the late Mufti Raza Ansari, of Firangi Mahal, a centre of Islamic learning in Lucknow. I first met him in Aligarh, where he lectured in the Department of Theology, and I have several cassettes of my recorded interviews with him, a selection of which I should one day like to publish. A more courteous, considerate, and tolerant man, it would be difficult to find. Secure in his beliefs, which *were* beliefs and not mere prejudices, he could talk calmly, attentively, and with respect about my often very different views. I found the same qualities later in several Jesuit priests whom I got to know (one of them learnt Urdu from me, and through him, I met others). What they and I have in common is a humanist morality, though theirs is religiously based and mine is not.

Handling Differences

I have always operated on the principle that one builds on what common ground one has with anyone, and in normal circumstances, attaches more importance to that than to the areas where no such common ground exists, no matter how extensive these may be. This applies when meeting

AN INFIDEL AMONG BELIEVERS 63

an individual from a similar background to mine—language, cultural, political, or any other—and equally when I am with someone from a different culture or religious belief. But this does not mean—in either case—that I pretend to agree with them on everything. I have never, except in exceptional situations of short duration, concealed the fact that I am an atheist and a communist, or hesitated to defend my beliefs—calmly and good-humouredly, I hope—against anyone who cares to attack them. But I don't generally initiate such discussions.

Many of those who wish to foster understanding between people of different religions feel they can never say anything that could give offence, and this severely curtails the usefulness of what they have to say. It is a wholly admirable approach to concentrate on seeking common ground; but we cannot get away from the fact that there are millions who seek not to foster understanding but to stir up suspicion and hostility; and in my opinion, anyone who wants to foster understanding needs courteously, but openly and vigorously, to challenge those who do the opposite. A starting point is to constantly remind those making hostile generalizations that there is no *one* Christianity and no *one* Islam. In Christianity, during the twentieth century alone, there have been wildly opposing trends, even within the Catholic church—the *Opus Dei* of the Jesuits, who found Christian grounds for supporting the worst excesses of the Franco regime in Spain; and Latin American Jesuits whose interpretation of Christian belief moved them to support the liberation struggles of Latin American peoples. Similarly, there is the Islam of Khomeini, which led him to condemn Rushdie to death, and the Islam of others who emphatically deny that their religion required any such thing. Christians who want to help build an inclusive, tolerant society need to challenge fellow Christians whose stand is opposed to theirs. Muslims need to do the same in the Muslim community.

While, obviously, one should always speak and write in a way that minimizes any offence given, the argument that no one should be permitted to give offence to the adherents of any religion is quite untenable. There are, in any case, in every religion fundamental beliefs that are in themselves offensive to adherents of other religions. Well, too bad. Everyone must learn to live with that. I may remark in passing that my own beliefs as an atheist, which I hold as sincerely as any religious person holds his or hers, have been assailed all over the world, and in the most intemperate

64 A LIFE IN URDU

language, but I have never felt that I had any right to demand that the writings of such assailants be banned.

Interplay of Cultures

Closely related to this is the question of cultural values. It is commonly said that modern communications have brought the peoples of the world into closer contact with one another and so made possible increasing tolerance and understanding between them. That is indeed the case, but anyone who contemplates what has been happening in country after country in recent years cannot fail to see that the opposite is also happening. Rejection of difference has hardened into mutual hatred, to the point where white people will kill black people simply because they are black, Sikhs will kill Hindus simply because they are Hindus, Hindus will kill Sikhs simply because they are Sikhs, and so on—the list could be extended almost indefinitely. When matters reach this stage, we will not get very far if our response is simply to say, 'We recognise that this is the expression of your culture, and we respect it'.

All cultures are in a constant process of change, and different outlooks contend all the time for general acceptance. Within Islamic communities, the humanist Sufi trend contends with the bigoted fundamentalist trend. Among white Britons, a narrow-minded national chauvinism is an authentically British cultural trait, but so also, thank God, is the detestation of flag-wagging jingoism. People of all communities are entitled to express their opinions on these two tendencies. We need to be constantly willing to re-assess our own culture's values, but that in no way implies that we may not apply the same critical approach to the cultures of others, or that they may not do the same to ours. A spurious 'respect' for what the most vociferous in all communities declare to be the one authentic expression of their distinctive values is positively harmful to all of us.

What is needed is the open interplay of diverse values, both within and between communities—to encourage the emergence not only of a willing tolerance of diversity but also of values that were once those of a particular section of society but have the potential to become the common values of us all. For example, nearly all South Asians (and not just Muslims) have a far more generous concept of hospitality, a far greater sense of responsibility for the care of the aged, and a far greater respect for patriarchal values than the white British have. I think that westerners would benefit greatly from rejecting those of their own traditional values, which make them less hospitable and less caring than the South Asians; on the other hand, I think that they should, equally avowedly, maintain their rejection of authoritarian patriarchal values.

Discussing Religious Issues

As I have spent most of my life in studying and teaching Urdu, it is with Muslims that I have had most occasion to discuss, and often to dispute, the validity of what they think their religion teaches them. I would obviously not be in a position to do so unless I were reasonably well-versed in Islamic beliefs and practices. I have been prompted over many years to become so—through my long association with Muslims, including periods spent living in Muslim households, and my reading to understand the context of a literature, much of which is grounded in Islamic traditions.

These discussions have been especially relevant since Khomeini's *fatwa* condemning Salman Rushdie to death. I should first say something about my own reactions to Salman Rushdie's writing. *Midnight's Children* made little or no appeal to me and I gave up after reading about a hundred pages. I have not read his subsequent books and feel no desire to do so. This is not because I do not respect him. On the contrary, some of his comments on public affairs (notably his critique of the 'British heritage' myths assiduously cultivated at the time of the Falklands war in 1982) have been perceptive, hard-hitting, and true; and the theme of his next novel *Shame* (1983) with its exposure of the repulsiveness of regimes like that of the late Zia ul Haq is one that I think admirable. It is, if you like, a matter of personal literary taste that his fiction does not appeal to me. The merging of fantasy with realism which characterizes his work is something I find profoundly unsatisfying, the more so because I feel that straightforward realism would be a much more effective way of combating the evils he seeks to combat. However, he and his publishers and his readers clearly do not share my taste in this; and of course, they have a perfect right to proceed accordingly.

66 A LIFE IN URDU

About *Satanic Verses* other questions need to be raised. Was it desirable to write things that would be deeply offensive to millions of people? And was it permissible to do so? My answer to the first question is: probably not. And my answer to the second question is: yes; desirable or not, it is most certainly permissible. No one, and no group of people, however large, has any right to demand that no one be permitted to write things that are offensive to them. They may express their anger and outrage at such writing, and organize others to do so, as vigorously as they like; they have no right to have it banned. The archaic blasphemy laws, far from having their scope extended, should be abolished.

So much by way of prelude. I want now to look at the character of the movement of protest, and how that reflected—or did not reflect—Islamic belief. All those who participated in the protests against Salman Rushdie were united in their abhorrence of the book (which, it is safe to say, most of them had, like myself, never read), and all declared that they were motivated solely by devotion to Islam and to the Prophet.

Let us assume that this was so. As in every movement of this kind, there will have been those for whom it was not so. But, as Muslims would say, only God knows which of them were sincere and which were not. There is no denying that, for example, Khomeini's death sentence on Rushdie strengthened his position both in the internal politics of Iran and in the Muslim world at large, but nobody knows for certain to what extent, if any, this formed a part of his motive. Similarly, there is no denying that my friend Maqsood Elahi Sheikh, the editor of the Urdu weekly *Ravi* to which I am a regular subscriber and occasional contributor, in sustaining a campaign against Rushdie enhanced the influence of his paper. But again, nobody knows how far this consideration motivated him. So let us consider the protesters' demands on the assumption that they were entirely sincere.

Most called for the banning of *Satanic Verses;* fewer approved of Khomeini's sentence of death on its author; but all claimed that their stand was consistent with the teachings of Islam. This claim was accepted by their supporters and by most of their opponents. With due respect to all concerned, I question it.

There were two common arguments advanced against Rushdie. The first is that he was an apostate—one who rejected the religion which once

AN INFIDEL AMONG BELIEVERS   67

he accepted—and that the punishment for apostasy is death. The proposition is commonly accepted by Muslims.

Muslims turn for guidance first to the Quran and then to the *hadith*—the duly authenticated accounts of the words and deeds of Muhammad in various situations which indicate to true believers how they should feel and act in similar circumstances. As far as I can discover, there is nothing in the Quran or the hadith which supports this argument on the punishment for apostasy. Quite the contrary. The much-quoted verse of the Quran (2: 256), 'Let there be no compulsion in religion' surely rules it out'.

The second argument was that whether he was an apostate or not, the punishment to be meted out to anyone who insults the Prophet, is death. This is, to me at any rate, a less familiar one, but I have been assured that it is so by a close and valued Muslim friend of more than twenty years' standing. Not having read *Satanic Verses*, I cannot say whether the charge that it insults Muhammad is a valid one, but let us assume that it is. Yet Muhammad himself felt quite differently from his present-day devotees. The Prophet's own response to insult was clear from a hadith that tells how a party of Jews asked, and was granted, permission to visit him. On being admitted, they greeted him not with *as salamu alaykum*—peace be upon you—but with *as samu alaykum*—death be upon you. The Prophet's wife Aisha, who was present, angrily replied, 'And death be upon you too', whereupon Muhammad rebuked her, telling her that God is kind and loves kindness in all things. She, thinking perhaps that he had not registered that they had said *samu* (death) and not *salamu* (peace), asked if he had heard what they said. He replied that he had.

Islam exhorts its followers to create in themselves, as far as is humanly possible, the attributes of God. God's attributes are many but it is surely significant that those which have always been most stressed are His compassion and His mercy. The anti-Rushdie campaigners could hardly claim that these qualities were much in evidence in their campaign.

In short, without suggesting that the campaigners were deliberately deceiving either themselves or anyone else, I deny that their stand was an authentically Islamic one. And if others believe that it was, let them produce authority that can stand against the message of the Quran and of the hadith I have quoted.

Who Can Challenge Who?

I am aware that many Muslims feel that only Muslims are qualified to make statements about Islamic doctrines, and many non-Muslims seem to think this too. The obvious unsoundness of this view should not need stating. If I quote a verse from the Quran and argue that certain logical consequences follow from it, the question of whether I am myself a Muslim is irrelevant. The consequences I state either do follow from it or they don't. If they do, accept them. If they don't, prove to me that they don't, through rational argument that Muslims and non-Muslims alike can accept as a proper means of arriving at the truth.

Muslim resentment against non-Muslim polemics against their beliefs is understandable, because it was for centuries engaged in by bigoted, self-styled Christians who vigorously supported every imperialist act of aggression against Muslim peoples; and such motives are still very much in evidence. But I condemn such attacks as wholeheartedly as Muslims do, and my own standpoint is a very different one—one which I think sincere Muslims can respect whether they agree with it or not.

Related to this is the question of whether Muslims themselves are willing to publicly challenge fellow Muslims with whose actions or interpretations of Islam they disagree. A brief but forceful hadith tells us that the greatest *jihad* (holy war) is to speak the truth to the tyrant's face. Another says that there are three kinds of jihad; the first is action to prevent wrongdoing; the second (if you haven't the courage to undertake the first) is the public censure of wrongdoing; and the third (if you haven't the courage to undertake the second) is to silently, in your heart, condemn wrongdoing. The third is the weakest jihad. For Muslims living in Britain, rather than, say, Iran, the second kind of jihad should not require much courage.

If Muslims are shocked and angered by non-Muslims' offences against the principles of Islam, should they not be doubly shocked by even greater offences committed by people who proclaim themselves to be Muslims? If a non-Muslim offends against these principles that may be reprehensible, but it is hardly surprising. If those who claim to be a Muslim, do so, one might expect true Muslims to react with a redoubled sense of outrage and anger. But when the Pakistan army invaded what was then East Pakistan and is now Bangladesh, killing, looting, and raping, Muslim opinion at large was unmoved. When Idi Amin committed his bloody atrocities, his fellow Muslim rulers of Libya and Saudi Arabia, far from condemning him, gave him support and protection. When Iraqi Muslims used poison gas, there was no Muslim protest. When Turkish Muslims, Iraqi Muslims, and Iranian Muslims all pursued policies of virtual genocide against the Kurds, again, the organs of Muslim opinion voiced no disapproval. True Muslims should regard the perpetrators of these crimes as a disgrace to Islam.

* * *

I regard it as a matter of great good fortune that I have been able to be close to people of different cultures. My own values and way of life have been partly shaped by my contact with them, as has my sensitivity to different ways of seeing things. Where they sincerely hold religious beliefs, I have tried to learn about them, and respect them, though I do not share them. For me, mutual respect and frankness go hand in hand, and in challenging anyone whose attitudes I disagree with, I attempt, without in any way concealing my own beliefs, to build upon common ground between me and them.

And that, I think, is why I, an infidel among believers, not only survive, but evoke, if I may say so, affection and respect.

PART II
ON URDU AND ITS LITERATURE

5

An Eighteenth-Century Satirist

1959

The poet Sauda is one of the first great names in the history of Urdu literature in northern India. He lived from about 1713 to 1780, and spent the greatest part of his life in Delhi, in a period when the Mughal Empire was in catastrophic decline. His reputation was once largely based on his mastery of the qasida, a poem of praise, which has long since ceased to appeal; and he was also a great exponent of the ghazal form. But the most vital part of his output is his satirical verse—vigorous, passionate, and often bawdy verse, in which he lambasts the weaknesses and vices both of individuals and of the society in which he lived.

Under four great emperors, from 1556 to 1707, the empire had seen an age of dazzling splendour, yet by the time Sauda reached his fifties, the picture had totally changed. The great provinces had broken away to become virtually independent kingdoms, and the emperor had lost all effective power except that of granting, under threat of force, legal sanction to the acts of his nominal 'subjects'. The English had established themselves in the east, in the empire's richest province, while the Afghans ruled a huge tract of what had once been imperial territory in the northwest, and repeatedly invaded and plundered the imperial capital itself. Within the domains still nominally part of the empire, unceasing warfare raged between the great nobles, and combined with the forces of plebeian rebellion to produce anarchy. Only one principle guided the actions of the great and powerful—that of naked self-interest; and that is generally conceived in the narrowest and most short-term sense. It was a degenerate age in which an old order was breaking up and no new one yet emerging to take its place.

People generally familiar with this background have often assumed that the literature of the period reflects this degeneration. It is a false

A Life in Urdu. Edited and with a Foreword by Marion Molteno, Oxford University Press. © Oxford University Press India 2023. DOI: 10.1093/oso/9789391050948.003.0005

74 A LIFE IN URDU

assumption, and nothing shows its falsity so clearly as do the satires of Sauda.

All poets of his day depended upon the patronage of the great nobles for their livelihood, but this did not prevent Sauda from speaking his mind with the utmost forthrightness, using his gifts as a poet to pillory that very nobility on whom he depended. Like many of his great contemporaries, he felt bitterly contemptuous of the incompetent, self-seeking men who now controlled the destinies of the empire. Here's a prose translation of a poem that expresses this:

> The ministers of the Empire have been summoned for consultation. See how they consult for the welfare of the state. The Imperial pay-master is thinking up some scheme to stay at home doing nothing and still draw his pay, while the Chief Minister has his eyes on the silver knobs on the poles of the royal tent, and is calculating how much they will fetch in the market. They are all of them strangers to any sense of shame.

One of his poems assails a rich noble for his meanness, a vice most detestable to one of Sauda's generous nature. This is how he introduces the subject:

> God filled the world with numberless good things
> That every man might eat and have to spare;
> Man lives in a vast orchard, fit for kings
> Laden with fruits enough for all to share.
> The ordinary man like you and me
> Gives thanks that He provides for us so well.
> But what is He to do with such as he
> Who figures in this tale I'm going to tell?

At one point, he puts into the mouth of the miser himself a passage in which he contrasts his own and his ancestors' thrift with the prodigal extravagance of his son, who had had the temerity to invite a friend to share a frugal meal with him:

> His grandsire was a great voluptuary
> But still, he was no spendthrift—no, not he!

He planned his operations like a soldier
And sent his servants, haversack on shoulder,
To beg from door to door for scraps of food
And bring them back to him; anything good
He'd pick out for himself. Then he would say
'The rest is yours'—and dock it from their pay.
That's how our family fortunes were amassed
And was it all for this, that he at last
Should leave us naked 'gainst the winter's blast?
I thought *myself* extravagant, but he
In reckless spending outdoes even me.
He'll rapidly exhaust our buried hoards,
Pull down the house, and sell the bricks and boards.
And all for senseless prodigality!
Well, since this thing is done, I'll have to see
Where lies the true responsibility.
His tutor should have taught the boy more sense,
So he shall pay the bill ...
On such a perfect nobleman, I say,
May God send down his curses night and day.

Many of his pieces are directed against self-important, ignorant frauds of one kind or another. Here is an example, aimed at a hakim named Ghaus. A hakim practises the traditional Greek system of medicine, developed by the Arabs and still practised today in countries with a large Muslim population. Ghaus is a common title of Muslim saints, as well as being a proper name, and Sauda makes use of this coincidence. In the poem, he also refers to Halaku Khan, the grandson of Chingiz ['Jengis'] Khan, and commander of the Mongol Hordes which overran the Muslim Abbasid Empire:

There's a hakim, the mention of whose name
Makes every good physician blush with shame.
Down in the main bazaar you'll find his house;
He looks like Satan, yet his name is Ghaus.
Since he took up his practice people say
Death works while Healing takes a holiday.

None whom he treated ever yet got well—
Worthy successor to Halaku Khan
He massacres Hindu and Mussalman.

There is never anything puritan about his attitude. He had an unquenchable zest for living, and a capacity to enjoy to the full the good things which life can offer, both physical luxuries and also the pleasures which come from a wide range of learning and an extensive reading of literature. His vigour pervades his writing, even on mundane topics. One poem attacks the excessive heat of summer, while another objects with spirited indignation to the hardships of an exceptionally severe winter:

This year it was so cold that people said
The sun himself rose shivering from his bed ...
The youngster who gets married in this season
Must hand his head in shame, and with good reason.
His bride lies with him in the bridal bed,
But he is forced to hug his knees instead,
So cold it is ...

In his many personal satires, the vices he assails are those which have in all ages and places been detestable to ordinary people; and he counts himself among them. This is how he describes himself: 'I am not like the rose in the garden, nor am I a thorn in anyone's path. I am not famed for virtue nor yet notorious for vice. I simply try to act as my best feelings dictate to me. I seek no one's favours, nor do I ask that anyone should seek mine. People may think well or ill of me as they please: I act as my nature prompts me'.

In his attitude, there is no suggestion of a 'holier than thou' approach. One of his best short poems is a spirited attack on self-appointed censors of other people's morals. In another, he tells how an acquaintance warned him not to make any man his friend, for none would prove true when put to the test. Sauda records his words and then writes:

I heard him out; then, smiling, said to him:
It is not good to speak so ill of men.
Who made *you* judge of others? You had best
Thank God that no one puts *you* to the test.

AN EIGHTEENTH-CENTURY SATIRIST   77

Indignant and angry at what he saw around him, he used every weapon in his exuberant nature, including ridicule, invective, wild exaggeration, and the coarsest and most ribald humour. One of his satires is directed against an aristocrat known for his gluttony. It is difficult to convey in translation the vigorous flow of Sauda's imagery, but here is a sample, partly in a rather free verse translation, and partly in prose:

> He only has to hear a saucepan rattle
> And like a soldier digging in for battle
> He'll take up his position by the door.
> Nothing can shift him then that god of war
> Rustam himself, might rise up from the tomb
> And try his strength against him. He'd stand firm.
> He'd fight to the last breath and never yield
> Until his corpse was carried from the field.

It is enough to catch a whiff of food cooking for him to fly to the place and sit there beating his head with both hands in an agony of impatience and looking like a great fly that sits on the food washing its face with its front legs. When food is set before him, he rushes at it as a soldier rushes to loot a house, feverishly gathering everything up in case anyone should come and disturb him before he can finish, and his hands flash back and forth between the plate and his mouth as nimbly as those of a fencer hard pressed by a determined opponent. So obsessed is he by the thought of food that it dominates his mind even when he is alone with his wife. He—

> Fixes his lady's bodice with a stare.
> 'Tell me,' he asks, 'What have you got in there?
> Are they two loaves? Or two delicious cheeses?'
> Or, if his hand should stray into her breeches,
> 'What's this I feel,' he cries, 'so soft and warm?
> Newly-baked bread? If so, it would do no harm
> To let me eat it. Why do you hide it from me?'

In Sauda's day, a satirist might legitimately blacken his opponent and expose him to ridicule, and the more outrageous the charges were, the greater would be the appreciation of his audience. The poet, audience,

78 A LIFE IN URDU

and victim alike accepted these conventions, though that is not to say that the victim of a clever poetic attack relished his position. There are parallels in other cultures. The comedies of Aristophanes in ancient Greece furnish a close parallel, and in modern times, the conventions which still govern the political cartoon approximately resemble those of Sauda's satires—the cartoonist is allowed considerable freedom in the means he employs to heap ridicule on the politician under attack, including ridiculing peculiarities of personal appearance and idiosyncrasies of personal habit. These approximate parallels may help a modern reader to understand the general atmosphere of Sauda's satires, and to enter into it. To say that Sauda's satires are not remarkable for their delicacy would be considerably understating the position: the crude and coarse element in them is no less prominent than it is in the writings of Rabelais, but they are pervaded with the same healthy, vital spirit as Rabelais is, and can be read with the same enjoyment.

Because satires of this kind form the bulk of Sauda's satirical verse, some have concluded that he was nothing more than a sort of poetically talented buffoon. This judgement is wide of the mark, and reflects an inability to see below the surface of his verse. Its mainspring—as in all truly great satire—is a deep compassion for humanity and a keenly felt sorrow and anger at the conditions of an age which deform and degrade people. This is true even of the most boisterous and Rabelaisian of his work, despite surface appearances. But there are other satires in which this deep feeling is quite apparent. Two in particular, in which he surveys the whole social scene of his day, show how keenly he grieved over the decadence he saw around him.

One of these concludes with a moving lament for the fate of Delhi (which he here calls Jahanabad), which had once been one of the most renowned cities in the world. I give it here in prose translation:

How can I describe the desolation of Delhi? There is no house from where the jackal's cry cannot be heard. The mosques at evening are unlit and deserted and only in one house in a hundred will you see a light burning. Its citizens do not possess even the essential cooking pots, and vermin crawl in the places where in former days people used to welcome the coming of spring with music and rejoicing. The lovely buildings which once made the famished man forget his hunger are in ruins

AN EIGHTEENTH-CENTURY SATIRIST   79

now. In the once beautiful rose gardens where the nightingale sang love songs to the rose, the grass grows waist-high around fallen pillars and broken arches. In the villages round about, the comely young women no longer come to draw water at the wells and stand talking in the leafy shade of the trees. The villages are deserted, the trees themselves are gone, and the wells are full of corpses. Jahanabad, you never deserved this terrible fate, you who were once vibrant with life and love and hope, like the heart of a young lover, you for whom men afloat upon the ocean of the world once set their course as to the promised shore, you from whose dust men came to gather pearls. Not even a lamp of clay now burns where once the chandelier blazed with light. Those who lived once in great mansions now eke out their lives amid the ruins. Thousands of hearts once full of hope are sunk in despair. Women of noble birth, veiled from head to foot, stand in the streets carrying in their arms their little children, lovely as fresh flowers; ashamed to beg outright, they offer for sale rosaries made from the holy clay of Karbala.

But Sauda, still your voice, for your strength fails you now. Every heart is aflame with grief, every eye brimming with tears. There is nothing to be said other than this: we are living in a special kind of age, so say no more.

The reference to the wells being full of corpses refers to women who, when armies were rampaging, threw themselves into the wells to escape being raped. These are not the words of a mere clown. They underline a point that Rabelais made to his readers, and which Sauda might well have said of his own writings:

You ... may not too easily conclude that they treat of nothing but mockery, fooling and pleasant fictions ... You must open this book and carefully weigh up its contents. You will discover then that the drug within is far more valuable than the box promised.

6

Rusva and Premchand: Stories of Courtesans

1970 and 2003

Two great prose writers of the late nineteenth and early twentieth centuries—Muhammad Hadi Rusva (1858–1931) and Premchand (1880–1936)—each wrote a novel with a courtesan as the central character. Rusva's *Umrao Jan Ada* was published in 1899, and Premchand's *Bazaar e Husn* in 1917.

The phenomenon of the courtesan is no longer familiar to either the English-speaking world or many in contemporary Urdu-speaking society. Like the hetaira of ancient Athens, she was the product of a society in which respectable women—the great majority of all women—took no part in public life, and even in their private lives, could form no friendly relationships with men, other than their fathers, husbands, sons, and other close kin. Pericles, the great statesman of Athens, in his speech in praise of the city of his birth, said, 'The greatest glory of a woman is to be least talked about by men, whether they are praising or criticising'. Intelligent, cultured men needed the company of intelligent, cultured women, and this is what the hetaira was. Pericles' own liaison with one, Aspasia, was well known, and he suffered no censure for it.

The courtesan also sold her sexual services and so could fairly be called a prostitute, although the most accomplished of them could be very choosy about who they offered these services to. 'Prostitute', and its Urdu equivalent, are pejorative words, while 'courtesan' is not unambiguously so. The accomplished courtesan had to be not only sexually attractive but also extremely well educated, and very commonly an accomplished singer.

A Life in Urdu. Edited and with a Foreword by Marion Molteno, Oxford University Press. © Oxford University Press India 2023. DOI: 10.1093/oso/9789391050948.003.0006

Rusva and *Umrao Jan Ada*

Rusva was a man of extraordinarily wide interests and talents. His works include long theological treatises, translations from English, cheap thrillers written to earn money, and three serious novels. *Umrao Jan Ada* was his greatest work, and also the first real novel in Urdu literature, in the generally accepted modern sense of the term.

In the introduction to one of his earlier novels, Rusva said that the fiction writer is a kind of historian, and in a way fiction is of greater value than histories, better able to give an overall picture of reality. Elsewhere he wrote 'My novels should be regarded as a history of our times, and I hope it will be found a useful one'. In *Umrao Jan Ada* he showed, considerably more than in his other novels, that he could apply these principles in practice.

Set in his birthplace, Lucknow, which he knew intimately, it is the life story of a Lucknow courtesan, whose name forms the title, and there are some grounds for thinking that in essentials it is a true story. The story spans the years 1840–1870, that is, the decades spanning the watershed of the great rebellion of 1857. In those decades, courtesans of Umrao Jan's class, besides being expert singers and dancers, were also highly educated in the traditional culture of the day and were quite often poets, as Umrao Jan herself was—Ada is her *takhallus*, her poetic name. They played a significant role in Lucknow society, and through her experiences, one really does see something of the social and cultural history of the times. Cultured men who could afford it commonly kept a courtesan mistress as well as a wife. The courtesan would move freely in a cultured society, and through her experiences, one could see something of the social and cultural history of the times. He shows Umrao herself as being aware of the relevance of her experience to an understanding of the historical period through which she lived. Each chapter begins with a verse; the one where she starts to tell her story begins:

> Which is the story you would rather hear?
> The story of my life or of my times?

The story is beautifully told and extraordinarily well constructed. The characterization and dialogue are excellent, and the story has a proper plot and real development. Rusva begins with an account of how it came to be written. He had a friend from Delhi who was very fond of Lucknow and frequently came to stay there for long periods. On these occasions, he would rent a small house, and would often invite his friends there to spend the evening with him. The room where they used to sit together, talking, and reciting their verses to one another, was separated by only a thin partition wall from the house next door. In it was a sort of hatch, the shutters of which were always kept closed. They had been given to understand that the occupant of the house on the other side of the wall was an elderly courtesan, but she was a quiet and unobtrusive neighbour. One evening, the host arranged a small informal *mushaira,* a gathering at which the guests turn by turn recite verses they have composed. On these occasions, the expression of appreciation is loud and uninhibited, and on this particular evening, Rusva has just recited a verse when the company is surprised to hear an exclamation of approval coming from the other side of the partition wall. The host smiles and calls out, 'Come in and join us. It's not proper to call out from there'. But there is no reply. A few minutes later, a maidservant appears and asks, 'Which of you is Mirza Rusva?' Rusva identifies himself and the maid says that her mistress is asking to see him. The other guests are quick to note that the lady next door knows Rusva well enough to recognize him from the sound of his voice, and there is some chaffing at his expense. He excuses himself, goes out with the maidservant, and is taken in to see her mistress, whom he at once recognizes as Umrao Jan. Knowing her accomplishments as a poet, he urges her to return with him and take part in the *mushaira,* and after some demur, she does so. Her verses are much appreciated, and after that evening, she frequently visits the house to take part in gatherings of this kind.

One evening she and Rusva are talking with their host after the other guests have gone, and they ask her if she would relate to them the story of her life. Rusva is particularly insistent; and in the end, she agrees to do as they ask. The rest of the book is an account of the successive meetings with Rusva in which she tells him her story. After each occasion, unbeknown to her, Rusva writes it all down, including the occasional exchanges between them with which her narrative is interrupted—a device that very effectively enhances the illusion of reality. She begins with her childhood recollections, until at the age of seven, she is kidnapped by a

RUSVA AND PREMCHAND: STORIES OF COURTESANS   83

sworn enemy of her father and taken to Lucknow to be sold into a brothel. She then recounts all her changing fortunes during thirty years until she retires quietly to spend her old age alone in the house she now occupies. When her story is complete Rusva hands her his manuscript and asks her to read it through and correct any mistakes he may have made—a deeply emotional experience for her.

We are not left in any doubt that Rusva's deepest sympathies are with Umrao Jan, whom he sees as a victim of others' sins against her. Their easy companionship is realistically portrayed—whenever he is talking to her about herself, it is in a half-serious, half-bantering tone. Yet his approach to her is unsentimental, and on one occasion, he speaks with a bluntness that is almost cruel. She has been relating an incident when she was treated with contempt by an older respectable woman, and after the lapse of all these years, Umrao Jan still feels angry about it. Rusva cuts her short and tells her bluntly that she could not expect anything different—

> Think of their position—poor women, they spend their whole lives imprisoned within their own four walls, and have troubles without end to endure. When times are good anyone will stand by a man, but these stand by him in good times and bad alike. While their husbands are young and have plenty of money, it is usually other women who get the benefit of it. But when they grow old and have nothing, no one else so much as asks after them, and it is the wives who go through all manner of distress, and trust in fate to revenge them on the others. Don't you think they are right to pride themselves on all this?

Umrao's own attitude towards herself is equally unsentimental. She knows that a woman like herself who has been a courtesan would be deluding herself to think that any relationship which demands of others that they love and trust her would be possible for her. She must live her own life and rely on no one but herself. She obviously regrets that this should be so, but she adds, with characteristic realism, that the suffocating atmosphere of purdah would now be unbearable to her. But all this is said in a matter-of-fact way, and with a complete absence of any maudlin self-pity.

Umrao Jan Ada was an immediate success and has remained popular ever since. When I started teaching Urdu at SOAS in 1950 and made proposals to the then head of department, Harley, to revise the syllabus,

84   A LIFE IN URDU

Umrao Jan Ada was among the set books I proposed to include. Harley was alarmed at the idea—'Some of the students' parents might object', he said. I had never before heard of parents to whom it would occur to try and censor a university syllabus, but Harley was not alone. Later, Indian and Pakistani university teachers expressed surprise at its inclusion. 'Do you teach it to your *girl* students too?' they asked.

In fact, during those first years of teaching, my most interesting student was a young woman from Delhi, Amina Ahmad, and I have vivid memories of reading it with her. She was the daughter of an English mother and an Indian father, and spoke Urdu fluently but had read very little Urdu literature. Her spoken Urdu, she had learnt mainly from family servants and from Urdu-speaking children during her childhood in Delhi. In reading it together, I told her the meanings of literary words she did not know, and she instructed me in the colloquial idiom that I didn't know.

It remains one of my favourite books. It is also one of the most accessible Urdu books for a non-Urdu-speaking reader. It's unfortunate that the only English translation, published in India in 1961, fails to do justice to the original, and gives a very inadequate impression of its true worth.

[Editor's note: You can read 50 pages of Ralph's translated extracts from *Umrao Jan Ada* in *A Thousand Yearnings*. A full translation by David Matthews was published in 1996.]

Premchand and *Bazaar e Husn*

Premchand was one of the greatest writers of twentieth-century India. He has two special distinctions: firstly, he was one of the very few non-Muslim writers who stands in the first rank of the writers of Urdu literature; and secondly, he is a figure of equal importance in two literature—that of Urdu and that of Hindi.

Among the Hindus of the Urdu/Hindi speaking area, two groups were thoroughly at home in the Muslim milieu. One was the Kashmiri Brahmins—Kashmiri in the sense that they had originally come from Kashmir to settle in their new homeland. The other was the Hindu Kayasths, a caste of people whose traditional profession had been service in the middle and lower ranks of the Mughal administration. This had made them fluent in Persian, and when Urdu replaced Persian, in Urdu

RUSVA AND PREMCHAND: STORIES OF COURTESANS   85

too. Premchand was a Kayasth, and began his literary career as a writer in Urdu. He continued to write in Urdu all his life, though he soon began writing in Hindi too, and produced his own versions in both languages of almost everything he wrote.

He was extraordinarily prolific, producing altogether nearly 300 short stories and 12 novels. In them, one finds an unparalleled picture of the life of the Indian people. His first stories were published before the First World War, but it is those from the 1920s and early 1930s that are the basis of his fame. Through his stories, one can trace his development from that of a rather naive nationalist, through being influenced by Gandhi's concern for the poor, to a many-sided realism about the social conflicts of his time, clearly influenced by the theories of socialism.

A deeply humane man, he was free of class, religious, or male prejudices, and his novels and stories are remarkable for the range of their themes. He writes vividly, with keen observation, a sympathetic interest in the lives of ordinary people, and a wry, affectionate humour. His great achievement was to bring into the pages of literature the ordinary people of India, and particularly that large majority of them who live in the villages in which he himself spent much of his life and which he knew so well.

Bazar e Husn—the title literally means 'market place of beauty'—is one of his earliest works. It also happens to be one of the first works of Urdu prose literature that I read when in 1946, I began my university course in Urdu. I vividly remember the impact it made on me in the very first chapter, with its description of landlord oppression. It was obvious that no English person writing about India could possibly have made the impact that Premchand did, writing as he did from within Indian society and speaking of what he knew intimately from his own life experience. I at once thought, 'This should be translated into English', and looked forward to the time not only this book but much of his best writing could be available in good translations. When many years later, this began to happen, it was a matter of very great satisfaction to me.

Bazar e Husn is a fascinating book, for several reasons. It is a novel about interactions between men, respectable women, and courtesans, and all these relationships are vividly portrayed. Saman, the central figure, has been married to someone she feels is beneath her, because her family has got into debt. Premchand describes the gradual steps by which she moves

86 A LIFE IN URDU

from being a dissatisfied wife to a woman who is thrown out of her house by her husband and—threatened now with destitution—is taken in by a courtesan who enables her to train as a singer. There were courtesans who were not available for sex, but attracted a clientele by their other accomplishments, and Premchand seems to suggest that Saman was one such.

From that point, the story is told not so much through Saman's experiences, as through all those in 'respectable' society connected with her, and Premchand's wide sympathies enable him to enter into the often-conflicting feelings of the different characters. The story provides a powerful portrayal of the double standards applying to men and women. Men who resorted to courtesans might be regarded as less morally upright than those who (as far as anyone knew) did not, but society's censure of them was more formal than real. Predictably, the courtesans themselves were not accorded any such tolerance. They were immoral women, and it was only in the practice of their trade that they could appear in the company of respectable people—people who nevertheless thought it not only permissible by obligatory to engage them to provide entertainment on grand occasions like weddings. And yet, in the eyes of society, once a courtesan was always a courtesan, and a quick and lasting repentance, such as Saman's life exemplifies, made no difference. She was stigmatized for life.

If English readers feel, as they well may, that there is too much melodrama in the story, let me assure them that it is not in the least unrealistic. Leaving aside the question of how far this is still the case, at the time when Premchand wrote it, the Indian social scene was full of melodrama. A continuing theme throughout the book is that both men and women are up against powerful social conventions; that individuals may be motivated by human decency and a desire to show proper respect for their fellows, but frequently find that they lack the courage to do so.

Viewed purely as works of art, Premchand's novels are uneven, and his zeal sometimes clashes with, and prevails over, his sense of realism. There are also features in his narrative which are likely to jolt the preconceptions of English readers about what a novel should be. He, not infrequently, has passages with explicit moralizing over the words and actions of his characters—English readers are more used to narrative in which the moral is left implicit in the description of the incident being narrated. Some years ago, I was delighted to read a book by two Americans, Scholes and Kellogg, entitled *The Nature of Narrative,* in which they said that they aimed to 'put the novel in its place'. It is a very apt phrase, for they mean both seeing the novel in its setting, part of a long tradition of prose narrative fiction that has taken different forms in different cultures and times, and also demoting it from the unwarrantably exalted position that critics have claimed for it. The attitude that any narrative which does not fit into the currently accepted definition of a 'novel' is an imperfect striving to attain what a 'proper' novel ought to be, is decidedly limiting. So guard against any remnants of this attitude, and enjoy this excellent narrative for what it is.

Those who rightly admire Premchand's later work have been, in my view, too critical of his earlier stories. It is said that some of his 'good' characters are unconvincing and reflect naive idealism. In my opinion, this criticism is totally unjustified. Modern fiction in the west tends to fight shy of portraying wholly noble characters, but that does not mean that such people do not exist. G.K Chesterton has pointed out that there is a bias in modern novels to be interested only in unusual, complex individuals. There *are* people with the capacity behave as Premchand's 'too-good-to-be-true' characters do, and to accuse him of naivety or lack of realism because he chose to portray such characters is ridiculous.

It is useful in this regard to look at a few examples from his other work. In the story *Masum Bacca* ('An Innocent Child'), he honours the simple goodness of a servant whose innocence (in the best sense of the word) is mocked by his sophisticated master (the narrator of the story). The servant leaves his job to marry a destitute, homeless woman who has already been married three times and has three times run away from her husband. His master asks him whether he really thinks such a woman can ever be a good wife. He replies that she is a good woman:

Those people [her husbands] probably thought they'd done her a big favour by marrying her. They wanted her to devote herself to them heart and soul. But sir, you can't make another person yours until you make yourself hers.

Some months after their marriage, she again disappears. Her husband searches everywhere for her and ultimately finds her in a hospital in a distant city where, six months after their marriage, she has given birth to a

88 A LIFE IN URDU

son. He comes back radiant with joy to his old master, proudly carrying the child in his arms. His master says sarcastically that it's the first time he's ever heard of a child being born six months after marriage. The servant replies:

> Sir, I didn't even think about that. It was because she felt ashamed that she ran away. I said to her, 'Gomati, if you don't love me, leave me, I will go away at once and never come near you again. Anything you need, I'll do all I can to send you … I love you as much as I ever did … If you have not stopped loving me, come with me. I didn't marry you because you were a goddess but because I love you and I thought you loved me too. This is *my* child, my own child. If I'd bought a sown field would I abandon its crop because someone else had sown it?'

And he laughs out loud.

You feel that here is a man, as real as such men are rare, and that the narrator is right when this reply overwhelms him with shame at what has been his attitude to him.

By the early thirties, Premchand was not afraid to describe, without comment and without adverse judgement, characters who behaved in ways that most of his contemporaries would have condemned. In the same collection, he has a story *Nai Bivi* (New Wife) in which a young wife, Asha, is married to an elderly *banya* (grain-merchant-cum-moneylender). A young manservant feels a cordial contempt for his master, and motivated both by his sympathy for the young wife's plight and his own sexual desire for her, makes advances to her. The story ends with the words they exchange when her husband has gone out:

> [Servant speaking]: 'All the things you do for him are
>   things a mother would do. *That's* not what a wife is for.'
> 'What *is* a wife for, then?'
> 'I'm only your servant. Otherwise I'd tell you.'
> They heard the sound of a car stopping. For some reason
>   Asha's *anchal* [the end of her sari] had slipped off her
>   head onto her shoulders. She quickly drew it over
>   her head again, and as she went to her room she said,
>   'When he's had his meal and gone out again, come to
>   see me.'

RUSVA AND PREMCHAND: STORIES OF COURTESANS 89

Premchand makes no comment, and ends the story there.

As the range of his understanding of the society in which he lived extended, so did the range and quality of his writing. He trusted more and more to his readers to draw conclusions, and no longer thought it necessary to include among his characters even one who was wholly admirable. His greatest novel, *Gaodan* (The Gift of a Cow), written in the years between 1932 and 1935, and published in June 1936 shortly before his death, bears striking testimony to his maturity. Its central character is Hori—a poor peasant who has less than an acre of land. The story describes his relationships with his two brothers, his wife, and three surviving children, and the landlords, moneylenders, police, and others who ruthlessly exploit and oppress the village poor. His dearest wish is to own a cow, and he plans that when he dies, he will make a gift of it to a Brahmin, for this will guarantee his salvation. He manages to acquire one, but his brothers react with insane jealousy, and one of them poisons it. He sinks deeper and deeper into debt, and in the end, dies with only a few small coins in his possession, earned by making ropes. But if Hori is the hero of the book, and one for whom the reader feels a deep sympathy, his defects and undesirable qualities are also depicted quite frankly. The book presents a detailed picture of the life of the peasantry of Uttar Pradesh (then United Provinces) which it would be difficult to surpass.

Premchand's last story, *Kafan* (The Shroud), is even more powerful in its portrayal of how extreme poverty and oppression degrade people. The story opens with a father and son, belonging to the very poorest section of village society, conversing about the impending death of the son's wife in childbirth. You are struck by the matter-of-fact and unfeeling way in which they speak of the dying woman, with only an occasional conventional comment on her goodness. When she finally dies, they turn their attention to how to collect the money to buy a shroud, and having at length with great difficulty raised it, go into a liquor shop on their way and spend the money they have collected. The story ends with their half-drunken conversation as they come out of the liquor shop.

This story marked a new stage in the development of Premchand's social and political views, and his adoption of an outlook strongly influenced by modern socialism. A year later, he consented to preside over the first session of the newly formed Progressive Writers Association in 1936. For two decades before its foundation, he had blazed the trail for the best

90 A LIFE IN URDU

of the prose fiction that the PWA writers were to produce. It is a matter of profound regret that he died shortly after writing *Kafan*. If he had lived a few years more, I am sure he would have produced work markedly superior to the great work which we already have, and by which he will be remembered, not only in his country, but—as translations into other languages make his work available in other continents—throughout the world.

[Editor's note: A translation of *Bazar e Husn* was published in 2003, with the title *Courtesan's Quarter*. The translator is Amina Afzar, and Ralph wrote the Foreword.]

7

Popular Literature

1973

There are kinds of literature in Urdu that in my view, deserve more attention than they have hitherto been paid, either by Urdu speakers or by those of us in the West who are able to read them. For want of a better word, I call this 'Popular Literature'. Other kinds of literature are also popular, that is, widely read and appreciated; but this kind is popular in another sense, in that it appeals primarily to a plebian audience. Much of it is the written record, by anonymous writers, of stories that were current long before anyone wrote them down. At bus stations and on railway platforms all over North India and Pakistan, you can buy cheap booklets, printed on newsprint, with these kinds of stories.

Let me introduce what I am about to say by making a very broad and arbitrary classification of the literature of the whole world. Broadly speaking, there are three kinds. The first is classical literature (and in that, I include modern classics as well as ancient classics). The second is folk literature, produced by unlettered people—some very fine, very well worth reading, such as the folk tales of many countries and the compositions of folk poets. The third kind, which is perhaps something in between, has never had the attention from serious students of literature that I think it merits. In this, I would include, for example, in terms of modern English literature, the best kind of detective writing. Even in the most comprehensive histories of English literature, you won't find the works of Mary Kelly or of Agatha Christie, and I firmly believe that they should be discussed, for they are not just a part of literature but one which can appeal to all classes of society.

The fact that classical literature is much greater literature doesn't make these other kinds unimportant. It is an interesting thing that if popular literature is old and respectable enough, it *is* classed as literature. The

A Life in Urdu, Edited and with a Foreword by Marion Molteno, Oxford University Press. © Oxford University Press India 2023. DOI: 10.1093/oso/9789391050948.003.0007

92 A LIFE IN URDU

medieval romances of Europe are an example. There is no real plot, none of the careful characterization, none of the kind of things that the advocates of realism demand, but nevertheless, people accept it as literature.

Urdu has this kind of literature too, and in abundant supply. Its medieval romances appear in the *dastan*. The word means simply 'story' or 'tale', but it is used primarily for enormous cycles of medieval romance, the most famous being that which relates the exploits of the legendary champion of Islam, Amir Hamza. Like the Christian knight of medieval European romance, he rides through the pages of the tale fighting for the true faith against unbelievers, witches, and sorcerers, and emerging triumphant over seeming insuperable difficulties. Within this enormous cycle, the most popular section in India was a story called *Tilism-i-Hoshruba*, which means literally 'the enchantment which steals away the senses'. That story alone comprises seven tall volumes totalling 7,500 pages. (The totals for the complete *Tale of Amir Hamza* are 18 volumes of nearly 16,500 pages.) This work, which is quite outstanding in its way, is barely mentioned in any of the works on Urdu literature; and yet in my view, it holds a position of essential importance in the development of modern prose narrative in Urdu.

The stories on which the *dastan* is based seem almost certainly traditional in origin, going back several centuries. One Indian tradition was that the *Tale of Amir Hamza* was written in Persian by Faizi, the great courtier of the Mughal Emperor Akbar, but the stories themselves are almost certainly much older, and had been popular as oral literature long before the *dastan* assumed its present shape. In the second half of the eighteenth century, they were recited at the courts of the nobles but also before more plebian audiences, in much the same way as their Arabic counterparts were once recited in Egypt, and the rhythmical prose, with its rhyming phrases, surely owes much of its origin to this tradition of recitation. We owe our present versions in Urdu in part to the phenomenal memories of two of the most famous *dastan*-reciters of old Lucknow, Mir Muhammad Husain Jah and Ahmad Husain Qamar, and they were committed to writing at the instance of Newal Kishore, the founder of a press in Lucknow which has performed inestimable services to Urdu literature. According to the Newal Kishore Press, the reciters would come to the Press every day and recite the stories, and the scribes would write them down.

The appeal of the *dastans* in their own time is closely comparable to that of the romances of medieval Europe, which Cervantes parodied in *Don Quixote,* or stories like those in *A Thousand and One Nights,* which transcended cultures to become popular with readers of different ages and across continents. They can justly be called propagandist literature—everything is in black and white—the virtuous are all virtue and the vicious all vice. There are no three-dimensional characters, and very little realism of any kind. The storyline is a succession of episodes following one another in endless profusion. The *dastans* flowered in the second half of the eighteenth century, when the Mughal Empire was in headlong decline, and they probably had the appeal of escapist literature anywhere. At a time when every principle of conduct in the medieval code was everywhere and every day being violated, people who knew no other code (including those who were daily offending against it) could escape from the sordid reality around them into a world where everything was splendidly simple and where the true Muslim warrior not only behaved unfailingly as a true Muslim should, but by doing so achieved the most eminently satisfactory results. Moreover, the multiple authors of the *dastans* had made provision for pleasing changes in diet. In the *Tale of Amir Hamza,* the hero is accompanied and supported in his exploits by his trusty friend Amar Ayyar—Amar the Artful—who possesses magic powers and uses them to reinforce Amir Hamza's valour. He does this mainly through the use of his magic bag Zanbil into which he can cause almost anything to disappear and out of which he can cause almost anything to emerge. Very often, he uses his magic to make his enemies look ridiculous, and his function in the tale is thus, to a large extent, to give comic relief from the prevailing atmosphere of high seriousness. Relief of another kind is provided by episodes with a love interest, in which the Islamic warriors' amorous adventures are related, often in circumstantial and titillating detail. (Their conduct in these scenes is not quite perhaps that which strict adherence to Islam would permit, but everyone seems to have been too absorbed to notice this.)

I haven't read everything in those thousands of pages but I have read enough to be firmly convinced that there is writing of good quality in this huge work, writing of a degree of excellence and of interest that would appeal to an English audience.

94   A LIFE IN URDU

Another kind of popular literature comes in stories told about figures who might have had real originals in history, but have now become just familiar vehicles for often humorous anecdotes. The *Akbar and Birbal* stories often have a punch line in which Birbal, the Hindu minister of the Mughal Emperor Akbar, is presented with an apparently insoluble problem and turns the tables on his master. Similar are the stories of *Mullah Dopiaza* (Birbal's rival) and *Shaikh Cilli*. Some in the same genre are not attributed to any particular figure, but often celebrate, with great satisfaction, situations in which ordinary people have kept their end up, or even scored against those who exercise autocratic and arbitrary powers over them. Another popular theme is mocking the purveyors of superstition.

Then there is a work called *Qassas ul Anbiya*, Tales of the Prophets, said to be by Ghulam Nabi, but the stories he has written down come from much older, anonymous Persian originals. No doubt there are Arabic counterparts as well. The book has long been famous and continues to be very popular but has never been considered literature, and I think it is fair to say that even today, hardly anybody speaking about Urdu literature would consider it worthy of attention. I am profoundly convinced that it is. I think there are two reasons why it has not been so considered. The custodians of the Islamic faith have always disapproved of it. Considered purely as religious literature, one must respect their objections to it because it gives currency to all kinds of fanciful tales about the prophets. The historians of literature have given no attention to it partly because they share the feelings of the Muslim divines, and partly because they regard its readers as belonging to too low a class of Urdu speakers to be worthy of their attention. Well, I think that there is a lot in this book that would appeal if considered purely as literature. If selections from it were available in translation, English readers would put it in the same class of literature as the *Thousand and One Nights*. It is in fact a very interesting book—not, as it stands, a work of folk literature, but clearly bearing the marks of folk influences. Many of the stories add vivid detail to the outlined versions which one finds in the Quran, and supply answers to questions that the Quran's references may have given rise to in the ordinary Muslim's mind. It tells all manner of tales of all the Muslim prophets and includes amongst them some whom perhaps no true Muslim would consider as a prophet at all.

POPULAR LITERATURE 95

Many of these stories were well known to classical poets, and allusions to them are common in their work. One tells the story of the creation of Adam and the loss of Paradise, with the concept, central in Islamic belief, that Adam was created by God to be his *khalifa*—a word generally translated by the rather unusual English word 'vicegerent', one who 'acts for' the authority that appoints him. (Neither 'representative' nor 'deputy' nor 'plenipotentiary' conveys the exact sense.) In another of the book's long chapters, it tells the story of Alexander the Great, who in the Muslim world is known by the name of Sikandar. God knows where the person who first told the story got it from—it has nothing to do with religion, but it has nothing offensive to religion either. It's an interesting story, and has many kinships with the sort of episode you will find in European folk tales, for instance. Traditionally Sikandar is identified with the ruler whom the Quran calls 'Dhool Karnain', but these stories add much that is not found there, especially the best known of all the Sikandar stories, that of his search for the water of life with someone called 'Khizar'. Khizar is generally identified with an unnamed person who appears in a passage in the Quran immediately before the account of Sikandar, and who explained certain of God's actions to Moses.

An interesting indication of the popularity of this kind of literature is given in Ashraf Ali Thanavi's book *Bihishti Zewar,* in which he sets out to tell the average Muslim woman everything she needs to know, from how to write, keep household accounts, and treat simple illnesses, to the doctrines of her faith—and lists of books which she should on no account read. This last is especially interesting because it shows how widely these books *were* read and how great was their influence. They are still very popular and you can buy them, for example, in any small shop in Delhi in the region of the Jama Masjid. Some idea of the extent and depth of its influence is given by the fact that at one time, a copy of *Bihishti Zewar* commonly accompanied the Holy Quran as part of a young Urdu-speaking wife's dowry.

On my first study leave in India, 1949–1950, I encountered another immensely popular form of short literature, the writings of Kwaja Hasan Nizami (1878–1955). This remarkable man was the spiritual successor of the medieval saint Nizam-ud-Din, and as the incumbent of his famous shrine on the outskirts of Delhi, he was the spiritual guide to hundreds of thousands of men and women from all walks of life. They looked

96   A LIFE IN URDU

unquestioningly to him for guidance in every aspect of their lives, and he provided this in a stream of pamphlets on an enormous range of subjects. Their purpose was didactic, but the moral tales were embodied in lively stories about everyday things, sometimes starting out as radio broadcasts.

Few scholars of Urdu would consider his writing 'literature', but the examples I have seen have qualities that make them definitely worth reading. They are full of lively accounts of situations most people can relate to, and because he always bore in mind that he needed to reach a mass audience, he expressed himself forthrightly in simple, but extremely effective language in the pure idiom of Delhi, which it is a joy to read. A typical example was given in a letter he wrote to me in response to a report he had seen in *Nai Roshni* of a talk I had given, with what, at that stage (aged 31), I thought were profound thoughts on the future of Urdu. He thought that I was too pessimistic and said that 'his tongue was not harmed by the action of the thirty-two teeth that enclosed it, and the dangers to Urdu were no greater'. He said, 'I am now 74 years old, but even now I write a book of 16 pages every day, and have announced that before I die I will write 100,000 books'. In view of the immense number, he had already written this did not seem too unrealistic an aim.

I have long felt that it was high time that people like me, and others with the expertise to undertake translation, presented something of this kind to the English-reading world.

[Editor's note: You can read examples of each of these kinds of literature in Ralph's translations in *A Thousand Yearnings*. In 2007, a year before his death, an unabridged translation of *Dastan i Amir Hamza* was published for the first time. See Sources & References.]

8

Remarkable Women—Two Memoirs

2002–2006

Anis Kidwai: *Adazi ki Chhaon Mein*

This is a memoir by a remarkable woman of the dramatic and tragic times she lived through and participated in. It relates the harrowing events of 1947, in which she played a part. She was forty years old at the time; it was another twenty-seven years before the original Urdu was published—1974—but it is based upon her own write-up of the numerous notes she had made from day to day in the course of her activities, which gives it a fresh, immediate quality. It's a wonderful book—an account of her constant, unceasing efforts to help all the people—Muslims, Hindus, Sikhs, and everyone else—who suffered so terribly in the riots of 1947 and the days that followed. Her deep human sympathy is evident throughout, and her narrative impresses me as completely honest. Her sympathy for Hindu and Sikh refugees from Pakistan is no less than her sympathy for the Muslim victims of Hindu and Sikh violence.

I first heard about it in 1998 when my friend Urvashi Butalia, from the publisher Kali for Women, asked me if I would undertake the translation. Although I had never read it, I heard enough about it to feel that translating it would be a very worthwhile enterprise. I quickly read it from cover to cover, and as soon as I had finished reading it, I immediately started translating. I promised Urvashi I would translate it for her as soon as I could make time for it.

I had been asked to 'translate and edit' the book and acted accordingly. First, I eliminated some repetition, which arose from the fact that it was compiled from her original notes. (For example, there are two separate accounts of the fate of some of the villages near Delhi, and I have composited these into a single account.) Anis Qidvai has, like most Urdu writers,

A Life in Urdu. Edited and with a Foreword by Marion Molteno, Oxford University Press. © Oxford University Press India 2023. DOI: 10.1093/oso/9789391050948.003.0008

interspersed her narrative with Urdu and Persian verses, some of which have become proverbial (in which case it is rarely possible to trace their origin) while others are from famous Urdu poets. Urdu readers would at once recognize them and appreciate them, but I added notes for English readers who might be interested to know their source. Other notes were needed because the writer, quite correctly, assumed a knowledge of things with which her readers who had lived through the events she described would be familiar, but which would not be familiar to English readers, or even to South Asian readers who perhaps had not even been born at the time.

To give you some idea of the chaotic situation she and her friends were working in, here is a brief extract from my translation:

Jamila Begam was spending all day in an ambulance going the rounds picking up the sick and the wounded and taken them to hospital. Whenever a special train was ready to go to Pakistan the relative [of the wounded] would raise an outcry, 'Hand over our relatives to us right away. We'll take them along with us.' She had to keep with her a list of people whose relatives were lost or who had died so that she could read it out and tell people how many had died or what had become of them. Injured people came running to the hospital from the city. Sometimes the police or the army brought the injured to put them in the camp hospital. Then many people who'd been thrown from the trains brought their broken bones and injured bodies here. So both in the camp and in the city the hospitals were full.

One morning I too went with Jamila Begam. For some days both of us had been worried about the children. A lot of women came from the [Christian] missions and we thought that they must have collected the children. 'Why shouldn't we make some arrangement for the orphan children?' we thought. What was happening was this. On days when a train was leaving for Pakistan innumerable children would get onto it. Their parents were often left behind while the children, in their eagerness to make the journey, would go off on their own. Sometimes the parents would go off and the children would be left behind at the station. God knows what happened to these children when they got to Pakistan, or whether they got to their parents or died on the journey. Anyway, with this plan in mind we went to Irwin Hospital. There wasn't much time but we made a rough survey of the whole situation and noted how many children there were there.

The ambulance that had brought us had left and was due back in an hour's time after leaving patients at another hospital. So we thought that while we were waiting we should go down and sit in the office and plan what we could do. But before we'd even begun to talk about this a second ambulance arrived and lots of people got very agitated and began asking, 'When?' 'How?' When we enquired we were told that a health visitor, Dr Mufti, had been murdered while doing the rounds in Paharganj and it was the corpse's severed limbs that were being taken out of the ambulance. I at once sat down. A strange sensation ran through my body. Jamila, clutching her head with both hands, was saying, 'It's the limit. It's too much. They've even killed someone who's a servant of the Government of India.' But God knows what she was saying after that—I couldn't hear it. Now it was impossible for me to stay any longer. I implored Jamila, 'Please, for God's sake, phone my home and tell them to send a car. God knows when the ambulance will come. I can't bear to stay here any longer.' In our agitation we repeatedly got the wrong number, but eventually we got through and a car came and took us away.

I was so affected by this incident that for several days I couldn't summon up the courage to think about the children. And we were faced with another major difficulty. If we took the children where would we keep them? Jamila Begam's home was empty and she suggested that we get the government to give us a guard from the army and we could keep the children there. But we had no friends and no women helpers to whose care we could hand them over.

One cannot be otherwise than shocked by the harrowing events that the book relates. But a reader who knows Urdu can also not fail to enjoy the beautiful Urdu in which it is written, and to admire the frankness with which she has told her story. She does not whitewash anyone—a quality which is found all too rarely in writing on these themes.

The book has been translated into Hindi, though not, I believe, into other Indian languages—but not yet into English. I much regret that I did not know of it long enough ago to produce a translation during Begum Anis Kidwai's lifetime. If a translation could have been done and

100 A LIFE IN URDU

published during her lifetime, it could have brought her the acclaim she so richly deserved from many thousands of people who are only now able to see her greatness.

[Editor's Note: Ralph left a typescript of 100 pages of his translation, but to his regret the project was never completed. After his death the book was translated by Ayesha Kidwai, granddaughter of Anis Kidwai, and published as *In Freedom's Shade*.]

* * *

Shaukat Kaifi: *Yad ki Rahguzar*

This is a very remarkable book. It is a memoir, published in 2006, recounting the story of the life-long, loving and committed relationship between Shaukat Kaifi and her husband, the poet Kaif Azmi. For me, it has a special interest, which I should perhaps begin by declaring.

I knew of Kaifi Azmi from my first year's study leave in India in 1949–1950, and I first met him at that time. He was a leading Urdu poet in the Progressive Writers' Association, and in addition, there was the attraction that we were both members of our respective communist parties, and very dedicated members at that. Shaukat writes of him (p. 217) 'He always carried his Party card in his briefcase and would often take it out and say proudly 'This is my most valuable capital'. I last met him in the late 90s in Lucknow where we were both participants in a seminar on Faiz. I asked him then whether he was still a party member. He said, 'Yes, card-carrying'.

I think it relevant to say all this because, obviously, he looms large in this book. But until after his death, I never knew that he was married, or that Shabana Azmi, the famous film star, was his daughter. Even then, I did not know anything about his wife until I received this book.

I began reading it as soon as it arrived, and it held my interest to the end. Its most striking quality is a sort of naivety, a naivety of a very positive and admirable kind. It seems that Shaukat has never been a communist party member, but to me, this doesn't matter—I realized more than fifty years ago that (obviously) not every good person is a communist and (much more important) that not every communist is a good person. It's the good people who are to be valued and Shaukat is emphatically one of these. Like Kaifi, she has had a lifelong commitment to a sincere and honest life in which she exploited no one and worked constantly for the well-being of the common people, and against those who oppress and exploit them. For her, this is what politics is all about. In her long and active life, she has known scores, if not hundreds, of well-known left-wingers, but she makes no 'party political' (so to speak) judgements of any of them, because it is their personal qualities and the way they relate to her that concerns her. For instance, in the terrible days of Ranadive's domination of the communist party (1947–1950), she expresses no opinion of the political line, but speaks of the way in which in that period, everyone came to suspect everyone else, and of the distress this caused her. Incidentally, the book gives a vivid picture of communist party life before Ranadive's advent to power, a way of life which I myself witnessed at close quarters when I was in India both in 1943–1945 and 1949–1950. Joining Kaifi in this involved considerable material sacrifices on her part, but she did so as a matter of course.

An early part of the book gives a vivid picture of her girlhood and youth in Hyderabad (in Andhra Pradesh) and goes on to describe how she fell in love, virtually at first sight, with Kaifi and he with her. No other book that I know of has done anything like this, and the picture is a fascinating one, in which one sees the mingling of traditional, conventional social Muslim values with the intense romanticism which these produce in those who break with them. Thus, before Kaifi even declares his love for her, he responds to her speaking of a marriage that has been arranged for him by telling her (p. 40) 'I will never marry', without adding the unspoken words 'anyone but you'. And she tells us how soon after this she wrote to him, 'I love you Kaifi, I love you boundlessly. No power in the world can stop me coming to you—no mountain, no river, no sea, no people, no sky, no angel, no God'—adding, with a touch of humour, 'and God knows what else'. Later, when, not knowing that her letters to him had been intercepted by her family, he feels that she is no longer writing to him and no longer loves him, he cuts his wrist and writes her a letter in his blood. Their marriage caused a breach between her father and her

102   A LIFE IN URDU

mother. Her mother, as a believer in traditional values, never expresses in words her strong disapproval of her husband's support for their daughter, but does not speak to him for a whole month.

To those who do not know that supremely popular genre of Urdu poetry—the ghazal—the extravagant romanticism of this story may seem a bit over the top. To those who do know the ghazal, it presents a wonderful picture of the love which the ghazal portrays, brought fully to life, so to speak, with all the main ghazal characters identified and introduced to the reader—the lovers, their sympathizers, and the stern upholders of convention (in this case Shaukat's own family) who do all they can to thwart the lovers.

Kaifi and Shaukat are both communists—that she is not a part member is not significant—and live their lives in accordance with communist principles as they understand them. Shaukat writes (p. 210): 'Kaifi was not only my husband, he was my friend who never imposed his own wishes on me and never made me do anything I didn't want to do. He always respected my wishes and my desires. He always tried to help me to go forward, achieve fame, be independent, and win people's praise'.

Shaukat is an actor, and has a long career both on the stage and in films from 1944 to 1988, and Kaifi is fully involved and fully supportive of her. Occasional disagreements are not concealed, and are resolved by happy compromise. Thus, when after many years, they acquire a house of their own, they discuss how it is to be furnished (p. 148). Shaukat thought Kaifi's suggestions were absurd, and, she writes, 'He thought mine were. Kaifi was a keen gardener and we agreed that he should do what he liked with the garden and I should do what I liked with the house'.

Sometimes they seem to have been guided, perhaps quite unconsciously, by more traditional values. Shaukat is not a conventionally religious person, but she believes in the power of prayer. In 1973, when Kaifi suffered an attack (which eventually left his left arm paralysed) and his life was in danger, she says (p. 55), 'Of all his many friends, Muslim, Hindu and Sikh, there was not one who did not go to his mosque or temple or gurdvara to pray for him, and it was the effect of their prayers that he gradually recovered consciousness'. Much later on in the story, when Kaifi decides that they should leave Bombay and spend the rest of their lives in Mijwan, the extremely backward village in which Kaifi had spent his boyhood and youth, one wonders whether it is only their great mutual love which determines what they do. She says of this decision (pp. 199–200): 'The object of his life was to change the world, to banish poverty, hunger and ignorance. But when he saw that to change the whole world would take a very long time, he turned to his village. And there he did indeed achieve a huge transformation.'

Anyway, the husband decides and the wife accepts. Shaukat merely comments (p. 187): 'I was living very comfortably in Bombay, and besides, I had always been a town dweller and the thought of living in a village filled me with dismay. But I knew that Kaifi would never change his mind. What could I do?' So that was that. She did live in Mijwan and worked shoulder to shoulder with Kaifi to achieve improvements in village life which in quality and quantity seem almost miraculous. And in all this, their unflagging efforts were paralleled by an equally unwavering patience. She clearly concurs with Kaifi's words to their daughter (p. 217), 'When you are working for change you must realise that the change may not come in your lifetime, but even so you must keep working for it.'

There is much else in this book that will interest readers, including her relationship with their two children, which is also determined both by her traditional and modern values. Those more knowledgeable than I about her career as a famous actress will find the full list of the plays and films in which she has performed.

When I first read it in the Urdu original, I learned from the foreword that Nasreen Rahman had translated it into English, but I had not seen the translation. Now I have. It is an excellent translation, and I am very happy to have had the opportunity, at the translator's own request, to sit with her and help her finalize it. I am delighted that through it, Shaukat's story will be available to a much larger audience than the Urdu original could reach.

9

Urdu Poetry Versus the Fundamentalists

2001

In the wake of the appalling terrorist attack on America, there are millions of people who think that the 'enemy' is not only Osama bin Laden and the Taliban but Islam itself. It isn't. Edward Said wrote in an article published immediately after 11 September that there is more than one Islam (and more than one America). Indeed there is, and it is on this that I want to comment.

In Urdu poetry, there is an Islam that runs clean counter to the Islam of the Taliban. I am not a Muslim, but I have spent long periods of my life living amongst Muslims in India and Pakistan and the greater part of my life studying Urdu, the vehicle of one of the greatest branches of their literature. In the course of it, I developed a great love and regard for its poetry and for the major values which that poetry expresses. It is rarely concerned with propaganda for Islam, and where it is, it is for an Islam as different from that of the fundamentalists as chalk is from cheese. Its values derive from the tradition of Sufism—Islamic mysticism—a tradition almost as old as Islam itself. Sufism preaches the religion of love, of which love of God and love of His human creation are two facets of the same thing.

The most popular part of Urdu poetry is the ghazal, which is infused with these concepts. Thanks largely to Hindi films, ghazal poetry is loved by millions of non-Muslims and millions of non-Urdu speakers. It deserves to be. Its message is one of vigorous humanism and of loathing and contempt for fundamentalism.

It has a long pedigree. Its classical forbear was Persian, as Latin was the classical forbear of the languages of Western Europe, and already in the thirteenth century, the great Persian poet Sadi was declaring:

A Life in Urdu. Edited and with a Foreword by Marion Molteno, Oxford University Press. © Oxford University Press India 2023. DOI: 10.1093/oso/9789391050948.003.0009

URDU POETRY VERSUS THE FUNDAMENTALISTS 105

The religious path is nothing but the service of humanity.

A century later, the even more celebrated Persian poet Hafiz wrote:

Do not distress your fellow men and do what else you will
For in my holy law there is no other sin than this

And a verse well known in Iran, sometimes attributed to Hafiz, says

Drink wine, learn the Quran, throw fire into the Kaba
Dwell in the temple of idols—but do not harm your fellow men.

Mir, the eminent eighteenth-century poet of Urdu, echoes Hafiz's words:

Go to the mosque; stand knocking at the door
Live all your days with drunkards in their den
Do anything you want to do, my friend
But do not seek to harm your fellow men.

Exaggeration of this kind is common in Islamic poetry. Of course, the poet does not mean that he wants you to do all these things—but he wants you to realize that harming your fellow men is a greater sin than any of them. Muslims know they are carrying out their religious duties if refraining from drinking wine, revere the Quran, and if possible, perform the pilgrimage. But if along with all these things they distress others, then all those virtuous deeds cannot atone for the single sin of causing distress to their fellow men.

It may be useful to say something about the background to all this. Ghazal poetry grew out of the traditions of Islamic mysticism, and the ghazal poets were the spokesmen for the mystics. To the true mystics, the formalities of religion are unimportant. Love of God and of God's human creation is all. There are points of connection with almost all other religions, such as the Hindu tradition of *bhakti* and the forceful poetry of Kabir. For Christians, the message of Islamic humanism has exact parallels in the Bible—'For all the law is fulfilled in one word, even in this: Thou shalt love thy neighbour as thyself' (Galatians, 5.14). And St Augustine's

106 A LIFE IN URDU

succinct 'Love, and do what you will', uncannily prefigures the couplet of Hafiz, which I quoted previously.

In the vocabulary of ghazal poets, fundamentalist doctrines are attacked through the person of the 'shaikh' and his colleague, the 'vaiz'— the preacher—who disseminates them. From Mir's time onwards, both shaikh and preacher have been the object of ridicule and contempt. Mir writes:

> If pilgrimage could make a man a man
> Then all the world might make the pilgrimage.
> But shaikh-ji is just back, and look at him
> As ass he went: an ass he has returned.

The man is such a dunce that he cannot even understand what Mir is telling him:

> Mir's every word has meaning beyond meaning
> More than a worthless shaikh can understand.

The preacher too comes under attack:

> I grant you, sir, the preacher is an angel.
> To be a man now—that's more difficult.

The shaikh has his counterpart in the Hindu Brahmin. Keep away from them both, says Mir:

> Mir, quit the company of shaikh and Brahmin
> And mosque and temple too—leave them behind.

Prayer, fasting, pilgrimage, and so on (the 'five pillars' of Islam) are in Islamic theology called *huquq ul Allah*—the rights of God. But there are also in Muslim theology *huquq ul ibad*—the rights of God's servants, i.e. of humankind—which may be summed up in the golden rule that you must treat your fellows as you would wish them to treat you; and that is to *all* your fellow human beings, Muslims, Christians, Jews, Hindus, Sikhs, and atheists. It is orthodox Islamic teaching that God may forgive shortcomings in giving Him His due, but will not forgive shortcomings in giving His servants their due, until they whose rights have been violated grant *their* forgiveness.

Linked to this concept is another very important one—that if, for example, you say your prayers and perform the pilgrimage, these actions in themselves have no importance—they matter only if you love God, and this love obliges you to worship God by these means. If saying your prayers means no more than repeating Arabic words you have learnt by rote and performing certain movements of your body, or if you say your prayers to show that you are a much better Muslim than others, then your prayers are not only useless but harmful, and have nothing to do with true Islam. This is the idea behind these verses of Mir:

> He went to Mecca and to Medina and to Karbala
> —and came back just the same as he had gone.

And:

> Don't be deceived by shaikh-ji's prayers
> He is just setting down a burden he's been carrying on his head.

Let me again stress that the poet doesn't mean that you should not say your prayers or not go on the pilgrimage. He means that the value of prayer—or fasting—or any other of the duties binding upon Muslims depends on the emotion you feel when you do these things. Someone who prays with a feeling of superiority to others and to 'prove' how devout they are, in a way insults God, because this outward observance conceals a feeling which can in no way be regarded as justified by Islam.

These attitudes are also expressed through what one might call the inclusive humanism of the Sufi concept of Islam—that is, that 'man'— for which read 'humankind'—all people are God's creation—and to be valued, regardless of who they are or what religion they adhere to. Mir has many verses of this kind:

> What have the angels got to do with man?
> The highest rank belongs to him alone

108   A LIFE IN URDU

And

> Man, formed of clay, gave lustre to this mirror.
> No one would have looked into it but for him.

['this mirror' being the universe, which is the mirror of God's beauty]
A century later, Ghalib wrote:

> The object of creation was mankind and nothing else.
> We are the point round which the seven compasses revolve.

[the 'seven compasses' refers to the 'seven skies', whose revolution was thought to determine our fate.] And this is not 'just poetry'. In one of his letters, Ghalib writes: 'I hold all mankind to be my kin and look upon all men—Muslim, Hindu, Christian—as my brothers, no matter what others may think'.

Half a century later, Hali wrote:

> The first lesson of the Book of Guidance was
> The whole human race is God's family.

Through into the twentieth-century poets continued to stress that all true lovers of God are a single community, regardless of the name by which they call Him. Akbar Ilahabadi writes:

> His radiance fills the Kaba, He lies hidden in the temple
> It is to Him we cry, whether as Allah or as Ram

And Iqbal, by far the most popular Urdu poet of the twentieth century, says:

> The infidel with a wakeful heart bowing before his idol
> Is better than the religious Muslim asleep in the mosque.

And so on and so on, and—as far as I am aware—up to the present day.

Mainstream orthodox Muslims have always been, and still are, uncomfortable with the Sufi tradition. Fundamentalists and revivalists like those of the Tablighi movement, in exhorting people to be good Muslims, lay almost exclusive emphasis on Islam's external observances. Sufism stresses, and very strongly too, that the formal observances of Islam are worthless unless they are inspired by the love of God, a love which necessarily involves love for God's creation, humankind—all humankind; not just the Muslim section of it—and not by a self-seeking desire for human approval. There is nothing unorthodox about this, a fact that the theologian al-Ghazali (AD 1058–1111) demonstrated to the satisfaction of most Muslims centuries ago.

I have given examples from the poets of Urdu and Persian, and primarily from the classical poets, because those are the ones I know best. But these are themes in many of the languages of the Indian subcontinent. In Pushtu, Sindhi, and Punjabi poetry, the mystic, humanist concept of Islam is all-pervasive, and millions upon millions of people, literate and illiterate alike, are familiar with it and influenced by it. To which, regrettably, one must add that though most of them like this message, they don't allow it to have much impact on their daily lives—rather like Christians who have for centuries sung the praises of God because 'He hath put down the mighty from their seat and hath exalted the humble and meek', but continue to support the mighty in their seats and have no sympathy with those who seriously commit themselves to exalting the humble and meek. And of course the shaikhs are still playing their accustomed role of intimidating those who do not toe their line.

Muslims familiar with this heritage of humanist values in the poetry that they love need to publicly champion these values. Fundamentalists use (and misuse) Islamic sources to justify their actions—and Islamic sources must be used to combat and defeat them. There is material in abundance, aside from all the sources in Islamic poetry—in the Quran, Islamic theology, and the Hadith (records of the words and actions of Muhammad). I have said more on this in my article 'An Infidel Among Believers'.

Some years ago, I made these points in a series of letters published in the UK Urdu language daily newspaper, *Jang* (December 1980–January 1981.) Numbers of my Muslim acquaintances, some of them in quite influential positions in their community, congratulated me on these letters and declared their complete agreement with them. To which I must regretfully add that not one of them was willing to declare this publicly, in

110 A LIFE IN URDU

print. The nearest response that I have seen was expressed in articles by Akbar S. Ahmad. These stressed the importance of the Sufi tradition in Islam with its doctrine of love for all humankind; what he did *not* do was tell his readers how forthrightly many of the adherents of this tradition had, over the centuries, attacked their bigoted co-religionists. Yet such a forthright attack cannot be avoided if the message of mutual understanding and mutual tolerance is to prevail.

As for non-Muslims, it's important to be aware of this humanist Islam, and deeply appreciative of it—and to do all we can to make those around us familiar with it. And while they are about it, both Hindus and Christians would do well to reflect too that they have a fundamentalism nearer home, a bigoted Hindu or a bigoted Christian fundamentalism, which needs to be combatted with the same zeal as we should combat Muslim fundamentalism.

10

On Translating Ghalib

1969

Ghalib, the 'Difficult Poet'

In one of his verses, Ghalib described himself as 'collyrium for men's eyes', freely offered to them to make their vision cleaner. In the century and more since he spoke this verse, many thousands of his fellow countrymen have accepted this gift from him, and given him in return the only gift he asked—the knowledge that his fit had indeed sharpened their vision and enabled them to see things they had not been able to see before.

From the time of his death, those who have loved his work have sought ways to make the wealth that he offers more widely accessible. The task has not been easy. There is no denying that Ghalib is, on the whole, a difficult poet. He himself knew this well, and even in his own day, much of his poetry was inaccessible to his contemporaries. One reason—but far from the only one—is that he wrote much of his work, both prose and verse, in Persian. In the days when Persian was the language of culture of the greater part of the Islamic world, this would have given him an audience over a vast area; but in his day, people beyond the borders of India had ceased to be greatly interested in what Indians produced, while within India Persian had already yielded place to Urdu as the favoured medium of poetry. Men whose fathers and grandfathers would have approved of Ghalib's choice of medium no longer possessed the literary taste, or indeed, even the knowledge of the language to appreciate what he wrote. When he wrote in Persian, he wrote for a few, and he never ceased to lament that even to these few, much of what he wrote went uncomprehended and unappreciated.

What he wrote in Urdu—his own and his fellows' mother tongue— sometimes struck his audience as equally difficult to follow. Both his

A Life in Urdu. Edited and with a Foreword by Marion Molteno, Oxford University Press. © Oxford University Press India 2023. DOI: 10.1093/oso/9789391050948.003.0010

112   A LIFE IN URDU

thought and the language in which he expressed it were often complex. And finally, even when his language was clear and simple, what he had to say was often beyond the imaginative reach of his listeners in his own day. Here, and here alone perhaps, we in a later time have the advantage over his contemporaries. For much of Ghalib's thought is remarkably modern, and there are important elements in it which we can expect to understand more readily than they could. Ghalib knew this, and prophesied the fate of his poetry in much-quoted Persian lines, which I have translated as:

> Today none buys my verse's wine, that it may grow in age
> To make the senses reel in many a drinker yet to come.
> My star rose highest in the firmament before my birth
> My poetry will win the world's acclaim when I am gone.

In Ghalib's own lifetime, much of his reputation rested more on what was known about his character than on a direct appreciation of his poetry. People knew about his personality from countless anecdotes of his wit and humour, which circulated orally long before they were written down. In the year of his death, the publication of the first collection of his informal letters to his friends enhanced his popularity still further, and for years these letters were the foundation of the regard in which he was increasingly held. Hali, his friend and younger contemporary, says, 'Wherever one looks, Ghalib's fame throughout India owes more to the publication of his Urdu prose [i.e. his letters] than it does to his Urdu verse or to his Persian verse of prose. True, people generally already regarded him as a very great Persian poet and thought of his Urdu verse too as the poetry of a high order beyond the comprehension of the ordinary reader; but these opinions were based on hearsay and not on their own reading'.

Hali's *Yadgar i Ghalib* (Memoir of Ghalib)—a book justly regarded as a classic of Urdu literature—published in 1897, nearly a generation after Ghalib's death, contributed further to this process. In it, he relates the story of Ghalib's life briefly, enlivening his account with an abundance of anecdotes that reveal Ghalib's personality so vividly. The *Memoir* also includes a sustained essay on Ghalib's Urdu poetry, illustrated by numerous quotations with detailed explanations and comments, and it was probably now for the first time that many of Hali's readers ventured to read some of the poetry themselves and tried to understand it. Since then, many others have contributed to the process Hali started, one of the earliest being Abdur Rahman Bijnori's vigorous essay *Mahasin i Kalam i Ghalib* (Beauties of the Verse of Ghalib), with its oft-quoted dictum that India has produced two inspired books—the *Vedas* and the divan (collection of verse) of Ghalib. Commentaries which explain every couplet in his divan have long been available and it is safe to say that almost all those who have read Ghalib's verse have needed to use these commentaries when they first began to study him.

To most of Ghalib's admirers, his Persian work is still a closed book (or to be more precise, two closed books, for his Persian verse and his Persian prose each occupies a substantial volume). In 1957, the centenary of the great revolt of 1857, stimulated the production of two Urdu translations of *Dastambu*, Ghalib's journal of 1857–1858, and since 1969 Urdu translations of much of the rest of his Persian prose have been published; but the task of making Ghalib's Persian verse accessible to Urdu readers was not undertaken until Sufi Tabassum wrote his commentary on the Persian ghazals.

When it took so long to introduce Ghalib adequately to his own intended Urdu-speaking audience, it is understandable that efforts to break through the language barrier for non-Urdu speakers came later. Most of those efforts had an intended audience of English-educated Indians and/or Pakistanis. Let me say first, that I do not think that these English versions are, in general, such as would fully satisfy an English-speaking public in countries where English is the mother tongue, and secondly, that this judgement by no means implies any hostility to them on my part. On the contrary, I consider that even the least adequate of these attempts deserves praise and appreciation. The best, in my view, is that of Muhammad Mujeeb, but anyone who has contributed something to the task of bringing Ghalib to a wider audience deserves praise.

I first made the acquaintance of Ghalib in the years 1946–1949 when studying for a degree in Urdu at the University of London. Although there was much in his verse that I didn't understand, I liked it from the start and from that time onwards, I hoped one day to make an attempt to introduce him to the English-speaking world. I count it my great good fortune that I met Khurshidul Islam only a year later and formed a close friendship with him that continued for the most part of forty years. My own work on Ghalib has been done in closest collaboration with him.

We have for many years believed that if once the barrier of language could be satisfactorily surmounted and Ghalib's prose and verse made available to a world audience, his work would win him a place in world literature which historical circumstance has hitherto denied him; and it is this belief which inspired us to make our own contribution to this. In translating, where every nuance of every word and phrase, in both the language of the original and that of the translation, can be important, we could do together what neither of us could do alone, for both of us know both languages well and each of us has one of them as his mother tongue. We could therefore hope to understand fully what the Urdu intends and to convey that intention as fully as English allows.

Together we aimed to enable an English reader to travel towards an understanding of Ghalib along much the same route as his fellow countrymen had traversed—that is, first through his letters and other prose writing, getting a picture of his life and personality, and only after that moving on to his poetry; and in both prose and poetry we have included both his Persian and Urdu work.

'Ghalib: Life and Letters'

The first outcome of our joint work was *Ghalib: Life and Letters*. In this, we sought to include everything of significant interest in his published prose, Persian and Urdu, excluding only those elements which are meaningful only to those with specialized knowledge. We tried wherever possible to let the story of Ghalib's life emerge from his own words. This was particularly possible for the last twenty years of his life, when there was a steady flow of Urdu letters and other writing which could tell their own story. In the earlier years, when there was less of Ghalib's own writing to draw on, we filled out the picture by drawing on Hali's near-contemporary *Memoir,* supplemented with material from more recent scholarly work. Where anything that Ghalib or Hali says requires elaboration if it is to be fully intelligible to the general reader in the English-speaking world, we have supplied it at once in the main text, including giving the historical background to events. We have as far as possible separated text from comment.

We have departed from tradition in the order in which we have arranged translations of the original material. Published collections of Ghalib's letters have always been arranged in such a way as to give all the letters to one person in a single block. Hali's materials are anecdotal, and the incidents it relates are not, for the most part, placed in any sort of historical order. As our aim was to enable all these materials to throw light on the development of Ghalib's life and thought, we have rearranged all this material in order of date.

The bulk of Ghalib's Urdu prose that has come down to us is in the form of letters to friends, and they are almost conversational in its style—informal and vivid. His colloquial Urdu presents its own problems for the translator, which I will not go into here, but what foreshadows more closely the problems of translating his verse is his Persian prose. Even when he used it for letters to friends, his Persian writing is of a highly formal, stylized kind, to which he devoted as much care as he did to his poetry. Hali begins his review of Ghalib's Persian prose with the remark that it differs from verse in only one respect— that it lacks regular metre, and that this enables it to be called 'prose' only in the Asian sense of the term. 'Otherwise, the poetic element in it appears more prominent than it does even in his verse'. There is a measure of exaggeration in the statement, but there is substance in it all the same. Ghalib imposed upon himself the most exacting standards when he sat down to write Persian prose, and his concern for appropriate diction, rhyme, rhythm, assonance, alliteration, and all kinds of verbal conceits is as evident as it is in his verse.

Critics have all too often assumed that because his language is carefully crafted, it is somehow lacking in sincerity and in natural appeal. That is a view that I emphatically do not share. Since Ghalib chose to write his Persian in this way, for me, it follows that as his translator, I should reproduce in my translation all those features which he valued in the original. But this is a matter of conscious choice. Translators can, if they think fit, disregard all this and translate into straightforward modern English. (For instance, Robert Graves did this in his translation from Latin of *Metamorphoses* of Apuleius, which he titled *The Golden Ass*.) I have tried to do just the opposite, reproducing in my translation all those features which Ghalib valued in the original. Two examples, that readers may turn to if they wish to see the results, are the letter with nostalgic memories of his youth in Agra, and the one in which he describes his reaction to his beloved's death (on pp. 29 and 43 of *Ghalib, Life and Letters*).

An age-old controversy in what may be called the theory of translation is involved here, well illustrated in the various English versions of *The Thousand and One Nights*. I am an unabashed champion of Richard Burton, who tried to give his English readers everything which the Arab audience found admirable in the Arabic original—and succeeded astonishingly well. The rhyming prose, the delight in the sheer exuberance of language, the repeated quotation of good, bad, and indifferent verse—are all there, and to remove them is to emasculate the work no less than the removal of the ribaldry does. Leaving aside the ribaldry, in which other issues are also involved, one can respect the decision of translators who consider that it is the essential content of the original that should be conveyed, and fear that if this is presented in unfamiliar trappings, it may prove an insuperable obstacle to the readers' appreciation. So they use an idiom and style familiar to the audience. What one cannot excuse is the amused contempt with which such translators have tended to speak of those who find that the styles of the original also appeal to them.

In medieval societies, writers and readers tended to think that written prose of the kind that moderns write, modelled essentially on the patterns of speech, was not worthy of consideration as literature. But modern readers may be guilty of the reverse prejudice if they reject all literary prose not written in the modern style. For myself, I can enjoy both kinds of writing and it seems to me that a cultivation of the ability to enjoy both is much to be desired and encouraged. Certainly, if the best products of the literature of all nations are to be enjoyed all over the world as they deserve to be, readers in both the east and the west will need to develop a broader taste, and break through the limitations which enable them to enjoy only what they have been taught it is permissible for them to enjoy.

It is these considerations that motivate me in formulating my own principles of translation. I applied them to the best of my ability in translating Ghalib's Persian and Urdu prose, and now do so in translating his verse.

On Translating Ghalib   117

Translating the Ghazal

Ghalib wrote poetry in several genres, but it is as a ghazal poet that he is best known, and the problems of translating the ghazal are formidable.

Many of the difficulties stem from the nature of the ghazal, and the restraints of the ghazal form. I know that there are admirers of Ghalib who do not think it is necessary to be bound by these considerations of form in their translations, and I can conceive that they can produce good translations of the essential meaning of a ghazal couplet on that basis. But I would also hold that such a translation would be less adequate than one which conforms at any rate to some of the basic features of the ghazal form. A translator tries to get as close as possible to an unrealizable ideal and to produce in English what Ghalib would have written had English, and not Urdu, been his mother tongue. Ghalib took it for granted that to write poetry meant to work within the strict forms that tradition had prescribed, and in my view, any translator who wants to do the fullest possible justice to him cannot ignore this. We too must write as far as possible within the limits of fairly clearly defined forms.

Having said that, let me at once add that a good deal of compromise is essential. To point the point in the most general terms, you must seek to impose the restrictions of form, but never to the point where the restrictions choke the poetry; and when in doubt, you should discard the restriction rather than injure the quality of the poetry.

How does this work out in translating the ghazal? The first thing to consider is that a ghazal consists of separate couplets, independent of each other where content is concerned, but cast in identical metre and bound together by a rhyme scheme that runs through that particular ghazal. Ideally, I would like to translate it into a form that maintains these features. But at each point, problems arise.

First, since the couplets are independent in meaning, do you have to translate whole ghazals? When translating into English from a language that uses similar genres of poetry, one would normally assume that one should translate the whole poem, because of its inherent unity of theme. Many translators from Urdu have assumed that they need to do this too with the ghazal.

We did not. In most cases, we have selected for translation what we feel to be the best verses and have left the rest. Does this matter? I think not.

118   A LIFE IN URDU

Hali—the first critic to bring to Urdu poetry both the expertise of an accomplished poet and the courage to assess his poetic heritage in the light of freshly thought out general values (however limited his attitudes may seem to us today)—said bluntly that ghazal poets were quite satisfied if they could compose two or three good verses to a ghazal, and were content not to spend much effort upon the rest. Ghalib himself treated his ghazals in the same way, discarding in later year verses which his mature judgement rejected as inadequate, and the residue still formed a ghazal. There is no good reason why we should not do the same.

Challenges of Switching Languages

Within each couplet, it is my job as a translator to change Ghalib's Urdu into English, but to change nothing that does not need to be changed—to leave nothing out, and to add nothing. This is a lot more difficult than it sounds.

A basic problem comes from the many nuances a word may carry, in any language. A key feature of ghazal poetry is the extreme conciseness of expression, and the power of poetic effects is often achieved through skilful choice of words with multiple connotations, so that much is implied in a very brief way. For each such word, I need to try to find a single word in English with a similar range; and if no such word exists, I have to choose the nearest possible. An Urdu speaker reading such a translation may feel that there are nuances that are left out—and that may be inevitable.

The alternative—which you see in many attempted translations—is that all those extra levels of meaning are included by using far more words than the original. Ghalib, like all the great ghazal poets, is often at pains to say little and suggest much, and the translation should do the same. It is no part of the translator's job to explain what the poet does not choose to explain. There should be no words in the translation which are not there or strongly implied in the original. Any explanation that is felt to be essential to contemporary readers should be given separately.

I will give a few examples of these difficulties, and show how I have tried to deal with them. First, on the connotations of each word. Sometimes the difficulty of finding a word-for-word correspondence arises because of

ON TRANSLATING GHALIB   119

differences in context, so that a word will not 'mean' to an English speaker what it 'means' to an Urdu speaker. Look, for instance, at the following couplet:

khushi kya? khet par mere agar sau baar abr aave
samajhta hun ki dhunde hai abhi se barq khirman ko

In trying to give in English what is conveyed to Indian and Pakistani readers by 'though clouds should come'—I could have used the literal translation of '*ave*' and said 'though clouds should *come*'; but in much of the English-speaking world there are nearly always clouds in the sky, so to get the sense of growing build-up which the original conveys, I have used the word 'mass'—

I feel no joy, though cloud should mass a hundred times above my
    fields—
To me it means that lightning seeks already to find out my crop

Then there are grammatical patterns. Ideally, I try to keep these as close as possible, given the differences between the languages. For example, a question form in Urdu should always be translated as a question in English. I would where possible follow similar word order, where the different natural patterns of word order in the two languages do not preclude this.

Sometimes a significant change in the obvious wording of the translation is needed to convey more adequately the tone and emphasis of the original. In the following couplet:

yih na thi hamaari qismat ki vasaal i yaar hota
agar aur jite rahte yihi intizaar hota

I could have translated the second line:

If I could have gone on living, I should even now be waiting

But this seems to me weak and lame in comparison with *yihi intizaar hota*. For a start, 'hota' grammatically suggests something that regularly

120   A LIFE IN URDU

happens, keeps happening; and the English 'waiting' cannot carry the
load that the long, single drawn-out *intizaar* can. So to try to get a similar
effect, I repeated the word 'waiting'—and this feels a truer equivalent:

> This was not to be my fate, that all should end in lovers' meeting
> Even had I gone on living, I should still be waiting, waiting.

Other poetic effects are achieved through deliberate patterning like assonance, alliteration, or the rhythms of particular phrases. Each language
will have its own, so these may seldom be possible to achieve in translation, but it's a joy when you can get something like it. In this ghazal, there
is deliberate patterning of sound across two couplets:

> *nahin nigaar ko ulfat, no ho; nigaar to hai*
> *ravaani e ravish o masti e ada kahiye*
> *nahin bahaar ko fursat, no ho; bahaar to hai*
> *taraavat e caman o khubi e hava kahiye*

which is echoed in the translation:

> The fair are cruel? What of it? They are fair
> Sing of their grace, their swaying symmetry
> Spring is soon fled? What of it? It is spring
> Sing of its breezes, of its greenery

Although some latitude and compromise are inevitable, it's important to
resist any temptation to 'improve upon' the original. To give an example:

> *nakarda gunaahon ki bhi hasrat ki mile daad*
> *ya rab, agar in karda gunaahon ki saza hai*

I have translated this as:

> Note too how I regret the sins that I could not commit,
> O Lord, if you would punish me for these committed sins

Ghalib-worshippers will be shocked at my impertinence, but I could not help thinking that it would strike the reader with greater force if the punch came in the second, and not the first line. So I felt sorely tempted to reverse the order of the two lines by translating them as:

O Lord, if you would punish me for these committed sins
Note too how I regret the sins that I could not commit.

(In that case, of course, the line could not find a place in this particular ghazal, but I am speaking of it for the moment as an isolated couplet.) However, the order I prefer is not the one that Ghalib preferred, and as a translator of Ghalib, I am not entitled to assert my preference over his. I therefore keep the original order.

Rhyme and Metre

The two features of a ghazal that are essential to its form are rhyme and metre, and both of these are a challenge to reproduce in translation. To take first the matter of rhyme. Ghazal rhyme often has two parts: the actual rhyming word—the *qafia*—is followed by the *radif* (sometimes translated as 'end rhyme')—which is not actually a rhyme but an identical sound. For example, in this couplet:

na tha kuchh to khuda tha, kuchh na hota to khuda hota
duboya mujh ko hone ne, na hota main to kya hota?

In the translation, I managed to get an echo of both the *qafia* and *radif*:

When nothing was, then God was there; had nothing been, God
would have been
My being has defeated me: had I not been, what would have been?

In translating several couplets of the same ghazal, I try to at least echo the rhyming pattern in the original. In those relatively few ghazals that have a certain unity of theme or of mood, a series of verses can sometimes be

122   A LIFE IN URDU

translated into a continuous piece of English verse that I feel will convey something of the effect of the original. For example, the couplets:

> *rahiye ab aysi jagah calkar jahaan koi na ho*
> *ham-sukhan koi na ho, awr ham-zabaan koi na ho*
> *bedaar o divaar sa ik ghar banaaya chaahiye*
> *koi ham-saaya no ho aur paasbaan koi na ho*
> *pariye gar bimaar to koi na ho timaardaar*
> *aur agar mar jaiye to nauhakhaan koi na ho*

The English hints at the rhyming effect by the recurrence of the word 'me':

> Now let me go away and live somewhere where no one else will be,
> Where there is none that knows my tongue, where there is none to
>   speak with me;
> There let me build myself a house with, so to say, no doors, no walls,
> And live there without neighbours, and with no one to keep watch
>   for me.
> If I fall ill, then there should be no one to come and visit me
> And if I die let none be there to weep and wail and mourn for me.

To say that it is not always possible to achieve this effect would be a considerable understatement—it is hardly ever possible, and there is nothing to be done about it. For any translator is faced with the stubborn and unalterable fact that Urdu has rhyming words in plenty and English does not; and translations that sacrifice meaning to achieve a rhyme do the poet no service. But where I am translating a single couple, it is not always much of a disadvantage. Even in Urdu, the linking rhyme throughout the ghazal is very important when a whole ghazal is being recited and listened to, but when people quote one couplet on its own, in conversation with friends, the rhyme is only detectable if it happens to be the first couple of that ghazal.

So I try to reproduce rhyme when translating the first couplet of a ghazal, or a series of couplets from one ghazal, but not if I am translating individual couplets. Even when translating several couplets from one ghazal, I avoid disturbing the natural order of words solely for the

ON TRANSLATING GHALIB   123

purpose of making a rhyme. I know Ghalib feels no inhibition about this, and it's a common feature in ghazals, but it does not make for natural English.

Metre is a different matter. This is one of the areas which I feel is least satisfactorily handled in many translations I have seen. In Urdu, it is absolutely essential that each line of a ghazal is in the same metre. This has such a powerful effect when recited that, if a line is not in correct metre, a listener will know immediately that it must be in some way have been misquoted. Urdu metre has a basis quite different from that of English metre and there are far fewer regularly used metres in English, so it is unrealistic to expect to be able to reproduce the *same* metre in translation. But I believe that one can, and should, always try to convey in English at least something of the effect of the Urdu metre.

The starting point is to be consistent about the number of syllables in the line. For instance, this ghazal has sixteen syllables:

han vuh nahin khuda parast, jao vuh bevafa sa-hi
jis ko ho din o dil aziz, us ki gali men jae kyon?

My English translation also has sixteen syllables, with a similar rhythm:

No, she does not bow down to God. Yes, she is faithless too—now go!
If I had prized my heart and faith, would I have gone into her lane?

[Incidentally, this translation also gives an example of where natural speech patterns in English require some departure from a word-for-word correspondence. Keeping the word order of '*din o dil*' in the translation would be '*faith and heart*'; but '*heart and faith*' are the natural English order, though I could not say quite why. Similarly, English idiom is '*No, she does not*' rather than a literal translation '*Yes, she does not.*']

Where the rhythm of the original is not, to my mind, adaptable to any natural English stress pattern, the best one can do is to produce an English line that has the same number of syllables and moves with a discernible rhythm of its own.

You will have seen from these examples how I interpret the need for compromise in presenting the ghazal. The first priority is meaning—to convey what Ghalib intended to convey. A key part of this is faithfulness

124 A LIFE IN URDU

to the original—nothing added, nothing taken away; and the attempt to replicate form should never distort that. Natural word order in English, an evenness of tone, and a rhythmically patterned line—the identifiable feature that makes it a poem, intended to be spoken. Rhyme (or at least a hint of rhyme)—if at all possible in rhyming couplets (the first of each ghazal); otherwise, only where it can be done without sacrificing meaning and naturalness. And an essential underpinning of regular metre.

I should say, finally, that it's only occasionally possible to achieve all that one would want in a translation—a total correspondence between the two languages, and a verse that has a similar length and clear metrical pattern. Here is one translation of a couplet that satisfies me because I feel it does this:

Ya rab, vuh na samjhe hain na samjhenge miri baat
de aur dil un ko jo na de mujh ko zabaan aur

O Lord, they do not understand, nor will they understand, my words
Give them another heart, or else give me another tongue

* * *

In concluding this discussion of the principles of translation that guide me, I want to say that I am fully aware that some choices I make as a translator are a matter of personal taste—prejudice, if you like. For example, I don't use 'thou' or 'thee, though I think a hypothetical English-writing Ghalib might well have used them. I don't say that I would never use them: there might be contexts that would seem to demand them, and there I would meet that demand. Nor do I much like 'I'll' 'You'll', 'He'll' and so on, preferring 'I will' ... except where the language of the original is quite obviously, markedly, and deliberately colloquial. Others may have different feelings about these forms, but the key thing a translator needs to aim for is a measure of consistency of diction. If you are going to use 'thou' and 'thee', keep to it—i.e. don't use 'thou art' and 'you are' indiscriminately and interchangeable, or the colloquial 'I'll go' and the archaic 'Twas not' in the same couplet.

I know that the range of diction of the ghazal is wide. Poets at a mushaira are speaking classical verse with an ancient pedigree, hence they can use archaic, gorgeous language. But they are also often reciting in a gathering of people of whom they know personally, hence they can lapse into informal colloquial. When you translate you need to match like with like, so the language of your translation will show the same wide range. But this does not give you licence to juxtapose widely differing styles right next to each other in the way that some translators do.

One hopes that readers who know both Urdu and English will not condemn particular versions simply because they are not to their own particular taste. Ghalib has something to say to many different audiences, each of which perhaps requires its own interpreter. It seems to me that his greatness demands of us all that we feel a common bond, and respect all those who have worked honestly and conscientiously at their task, enabling him to speak to ever new audiences.

PART III
ON LANGUAGE AND LITERARY HISTORY

11

Leadership in the Progressive Writers' Movement, 1935–1947

1977

When I was invited to contribute to a seminar on 'leadership', I was hesitant about accepting. I am concerned with the study of literature; I was (and remain) sceptical about the usefulness of the concept of 'leadership' as applied to literature; and I was therefore inclined to refuse. But then it occurred to me that I might usefully contribute a paper on the All-India Progressive Writers' Association (PWA). For the PWA, besides being a literary movement, was also, in the broad sense of the words, a social and political movement—the kind of movement to which the concept of 'leadership' is obviously relevant—and it made an impact sufficiently significant to merit serious attention. My own interest in, and knowledge of, India dates roughly from 1936, soon after the movement began. My own political beliefs were, throughout the period of its existence which I shall cover (and indeed still are), broadly in harmony with those of the PWA. Its influence on writers of Urdu—the subject of my studies—was probably greater than on those of any other language. For the last twenty years or so, I have been personally acquainted with many of its leading figures. And, finally, no very useful account of the PWA is available in English. For these reasons, I decided to accept the invitation.

I must stress at the outset that it is not my aim to make any evaluation of the literature which the movement produced; nor shall I attempt, even in outline, a history of the PWA. My aim is simply to study important features of the way the movement was organized and led during the first period of its existence, from 1935 to 1947. In Urdu, there are three substantial books covering the period I am dealing with. The one on which I have drawn for much of the specific detail of events is Sajjad Zahir's

A Life in Urdu. Edited and with a Foreword by Marion Molteno, Oxford University Press. © Oxford University Press India 2023. DOI: 10.1093/oso/9789391050948.003.0011

130 A LIFE IN URDU

Raushnai, published in 1956, a full-length account of the movement up to 1947. After the partition of the subcontinent and the creation of the new independent states of India and Pakistan, a new period began, and subsequent developments would require separate analysis and treatment.

First Steps: The Political Climate of 1935–1956 India

The first practical moves towards the formation of the Progressive Writers' Association seem to have been made in the Nanking Restaurant on Denmark Street, in November 1935, or perhaps in 1934: the date is not certain. It was here that a number of Indian students and intellectuals of political views ranging from the radical socialist nationalism of which Nehru was the main representative, to the communism of Sajjad Zahir, met, discussed and formulated its original manifesto, and made plans to establish the movement in India. They included Mulk Raj Anand (at that time one of the very few Indian writers in English to have made an impact upon the English reading public), Sajjad Zahir, Jyoti Ghosh, Promod Sen Gupta, and M.D. Tasir. Through friends, who after completing their studies in London, Oxford, Cambridge, Paris, and elsewhere had now returned home, contacts were made with sympathetic circles in India, and when Sajjad Zahir returned to India shortly afterwards—he was the first of the London circle to return—he set about establishing the basis for an organized movement there. He landed in Bombay, spent only a few days there, and then went straight to Allahabad, where his parents (originally from Lucknow) were living at that time. It was here that the first substantial steps towards organizing the movement were taken

The method was first to coordinate the efforts of all those who felt sufficiently committed to the formation of a movement to give a good deal of their time and energy to the practical work involved. At this stage, these were for the most part communists and fairly close sympathizers of the communist movement. The next step was to seek the support of writers and intellectuals who had already established themselves on the Indian cultural scene, and if possible to get them to sign the draft manifesto of the movement. This was, presumably, identical to the 'Manifesto of the

LEADERSHIP IN THE PROGRESSIVE WRITERS' MOVEMENT 131

Indian Progressive Writers' Association, London' dated 'London, 1935'. It is appropriate to quote this in full:

Radical changes are taking place in Indian society. Fixed ideas and old beliefs, social and political institutions are being challenged. Out of the present turmoil and conflict a new society is arising. The spirit of reaction, however, though moribund and doomed to ultimate decay, is still operative and is making desperate efforts to prolong itself.

It is the duty of Indian writers to give expression to the changes taking place in Indian life and to assist the spirit of progress in the country. Indian literature, since the breakdown of classical culture, has had the fatal tendency to escape from the actualities of life. It has tried to find a refuge from reality in spiritualism and idealism. The result has been that it has produced a rigid formalism and a banal and perverse ideology. Witness the mystical devotional obsession of our literature, its furtive and sentimental attitude towards sex, its emotional exhibitionism and its almost total lack of rationality. Such literature was produced particularly during the past two centuries, one of the most unhappy periods of our history, a period of disintegrating feudalism and of acute misery and degradation for the Indian people as a whole.

It is the object of our association to rescue literature and other arts from the priestly, academic and decadent classes in whose hands they have degenerated so long; to bring the arts into the closest touch with the people; and to make them the vital organs which will register the actualities of life, as well as lead us to the future.

While claiming to be the inheritors of the best traditions of Indian civilisation, we shall criticise ruthlessly, in all its political, economic and cultural aspects, the spirit of reaction in our country; and we shall foster through interpretative and creative work (with both native and foreign resources) everything that will lead our country to the new life for which it is striving. We believe that the new literature of India must deal with the basic problems of our existence today—the problems of hunger and poverty, social backwardness and political subjugation, so that it may help us to understand these problems and through such understanding help us to act.

With the above aims in view, the following resolutions have been adopted:

132   A LIFE IN URDU

(1) The establishment of organisations of writers to correspond to the various linguistic zones of India; the co-ordinations [*sic*] of these organisations by holding conferences, publishing of magazines, pamphlets, etc.

To co-operate with those literary organisations whose aims do not conflict with the basic aims of the Association.

To produce and to translate literature of a progressive nature and of a high technical standard; to fight cultural reaction; and in this way, to further the cause of Indian freedom and social regeneration.

To strive for the acceptance of a common language (Hindustani) and a common script (Indo-Roman) for India.

To protect the interests of authors; to help authors who require and deserve assistance for the publication of their works.

To fight for the right of free expression of thought and opinion.

Within a matter of weeks, it was clear that remarkably wide support for these aims would be forthcoming. Among those who expressed their sympathy were Pandit Amarnath Jha, then Vice-Chancellor of the University of Allahabad, and Dr Tara Chand, then secretary of the semi-official Hindustani Academy. And though this is anticipating a little, it is worth saying at this point that within months some of the most prominent writers of verse, prose-fiction, and literary criticism had declared their sympathies for the movement, including not only those on the left, but Congressmen of predominantly Gandhian outlook, men who, though sympathetic to nationalist sentiment, had held aloof even from the Congress, and men of not very articulate political views at all.

This wide support for a movement being formed by avowed communists looks more surprising in the 1970s than it did in the India of 1935. At that time, a political climate was forming to which the nearest parallel that the West could offer is perhaps provided by the years from mid-1941 to the end of the Second World War. In those years, the necessities of the war against fascist Germany, Italy, and Japan, fought in alliance with the Soviet Union and with a China in which nationalists and communists were formally in alliance, made communism respectable, and evoked ardent expressions of radical populism from even the most unlikely quarters. These were the days when *The Times* became what an incensed MP of the Tory rear-guard called (if I remember his

LEADERSHIP IN THE PROGRESSIVE WRITERS' MOVEMENT   133

words correctly), 'the fourpenny edition of the *Daily Worker'*—the daily paper of the Communist Party. (Those who are old enough to recall these years will recognize the correctness of this description, and those who aren't will discover its correctness if they turn back to the public speeches of British and American statesmen of the time.) India in the middle 1930s was in a situation where a fairly protracted, and on the whole inconclusive struggle with the British had produced among the politically articulate a dissatisfaction with Gandhian methods and a sympathy for more modern left-wing, Marxist-influenced political solutions. Nehru expressed these views very well, and his Harrow and Trinity education, and his closeness, through his father and through the now long-continued patronage of Gandhi, to the older established Congress leadership, further enhanced the range of his appeal. This was a period in which Congress, for good tactical reasons, committed itself to a programme of radical reforms, in which communists (including Sajjad Zahir himself) became members of the All India Congress Committee, and in which, in the elections of 1937, it gained victories which enabled it to take office in many of the Indian provinces.

The British, in general, could not bring themselves to recognize the extent to which it was gaining ground, but by 1935–1936 Indians, regardless of their own political persuasions, estimated the prospect more accurately, and to many of them, a preparatory avowal of the radical sentiments of future governments must have seemed to be only prudent. On the international scene, the Soviet Union, with its declared policy of support for colonial liberation, attracted the sympathies of many who were far from being on the left, for in a country aspiring to win its independence, politics is understandably dominated by this one central issue (sometimes, one feels, to the almost total exclusion of all others) and sympathy or hostility towards other countries is decided mainly by what is their attitude towards this one central issue.

Finally, the communist and near-communist pioneers of the PWA were able to take advantage, to some degree consciously and perhaps to an even greater degree unconsciously, of the remarkable class solidarity of the Indian privileged classes to which most of them belonged. I cannot speak for the rest of India, but the main organizers of the movement came from the Urdu-speaking intelligentsia of northern India; and in the vast region extending from Punjab in the west to Bihar in the east and from the Himalayas in the north to Hyderabad in the south, I think it is true to say that in those days if one was the son of a well-to-do family, distinguished by ownership of large landed estates and/or by eminence in the legal profession, if one spoke English well, and even more if one had completed one's education at a British university or in Paris, one was assured of an affable welcome from any other similar personage—no matter what one's political opinions might be. Besides, the pioneers of the PWA proposed to put their revolutionary beliefs into quite gentlemanly practice. This is quite clear from Sajjad Zahir's statement of the revolutionary ambitions which the small group of progressives had formed during their stay in England. There is an engaging naiveté in its tone. He writes (in 'Reminiscences', p.49), 'Most of the members of our small group wanted to become writers. What else could they do? We were incapable of manual labour, we had not learnt any craft, and our minds revolted against serving the imperialist government. What other field was left?' I would add that since all of them knew very well that no writer in an Indian language could make a living by writing, they must all of them have known what they proposed to live on while pursuing their chosen course. But Sajjad Zahir makes no reference to this sordid question.

Throughout the social stratum of which I am speaking, the assertion of one's modernity was felt to be very important, and the outward and visible signs of that modernity commanded more attention than the necessarily less tangible things of the mind and the spirit. The wearer of a good English-style (or better still, English-made) suit showed his modernity through his suit. The expounder of Marxist doctrine showed his modernity through his Marxism—for what, in 1935 India, could be more modern than Marxism? The two differed only in the medium they had chosen to display their modernity, and this difference was of relatively minor importance to them.

There is of course an element of mockery in this description: let me hasten to add, therefore, that I do not take the view that Indian politics in general, and the Progressive Writers' Movement in particular, was the creation of people who were all shams. Periods like the late 1930s in India and the early 1940s in Britain saw a remarkable growth of radical sentiment, extending over an exceptionally wide social range; and in such periods, one finds at all points on the spectrum men who are completely

LEADERSHIP IN THE PROGRESSIVE WRITERS' MOVEMENT 135

sincere, others who are the more or less willing victims of some degree of self-deception, others whose declared views are motivated by hard, cynical calculation, and yet others (perhaps a great majority) in whom all three of these things are mixed in infinitely differing proportions. All this is no doubt true of the political process in general—at all periods, and in all countries—but in periods like the late 1930s in India, at any rate when viewed in retrospect, it seems especially striking.

Sajjad Zahir's *Raushnai* gives a detailed account of the building of the PWA, in which the developments of the four months from December 1935 to early April 1936 occupy nearly a quarter of his book, and often illustrates the points I have made. I summarize here the account on pp. 36–44. When he and his fellow organizers reached Lahore, they went 'straight to the bungalow of Miyan Iftikhar ud Din ...' (a wealthy Punjab landlord and a prominent progressive, who later became well-known as the owner of the *Pakistan Times*). 'There his servants received us: they told us that Miyan Sahib and his Begam Sahiba had gone to a party, but had said that they would be back shortly'. They felt rather put out at this, and were even more put out when on their return, their hosts informed them that they were to spend the evening at an imposing dinner parry in Civil Lines given by Sir Abdur Rashid. (Sir Abdur Rashid later became the first Chief Justice of the Federal Court of Pakistan.) Iftikhar overcame their objections by arguing that he had already promised the host on their behalf, that anyway, there would be important people there (including Begam Shahnawaz) whom they could hope to influence favourably and whose influence would in turn be helpful to them in getting the PWA organized in the Punjab, and that they could leave early. Sajjad Zahir describes the scene at the party:

> I soon noticed that Lahore's 'high society' was in some ways higher than the Lucknow and Allahabad 'high society' of the English-educated. People here were not only healthier than us but wore better suits than us and spoke English with more style than us. In UP in those days many people wore *sherwanis* at such parties, but here everyone was wearing a suit. The women were perhaps no more beautiful than ours, but their complexions were fairer, and their saris more expensive: and they looked smarter than our women ... But the mentality of this class was practically the same in the Punjab as it was in UP.

136 A LIFE IN URDU

The friendly links with members of the big landlord class of UP are illustrated by the choice of Chaudhry Muhammad Ali Rudaulavi as president of the reception committee for the first PWA conference in Lucknow in April 1936. Sajjad Zahir devotes a page to describing him (pp. 92–93). He speaks of him as a *talluqdar*, one of the aristocracies of Oudh, who observes the etiquette and manners of that class, and writes in the attractive Urdu style of Lucknow's old traditions, but can also discuss Nietzsche, Marx, Freud, Tagore, and Iqbal. When he is with men of his own age, he discusses the problems of life after death, and landed property, and family affairs, while in the company of younger men, he will discourse on sexual problems in so a learned a manner that the eyes of even the most colourful among them open wider. Groups of beautiful young women attract him as surely as the magnet attracts iron. He has always looked upon progressive youngsters with a kindly and sympathetic eye.

I have gone into a measure of detail in order to make clear what at this distance in time is not always easy to get across—that the PWA was not at all the disreputable movement which, had I not dwelt at some length upon this, you might well have assumed it to be.

Winning the Established Writers

But the PWA was after all being organized as a movement of writers, though in fact its membership was not to be rigidly confined to them. And the main drive of the organizers was to win the support of the most prominent writers of their day, including those of the very highest reputation, whose association with the PWA would naturally attract the support of many others. It was remarkably successful in this. Above all, it won the enthusiastic and active support of Premchand, indisputably the most outstanding writer of novels and short stories, both in Hindi and in Urdu, in the 1920s and 1930s. Premchand's adherence to the movement therefore brought it a great accession of strength. His enormous prestige among both Urdu and Hindi speakers, his simple style of living, his unassuming nature, his closeness to the people of the villages, the pervasiveness of some of the most appealing of already familiar Gandhian ideas in his work—all these things brought strength to the new movement, and his death, only a few months after the Lucknow conference, was a heavy loss.

LEADERSHIP IN THE PROGRESSIVE WRITERS' MOVEMENT   137

Though assessment of the literature that the PWA produced is outside the scope of this essay, I may say in passing that just as Premchand brought strength to the movement, so did the movement bring strength to him; in his last work, his realism is noticeably less impaired by Gandhian preconceptions than it had been hitherto. An article which he wrote in Hindi at this time called 'Mahajani Civilisation'—Moneylender's Civilisation—throws light on the widely prevalent attitudes at that time. In it, the detestable features of capitalist society, which exalts the greed for money above everything else, are sharply contrasted on the one hand with the more humane relationship between man and man which, he says, preceded the impact of capitalism, and on the other hand (and even more strongly), with the new socialist society which he believes has been established in the Soviet Union, though he nowhere mentions the country by name.

At this early stage, very few Hindi writers other than Premchand declared support for the movement, though quite a number had expressed sympathy with its aims. It was amongst Urdu writers that the most striking headway was made. Iqbal was contacted, and his more active sympathy might perhaps have been won had a more prompt, persistent, and tactful approach been made. Sajjad Zahir describes (pp. 168–172) the one occasion when he and Dr K.M. Ashraf visited Iqbal at the beginning of the summer of 1937. The presence of another guest throughout this interview and Ashraf's sardonic loquacity had an inhibiting effect. Iqbal spoke of his interest in socialism, declared his general sympathy with the progressive writers' efforts, and asked them to keep in touch with him. Sajjad Zahir says that he resolved to have a more complete discussion with him when he next visited the Punjab, but Iqbal died (on 20 April 1938) before this could happen.

This is perhaps the point at which to remark that one reason why the progressive writers' movement achieved such widespread support so rapidly was that its aim of harnessing literature to social and political aims was not at all startling to the Indian public. In the Indian and the Islamic tradition alike, literature had always been didactic in one way or another, and indeed its readers would have been puzzled and surprised by any suggestion that it ought not to be. Moreover, modern Indian literature had come into being—about a hundred years earlier in Bengali and about sixty years earlier in Urdu—as the vehicle of modern, English-influenced

138 A LIFE IN URDU

ideas that it set itself to propagate, simultaneously conducting a polemic against traditional resistance to those ideas. By the 1920s, themes of revolt against imperialism, of nationalism, and of radical social reform were already common in literature (for example, both in the poetry of Iqbal and in the prose of Premchand), and the PWA represented simply the continuation and development of such themes. All of which shows, incidentally, how false is the picture which the movement's manifesto had painted, of a literature which 'since the breakdown of classical culture' had 'become anaemic in body and mind'. These rather curious words were introduced into the 1938 revision of the manifesto. Quite the reverse is true. Since the emergence of new, western-inspired literary forms in the nineteenth century, Indian literature had experienced a vigorous and healthy development, which the progressive writers were now to continue. Indeed, this continuity gave them an important advantage. It was the 'moderns' who developed somewhat in the wake of the progressives' rather than the 'progressives' themselves (I use terms that reflect the Urdu labels of the period) who represented a break with tradition, for it was they who insisted that literature harnessed to social and political ends must almost inevitably be inferior literature.

In Urdu poetry, the progressive movement won the allegiance of many of the big guns. They included Hasrat Mohani, perhaps *the* greatest ghazal writer of the first two decades of this century, and one who had been from his earliest days a fiery worker for India's full independence, and had by the mid-1920s deduced from Islamic premises that communism was the answer to India's and the world's needs. It also won two of the most eminent poets who had made their name after Iqbal—Josh Malihabadi, the self-styled 'Poet of Revolution' (*shair i inqilab*) and Firaq Gorakhpuri, who, like Premchand, was a man of eminence in the Hindi, as well as in the Urdu literary world.

In literary criticism and literary scholarship 'Abdul Haq, secretary of the long-established Society for the Advancement of Urdu (Anjuman i Taraqqī i Urdū) was the figure whose adherence to the new movement most enhanced its appeal. He was prevented by illness from coming in person, but Sajjad Zahir quotes extracts from the presidential address which he sent to be read out to the conference of Hindi and Urdu progressive writers held in Allahabad in 1937 (p. 182). In it, he exhorts the progressives to do for Indian society what the Encyclopaedists had done for France in the eighteenth century.

LEADERSHIP IN THE PROGRESSIVE WRITERS' MOVEMENT 139

There are many more famous writers who signed the manifesto. Ali Sardar Jafari, on p. 196 of his book *Taraqqi Pasand Adab* ('Progressive Literature'), lists all the major Urdu writers who did, but without annotation, they would not mean anything except to those who know a good deal about early twentieth-century Urdu literature.

From 1936 to 1947

The movement continued to register this sort of success in the years that followed, notwithstanding weaknesses in organization and, here and there, a loss of direction of which I shall briefly speak later. Even a hostile press felt obliged to devote considerable attention to it, most notably in 1936, after the success of the first PWA conference in Lucknow, when the Calcutta *Statesman* published in two long instalments an article, widely believed to have been government-inspired, attacking the movement as the product of a sinister communist conspiracy to subvert all that was fine and spiritual in India's ancient civilization, etc. It is arguable that this attack, in the climate of 1936, did the movement more good than harm. Certainly, defections from its ranks were negligible; some, like Amarnath Jha, who felt it necessary to withdraw public expression of support, continued to support it privately, and any losses were more than counter-balanced by the advances it continued to make.

It made the most solid gains in the Hindi-Urdu-speaking area, where in 1937, 1938, and 1939, it organized joint conferences of Hindi and Urdu progressive writers. The earlier aloofness of Hindi writers (other than Premchand) was to some extent overcome, and at the Allahabad Conference in 1938, one of the foremost poets of Hindi, Maithili Sharan Gupta, attended and read a poem. Nehru attended, and spoke at, this same conference, and the movement scored an even greater triumph when Sajjad Zahir succeeded in getting a declaration of support and a message to the conference from Rabindranath Tagore. His message is quoted at some length in *Raushnai* (pp. 191–192) and shows a change in Tagore's outlook somewhat similar to that in Premchand, which I have noted above, but even more striking. I re-translate from the Urdu:

140 A LIFE IN URDU

To live in seclusion has become second nature to me, but it is a fact that the writer who holds himself aloof from society cannot get to know mankind. Remaining aloof, the writer deprives himself of the experience which comes from mingling with numbers of people. To know and understand society, and to show the path to progress, it is essential that we keep our finger on the pulse of society and listen to the beating of its heart. This is only possible when our sympathies are with humanity, and when we share its sorrows ... New writers must mix with men, and recognise that if they live in seclusion as I do they will not achieve their aims. I understand now that in living apart from society for so long I have committed a grave mistake ... This understanding burns in my heart like a lamp, and no argument can extinguish it.

He then goes on to express in his own words the same sentiments as the PWA manifesto had expressed, calling upon writers to dedicate themselves selflessly to the service of their country and their people.

The strong move to the left in Bengal at this time also helped the progress of the PWA there. (It was in 1938 that Subhas Chandra Bose, at that time regarded by many as more to the left than Nehru, was elected President of the Congress.) Calcutta was chosen as the venue of the second All-India PWA conference, and this was held there at the end of December 1938. This conference opened with an address by Tagore; his advanced age and poor health prevented his attending in person, but he sent his opening address in writing, and this was read out. Among other things, the conference approved plans for better and more regular organization, adopted a new constitution embodying these plans, and resolved to issue a quarterly journal (in English) from Lucknow, with the General Secretary (now Abdul Alim as successor to Sajjad Zahir) 'as *ex offtcio* Editor, and an Editorial Board consisting of representatives of all the important languages of India'. The journal, entitled *New Indian Literature*, duly appeared in 1939, with an editorial board consisting of representatives of 'Hindustani [i.e. Hindi and Urdu], Bengali, Gujerati, Marathhi [*sic*], Tamil, Telegu, Malayalam, Kannada' and finally of four names under the heading 'English and General', including Mulk Raj Anand and Raja Rao. The first issue carried most of the major materials of the Calcutta conference.

LEADERSHIP IN THE PROGRESSIVE WRITERS' MOVEMENT   141

In practice, the aims set forth in the new constitution soon proved to be too ambitious. Some were never realized at all, and others only partially and temporarily, with local branches being formed, disintegrating, and re-forming at intervals and few achieving any consistent pattern of activity for any great length of time. But the journal, even if it could not be brought out at regular quarterly intervals, could probably have continued to appear had not the outbreak of the Second World War in 1939 put insuperable obstacles in its way. Two issues did appear in 1939; then Mulk Raj Anand left for a visit to England and was stranded there when war broke out. And in 1940, Abdul Alim and others were put in jail and the journal never appeared again.

The movement revived again in 1942, when the illegal Communist Party, after some months of internal discussion, finally took the line of support for the war, and the Government of India, after fairly lengthy secret discussions with its representatives, decided early in 1942 to grant it legality. With the arrest of the Congress leadership in August and the almost exclusive preoccupation of the Muslim League with the future of the Muslim community should the British transfer power, the communist and near-communist left had an unusually clear field, and its relative weight in the PWA increased. Accordingly, the PWA in this period made its greatest advances in Bombay, where the Communist Party had its oldest industrial base, where its headquarters was situated, and from where its weekly journals were issued—including one in Urdu, which was now in a position to employ some of the old PWA organizers. Bombay is itself a cosmopolitan city, with sizeable communities of, amongst others, Marathi, Gujarati, Hindi, Urdu, and Malayalam speakers, and here the PWA developed to some degree, in a way that had not been possible while its headquarters had been in UP, into a sort of microcosm of its ideal all-India form. But Independence ended alike the broad united front climate in which the PWA had grown up and the abnormal near-monopoly of free political activity on current issues which the communists had enjoyed in the period from 1942. The vigorous anticommunist offensive launched by its one-time Congress allies (and not least by Nehru) in 1946–1947, and the ultra-left line that the Communist Party itself adopted when Ranadive ousted Joshi from the leadership, radically changed the conditions in which the PWA must henceforth

142 A LIFE IN URDU

work, and initiated a new period which it is beyond the scope of this essay to discuss.

'Into the Closest Touch with the People...'

Even the shortest account of the PWA's activities would be incomplete without some reference to what it did to realize its aim, stated in its manifesto, 'to bring the arts into the closest touch with the people'. During its heyday, it scored some significant successes in this field. In the summer of 1937, the Punjab PWA had held its first provincial conference in Amritsar not only at the same time, but in the same meeting place—the historic Jalianvala Bagh—as the Punjab Peasant Committee ('Committee' in the Indian left-wing political sense which comprehends 'association' and 'conference' as well). Sajjad Zahir and K.M. Ashraf were there in the rather unlikely role of representatives of the peasants of UP. The decision of the PWA to meet there arose originally out of the refusal of halls to them—including a refusal by the authorities of Amritsar MAO College where one of them (Tasir) was Principal and another (Faiz) a lecturer! The peasants were thereupon approached and gladly agreed to let them meet in the dais of the big pandal in Jalianvala Bagh whenever it was not needed for the proceedings of their own conference: and this close contact was reckoned to be a great success. More significantly, in the summer of 1938, a very successful conference of peasant poets was organized at Faridabad, drawing in village poets from the area around Delhi and the easternmost regions of the (then) Punjab. Later, in the post-1942 period, similar activities were successfully organized in the rural areas of other provinces where communist influence was strong, very often (especially in Andhra) in almost indistinguishable association with the Indian People's Theatre Association, which was formed in those years on lines closely similar to the PWA but aiming at a much more predominantly plebeian audience, both in the towns and in the villages. In the same period, side by side with the development of peasant movements in the Punjab, UP, Bihar, and Bengal, there were developments of peasant poetry and folk song in these areas too.

In this same post-1942 period, the PWA made serious and successful efforts to organize activities that would appeal to the urban working class.

LEADERSHIP IN THE PROGRESSIVE WRITERS' MOVEMENT 143

In Bombay, a working-class poet Anna Bhao Sathe (a *man's* name), took up the traditional Marathi folk form called (if I have correctly deciphered Sajjad Zahir's Urdu script version of it) the *pavara*, and used it for the expression of revolutionary working-class themes. His poems, Zahir tells us (pp. 303–304), 'were recited before working-class audiences of thousands and were immensely popular. One on the Battle of Stalingrad was especially so'.

Similar success was achieved in organizing 'revolutionary mushairas'—the mushaira is the traditional poetic symposium at which Urdu poets recite their verse—of the Urdu-speaking industrial workers of Bombay. The writers of sophisticated (as distinct from popular, plebeian) verse also took part in these, and one—Kaifi Azmi—was very popular with these audiences.

The ancient mushaira tradition was developed in another way too, when meetings were held at which not only poems but short stories and other writings were read; thus, as Sajjad Zahir aptly says, reviving and developing the old tradition of *dastan-goi,* the traditional institution of recitation by professional story-tellers of the long romances of Islamic chivalry, romances from which, as late as the 1860s, an important element in the modern Urdu novel derives. The Urdu writers were particularly active in this period, and Sajjad Zahir gives an interesting account (p. 375 ff) of a successful 'Urdu literary conference and mushaira held in the town of Maligaon (in the heart of Maharashtra) two hundred miles from Bombay, where he says, the population consisted predominantly of Urdu-speaking weavers of homespun cloth, people who had originally come from the Banaras region of eastern UP.

The Processes of Leadership in the PWA

The processes of leadership which become evident as one studies the PWA and its development are not peculiar to India. Those who seek to start a new movement anywhere are likely to do three things. At the ground level, so to speak, they will both try to win the allegiance of people not yet committed to any cause and to gain in whatever measure may be possible the support of those whose allegiance is indeed pledged elsewhere but is not felt to be inconsistent with support for the new movement. At a more

144 A LIFE IN URDU

exalted level, it will seek to win over, or to ally itself with, men who are already established as leaders, who already have an important following, and who can be expected to carry that following with them when they accept the claims, or some of the claims, of the new movement. As we have seen, the PWA did all these things—the first two with the greatest success in the period when the left worked in the abnormally favourable conditions of the period from mid-1942, and the last in its early days, the period from the end of 1935 to 1939.

What does seem to me characteristically, though again not exclusively, Indian, is the extent to which its leaders went in the earlier period to accommodate themselves and their movement to a variety of social and political groups who already wielded influence in Indian society and the relatively great importance they attached to this method of building the movement as compared with the method of direct mass appeal for the support of the as yet uncommitted. A consequence of this was the blurring of the lines which, had they acted with greater consistency and in accordance with more sharply defined principles, would have demarcated them more clearly from other social, political, and literary groups whose claim to be regarded as 'progressive' was at least somewhat dubious. Sajjad Zahir's method of handling this sort of situation is one of some refinement, well illustrated by the account of the descent of him and his colleagues on Lahore in January 1936 from which I quoted extracts above. You start by describing, bluntly enough, the undesirable qualities of the men and women who constitute 'high society', in general; but it soon emerges that you are quite at home in this society and consider it quite proper to enter into relationships, both personal and political, with individual members of this high society' of a kind which could be justified, by your own declared principles, only if these individuals could be shown to be markedly and significantly different from their fellows; but no such marked and significant difference appears.

In less sophisticated progressives, this sort of free and easy opportunism is much more plain. The most amusing example in Sajjad Zahir's account is that of Krishan Chander's sterling efforts to organize the third All-India PWA Conference in Delhi early in 1942. Krishan Chander has always been, and still remains, one of the staunchest supporters of the progressive cause, and Sajjad Zahir is clearly at pains in his account to let him off as lightly as possible. But it is pretty clear that he must have

LEADERSHIP IN THE PROGRESSIVE WRITERS' MOVEMENT   145

reasoned along something like the following lines: 'The PWA has suffered heavily from government policies since 1939, but now, with its leaders once more out of jail, we have the opportunity of really putting it on the map again. So let's get as many big names to our conference as possible'. The result was that he sent out invitations to people who could not, by any conceivable stretch of the imagination, be regarded as sympathetic to progressive causes. Many of these, on their side, seem to have reasoned that the Communist Party, now legalized, was now quite respectable, and association with communist writers in a conference that would demonstrate (as indeed it did) support for the war effort, would attract the favourable attention of the British authorities. So they accepted. When Sajjad Zahir and Abdul Alim arrived in Delhi on the eve of the conference, having gladly accepted Krishan Chander's offer to do most of the organizing, this was the situation which confronted them. Alim solved it by organizing not one conference but two, running parallelly—a general 'Writers' Conference' and a Progressive Writers' Conference.

The same sort of ambivalence was often evident in the PWA's literary products too, and Krishan Chander again provides some of the clearest examples. He soon established himself as the most popular of the progressive Urdu short-story writers, and some of his work is extremely good. A great deal more would not rate very high by international standards, but has without any doubt served the progressive cause well and made a considerable impact on a wide readership. When in 1950, I criticized one of his most popular stories, he was not in the least offended, named two other progressive writers (Ismat Chughtai and Rajindar Singh Bedi) whose stories he thought would be more worthwhile translating into English than his own, but said that he had read this and other stories like it to mass audiences, that they had been very popular, and that he wished to continue writing for such audiences. It seems to me that this stand is quite unobjectionable. During the terrible Hindu-Muslim riots, he wrote many stories driving home the message that all decent men must abhor the communal killings and do their best to stop them. And if these stories are not great literature, it is to be hoped nevertheless that no thoughtful and humane man will wish to deny that he performed a service to humanity in writing them. It is another matter when he goes a step beyond this and seems to reason, 'I will give my readers what they like. If they like

146 A LIFE IN URDU

it, they will like me, and since I am a progressive that will mean that I am winning support for the progressive cause'.

If you want to see what remarkable results such logic can produce, you should read his *Seven Faces of London,* available under that title in an English translation in an Indian paperback series. (Marxists in the West who have close experience of their Indian counterparts must often have been struck by the very shallow quality of their internationalism at any rate where the nations of the West are concerned; and this, among other things, is evident in this book. I hasten to add that this judgement does not imply any complacent assumptions about Marxists in the West, whose attitudes to their Indian counterparts have also left a lot to be desired.) What apparently interests Krishan Chander most during his life in London is the discovery of an old Punjabi friend who is now a street trader in Petticoat Lane, and visits to strip-tease joints in the company of Indians employed in the BBC. The climax of the book is a fantastic story (presented as fact, with himself as one of the characters) in which he is lured to the palatial residence of one of his old English flames (portrayed in a strictly one-dimensional way as a filthy-rich *femme fatale*) who receives him at the side of her private swimming pool and, having been given the false impression that he cannot swim, manages to make him fall into the pool and goes off leaving him to drown. This kind of stuff, too, continues the old tradition of *dastan-goi* but not perhaps the best in that tradition, and not perhaps for any discernible progressive purpose.

Krishan Chander also included in his two-volume selection of progressive literature *Nae Zaviye* (vol. 1, p. 93), a poem by N.M. Rashid—a 'modern' rather than a 'progressive', but never mind—entitled *Intiqam* (Revenge). in which the Indian poet feels that he has taken revenge for India's subjection by having sexual intercourse with an English woman. The 'progressive' logic of this seems to be that the sovereign remedy for colonial slavery is mass copulation of the male slaves with the womenfolk of the enslavers. It was this same N.M. Rashid, whom the progressive poet Faiz chose to write the introduction for his first volume of verse, perhaps in the calculation that the avowed progressives would buy it anyway, and an introduction by a 'modern' might help to bring in the 'moderns' too. And Krishan Chander had written the introduction of Rashid's collection of verse *Mavara.*

It is perhaps worth saying something about the problems which face the leadership of such a movement as the PWA set out to be, considered in general, or, if you will, objective terms—problems, in other words, to which the strengths and the weaknesses of the leadership of the actual historical PWA are irrelevant.

The ambitious aims set out in the constitution of December 1938 seem to me to be such that no voluntary movement, however well-led, could have hoped to realize them. At the all-Indian level, it was forced to function in English—as, indeed, is still the case at that level with every countrywide organization. Yet it was concerned to promote the production of progressive literature not mainly in English (though, quite rightly, English was not excluded), but in the twelve to fifteen major Indian languages. For such a movement to retain any sort of continuing all-India coherence would have necessitated the prompt translation of at any rate the most representative work of every one of these languages into every other—a task of such formidable dimensions that only an organization financed by government funds could hope to make any headway with it. (In India, this is what has happened. The Sahitya Akademi—Academy of Letters—now undertakes this task.) It may be thought that progressive writers in English from the various regions could have imparted some of this all-India coherence and perhaps in addition to translations from their mother tongues into English, mediate between the different language regions. But of the writers in English who were associated with the movement in the early days, only Mulk Raj Anand stayed with it for more than a few years. The others, Ahmed Ali, for example, soon realized that even if they wrote in an Indian language (and Ahmed Ali did—in Urdu), at any rate, their English writing must be directed outside India, to the English-speaking world; and this turned their attention towards a field of interest which, for the PWA as a whole, could only be a subsidiary one; so that even if more of them had remained active in its ranks, this could hardly have altered the pattern of events very significantly. As for acting as translators, quite apart from any natural (and reasonable) reluctance they might have felt to devote to translating the works of others, time which they could otherwise spend on writing works of their own, it is a fact that very few Indians who possess sufficient mastery of English to make it their medium of literary expression possess anything like a

148   A LIFE IN URDU

commensurate mastery of their own mother tongue, and adequate translation from its literature would have been beyond the powers of most of them.

The one section of the PWA to attain anything like an inter-regional range was that of the Urdu writers. But this was not because the PWA's Urdu writers and Urdu-speaking organizers were more able than the rest, but mainly because Urdu itself is not, for the most part, a regional language, but the language of the Muslims, and more especially of the urban Muslims, distributed in towns and cities throughout the north, the north-west and the centre of the subcontinent, and in those days the preferred literary medium of the majority of writers from Punjab—Muslim, Sikh, and Hindu alike.

A further problem arose in pursuing the aim of bringing literature 'into the closest touch with the people'. The vast majority of the progressive writers were writers of sophisticated literature and wrote on themes, and in a tradition, and in a language, which was not very appealing to the uneducated, illiterate urban, and rural poor. The languages themselves have not attained the degree of uniformity that compulsory education, a widely circulating popular press, radio, and television have conferred upon English. Even in Urdu, where knowledge and appreciation of the sophisticated literary forms perhaps extend further into the mass of the language community than is the case with other languages, sophisticated poets had difficulty in getting across to the unsophisticated, and Sajjad Zahir's account rather suggests that only Kaifi Azmi learned how to do this really successfully.

Bringing progressive literature to the peasants, and evoking progressive literature *from* the peasants, presented even greater problems, well illustrated by the two examples from the 1937–1938 period which I gave earlier. When in 1937, force of circumstances brought the Punjab peasants and the Punjab progressive writers together to conduct simultaneous conferences in Jalianvala Bagh, the revolutionary zeal which each inspired in the other derived in the main from simple physical proximity and Sajjad Zahir, in his summing up of the conference (pp. 167–168) practically says as much. Mere physical proximity cannot, I think, be regarded as a very advanced form of communication, but the progressive writers could not get much beyond that. As writers, they spoke a different language (both literally and metaphorically) from the peasants and were

LEADERSHIP IN THE PROGRESSIVE WRITERS' MOVEMENT 149

ignorant both of the language and the popular forms of peasant literature. The one outstanding peasant conference which was a success by literary standards was that of the peasant poets held in Farīdābād in the summer of 1938. But this success owed almost everything to the efforts of one very exceptional man, Sayyid Mutallabi Faridabadi, of whom Sajjad Zahir gives a full account (p. 232 ff). An educated landlord who lived in the countryside, he had a knowledge and understanding of the local peasants and of their language and traditional cultural forms, which none of the writers of sophisticated Urdu literature possessed. In the communist-led cultural campaigns in the post-1942 period, in, for example, the Andhra region, it was song, dance, and popular drama provided by the Indian People's Theatre Association that made the greatest impact.

With the best will and the greatest skill in the world, it seems to me very doubtful whether the PWA could have made appreciably more headway than it did against these formidable objective obstacles that it faced. These are questions of really quite a different kind from those which arise about its methods of work in the areas in which it did achieve very notable successes. A full study of the history of the movement, pursued partly at least along the lines I have attempted to indicate in this essay, and based on a full study of the written materials supplemented by contact and discussion with its surviving leaders, would, I think, produce interesting and instructive results.

12

Aziz Ahmad and Urdu Sources on South Asian History

1983

I first got to know Aziz Ahmad in 1957, when he left Pakistan to accept an overseas lectureship in Urdu at the School of Oriental and African Studies, and thus became my colleague. At that time, he had already achieved distinction as a lecturer in English literature and a pioneer of new standards in the twentieth-century Urdu novel; after he left for Canada in 1962, he made his name in Islamic studies. He was also a talented translator from English into Urdu. For five years, we worked together closely and, let it be said, not always amicably, and came to know each other pretty well. Our disagreements, which were sometimes sharp and vigorously pursued, arose nearly always from what I felt to be his inability to adequately comprehend the difficulties and the needs of foreign students of his native language, and since the teaching of such students was a major part of his assignment, such disagreements were not infrequent. That being so, it surprised and puzzled him when he found that this in no way inhibited my whole-hearted praise of his talents and of his published work. (He came from a milieu where it is indeed rare for these two things to go together.)

Before he came to SOAS, I had already read his novel *Gurez* (published in 1940), whose setting describes the life of Indians under British rule. While he was at SOAS, I offered to translate *Aisi Bulandi, Aisi Pasti* (published in 1948) and for much of one summer, we worked closely together on the translation. He took the opportunity to make revisions in the original text, for the most part, omissions and abridgements of certain passages, but numerous minor changes as well. These were incorporated in

A Life in Urdu. Edited and with a Foreword by Marion Molteno, Oxford University Press. © Oxford University Press India 2023. DOI: 10.1093/oso/9789391050948.003.0012

the translation, which therefore diverges considerably from the published Urdu text. It was published a few years later as *The Shore and the Wave*.

He wrote many more novels. His craftsmanship is equal to the demands of his chosen literary form, and from those in the Urdu-speaking community who were alive to the importance of these things, he rapidly won well-deserved praise. But in most quarters, his novels earned him notoriety rather than fame, for his frankness, though quite unremarkable by western standards, aroused a good deal of shocked disapproval in his own country, for they were very generally regarded (often by those who hadn't read them) as 'obscene'. They are 'obscene' only by the standards of conventional Indian society. Nirad C. Choudhuri, in his *Autobiography of an Unknown Indian* (1951), tells us how in his youth, a fellow student of his had criticized a novel of that eminently respectable nineteenth-century novelist Bankim Chandra Chatterji for being 'flooded with eroticism', and comments, 'The flood was one solitary scene of kissing within wedlock'. Times have changed since then, but old traditions die hard; until recently, kissing was still taboo on the Indian screen.

These views not only do him an injustice, they have also impeded the assessment of his novels at their true worth. They have more to recommend them than their competent craftsmanship and their frank portrayal of things that the more conservative of his readers felt should have remained decently veiled. His command of both his own language and English was such that he spoke and wrote both with equal facility. Many of those who acquire that sort of command of English do so at the price of allowing their Urdu to rust. Not Aziz Ahmad. His novels showed that he could express in fluent and effortless Urdu all that he had learnt in his years of acquaintance with, and thorough study of, English and its literature.

Aisi Bulandi, Aisi Pasti is set during the Second World War in the fictional city Farkhundanagar, which is in fact Hyderabad, the capital of the large princely state (as large in area as Italy) in central India. It was criticized by some of his contemporaries on the grounds that he portrayed impermissibly, and in only thin disguise, the private lives of men and women easily identifiable by those who knew him and his acquaintances. This too was something that in the contemporary West would not have been regarded as exceptionable. In fact his close knowledge of the society he portrays is one of the strengths of the novel. The political–fictional

152 A LIFE IN URDU

disguise of 'Farakhundanagar' was never any disguise at all to anyone who knew Hyderabad. There is a twin city, 'Tabindanagar' (Secunderabad)—and the great lake of 'Shahid Sagar' (Hussain Sagar) lies adjacent to both. Overlooking the city is the hill of Kishanpalli, where many of the nobility and the wealthy families are having their homes built. The main characters of the novel belong to the families of three nobles who had been political rivals in Farkhundanagar half a century earlier; by the time of the story, these traditional family rivalries have been largely overcome by intermarriage. The world they inhabited was under pressure of change—the state itself survived under the aegis of the paramount British power until 1947, disappearing as a separate entity several years later when the redrawing of the boundaries of the Indian states on linguistic lines took different parts of it into different political units.

This was a social world Aziz Ahmad knew from the inside, for he had grown up in Hyderabad, and at the time when the novel was written had spent most of his life there. Through the lives of the characters, he gives a perceptive account of the 'three tides of westernisation' which had swept over the state, and describes in the period up to the eve of Independence the impact upon the educated, well-to-do sections of Hyderabad society, of the 'third tide'. All the same—as in those of his other novels I have read—though all the actions portrayed are plausible, the power to evoke deep human sympathy is somehow lacking. What is *not* lacking is a gallery of vivid pictures of many aspects of contemporary South Asian reality, painted by one who has absorbed the positive values of the West without losing touch with those of his own native tradition. And such a combination is rare.

* * *

This leads me to a consideration of the fact that there are many other works of Urdu literature that provide a rich source for the study of South Asian history. Prose fiction from the nineteenth century onwards offers valuable insights into understanding aspects of society, and how political developments impacted on people's lives, and of course, this is equally true for non-fiction. The trouble is that hardly anyone in the West whose professional task it is to study these aspects can read what these writers have to tell them, while those in the West who can read Urdu well are, for the most part lacking in the academic expertise of the professional historian and/or social scientist. And so important sources of study remain unutilized. For example, the problem of Kashmir has consistently been one of the major issues in the politics of the post-1945 period. An important element in determining the present situation was the internal political struggle of the 1930s and 1940s. Where can one find a vivid picture of Kashmir during those years? In Aziz Ahmad's novel *Ag*. But those who (if they knew about it) would like to read it for this purpose, can't. And those who *can* read it, aren't for the most part interested in doing so for this purpose.

The question naturally arises, what about historians and social scientists in Pakistan and India who write in English but know Urdu well? Don't *they* use these materials? For the most part, no. Why not? For several reasons. Some come in the category already described, of people who have acquired their English at the cost of letting their Urdu rust. Others may be unduly influenced by the absurd convention that a novel cannot be a worthwhile source for academic study (except of course for literary criticism.) Even where non-fictional writing is concerned, perhaps they think that works written in Urdu in that period lack the scholarly qualities of works written in English, and that therefore no self-respecting scholar pays any attention to them? Even if the premise were wholly correct (and it isn't), the conclusion doesn't follow from it.

Where historians are concerned, another factor is at work. In colonial times Indian history used to be divided into three periods, labelled the Hindu period, the Muslim period, and the British period. Since Independence, a sense of propriety has re-labelled them the ancient, mediaeval, and modern periods, but a good deal of the old content persists under the new labels, particularly where the modern period is concerned. There are still traces of the attitude sarcastically described by a historian colleague of mine, who said, 'Some historians think that for centuries Indians stood in the wings muttering the Urdu or Tamil equivalent of Rhubarb, Rhubarb! until such time as the British appeared on the stage and history could begin'. It is true that from, say, the 1820s to, say, 1918, it was British policy that largely determined the course of historical development, but from 1918 Indians themselves made the running, and major British policies were a response to their pressures. Even in the century or so of unchallenged British dominance, what various classes

154   A LIFE IN URDU

and groups of Indians were doing merits much more study than it has yet received—and this aspect of Indian history cannot be adequately studied without a knowledge of Indian languages.

For this purpose, Urdu has perhaps a wider spread than most languages, by which I mean that materials in Urdu treat of the history and the social and cultural life of a larger area, and over a longer period, than most other Indian languages do. In particular, there is material on the princely successor states to the old Mughal Empire (including those ruled by non-Muslims and/or inhabited by a majority of non-Muslims), and on the modern Muslim movements on a virtually all-India scale that arose in response to the impact of the British. I am not a professional historian, merely one who as a teacher and student of Urdu literature has an interest in all aspects of the history and the social and cultural life of the people who produced and still produce it. I do not therefore keep fully abreast of new contributions in historical writing. But unless I am out of date, there is no substantial history of Avadh (Oudh) in English, while there are two in Urdu—Najm ul Ghani Rampuri's *Tarikh i Avadh* (1909–1913) and Kamal ud Din Haidar's two-volume *Qaisar ut Tavarikh* (1896, written, as the author tells us, at the instance of Henry Elliot). Abdul Halīm Sharar's encyclopaedic work on old Lucknow *Guzashta Lakhnau* appeared more than half a century ago and has only recently been made accessible to English readers. There must surely also be volumes of Urdu material relating to the history of the Nizam's Dominions of Hyderabad.

On Muslim movements in response to British rule, the picture is similar. In Shaikh Muhammad Ikram's 'kausar' trilogy, the third volume *Mauj i Kausar* is a clear account of Muslim movements from the so-called Wahhabi movement of the early nineteenth century up to 1947. Major materials for the study of the Wahhabis (and their successors) are in Urdu—for example, Abdul Hasan Nadvi's *Sirat i Sayyid Ahmad Shahid* (1939, and later editions) and Ghulam Rasul Mehr's three volumes *Sayyid Ahmad Shahid* (1954), *Jamaat i Mujahidin* (1955), and *Sarguzasht i Mujahidin* (1956).

On the Aligarh movement that spans the second half of the nineteenth century, almost *all* the essential source material is still in Urdu. Graham's sketchy life of Sir Sayyid Ahmad Khan has been reprinted, and the major biography, Hali's *Hayat i Javed*, completed within a year or two of Sir Sayyid's death in 1898 and first published in 1901, has recently been published in an English translation by my colleagues Dr David Matthews and Dr K.H. Qadiri. But of Sir Sayyid's own, very voluminous work in Urdu, almost nothing has ever been translated into English. Of all the work of Nazir Ahmad, Sir Sayyid's important younger contemporary (to name only one of them)—the didactic proto-novels (as one may call them), a collection of lectures, and his religious writings—only one novel, I think, has been fully translated into English. Much the same picture could be presented for the period from 1900 up to the present day.

The importance of Urdu source material is even more striking when considering the specific features of South Asian Islam. While Aziz Ahmad's *An Intellectual History of Islam in India,* gives a very useful survey in English, almost all of the original materials through which an analysis of South Asian interpretations and reinterpretations of Islam can be made are in Urdu. This includes Sir Sayyid's own writings, Nazir Ahmad's comprehensive survey *Al Huquq o Al Farāaz,* the writings of Shibli Numani and of Abul Kalam Azad; and so on to the present day. For what Islam meant to a much wider circle of Muslims one can study Ashraf Ali Thanavi's fascinating book *Bihishti Zewar,* which among many other things tells a pious Muslim woman the doctrines of her faith. First published in instalments, from perhaps 1901 to 1903, it later appeared in book form (the earliest edition in the British Library is dated 1905), and has been reprinted many times.

I have been highly selective in naming both books and scholars—I am simply illustrating, not attempting a comprehensive review. But I do want to say that I am aware of encouraging developments, and ever hopeful that their exponents, in academic terms, may be fruitful and multiply. There are scholars in the West who *have* learnt the value of Urdu source materials, the necessity of using them, and, with varying degrees of accomplishment, the ability to read them for themselves.

Some of them, though not all, are in my view too timid in stating truths, and sometimes very important truths, that their knowledge of Urdu has taught them. I sometimes have the impression that in the field of Islamic studies more than most, scholars—both western and South Asian—feel a need to be 'diplomatic' (which, let us face it, is often only a polite way of saying 'less than completely honest') so that influential people will not be offended. Well, no sensible person would advocate giving offence unnecessarily, or stating honest conclusions in deliberately offensive language, but neither should one forget what Hardy, quoting St Jerome, stressed in his explanatory note to *Tess of the Durbervilles*, that 'if an offence comes out of the truth, better is it that the offence come than that the truth be concealed'.

Many writers on South Asian Islam know—and because it is very important, should therefore *say*—that the viewpoint of nearly all Muslim thinkers about the position of Muslims in the subcontinent over the past three centuries was that of Islamic chauvinism, which assumed that Muslims once occupied a privileged position among the inhabitants of the subcontinent, and that they should do whatever historical circumstances allowed them to do to regain it. That is a fact, and whether you approve, disapprove, or are indifferent to it, it is impermissible not to state it as a fact.

Aziz Ahmad was an example of a phenomenon of which we need many more—a man who united a thorough knowledge and a critical appreciation of his native traditions with the ability to view them through truly modern eyes and to a considerable extent to write frankly of what he saw and what he concluded. The qualification is because he himself (in my view) showed this all too common sense of diplomacy. In his book *Islamic Modernism in India and Pakistan, 1857–1964*, he gives a lucid summary of all the major Muslim thinkers of his period but fails to give any adequate indication—surely essential to a proper understanding of his theme—of the very widely varying impact of the different thinkers discussed upon the Muslims as a whole. This starts with not being clear what he takes 'Muslim' to mean. By implication, he defines it as a Muslim believer, and one, moreover, who is to some degree competent in traditional Muslim learning.

More than twenty years earlier, the Canadian scholar Wilfred Cantwell Smith, in a study on a similar theme, used a much more useful definition of 'Muslim' as 'any person who calls himself a Muslim'. The difference between this and any definition around religion is significant, for the main stimulus to Muslim rethinking in South Asia from Shah Wali Ullah onwards was not to do with reinterpretations of Islamic teaching, but with political considerations—the desire to find the prescription for the restoration of fallen Muslim fortunes. In other words, nearly all modern Muslim thought has had, amongst others, a political aim, and no study which does not give this aspect due prominence can be fully satisfactory.

For modern Muslim thought both embraces and transcends the bounds of modern Muslim *religious* thought. It does not belittle the religious thinkers to acknowledge that they too shared a political aim; while on the other hand, insufficient stress upon that aim makes it impossible—for instance—to give an adequate treatment of Jinnah's enormously influential role. Though Jinnah too may have been a Muslim in Aziz Ahmad's implied definition of the term, he sought the solution to Muslim problems not in a reinterpretation of traditional Muslim doctrine but in the study of modern politics.

All of this Aziz Ahmad knew very well, and it was for diplomatic reasons that he refrained from making it clear that he knew it.

* * *

The distorting effect of not using Urdu language sources is strikingly illustrated by the example of Iqbal, of whom there has been a curiously lopsided picture in the eyes of Western scholars. The earliest sustained poetical account of his philosophical views was written in *Persian*, which was a major reason enabling his work to make an impression, for a while, few scholars of Islam in the West knew Urdu, and several knew Persian. Iqbal's work in Persian aroused the enthusiasm of Nicholson to the extent that he asked, and received, the author's permission to translate it into English. Ever since then, it has been mainly through translations of his Persian work, and through his writings in English, that the world of Western scholarship knows him. But with all due respect to all concerned, it was not the fact that he so impressed Nicholson that made him a figure of major importance. What made him important was the sensational impact he made upon the Muslims of South Asia, and this impact owes relatively little to his Persian verse (which most of them could not and cannot read) and almost everything to his Urdu verse—to such poems as *Khizar i Rah*, recited, we are told, to an audience of something like 20,000 people in an atmosphere so emotionally charged that both poet and audience were often in tears. Nicholson wrote of *Secrets of the Self* that it 'took the younger generation of Indian Moslems by storm', and Arberry repeated this statement without comment years later (1966) in his introduction to his translation of *Javid Nama*. Yet neither of them gives any evidence that this was so, and the claim seems to me to be a

158 A LIFE IN URDU

highly implausible one. What *did* take the Indian Muslims by storm was, as I have said, Iqbal's *Urdu* verse. Yet the overall significance and impact of his Urdu verse have not been the subject of any really first-rate substantial study in English—and part of the reason is that those in the West who would be competent to write such a study if they knew Urdu well, don't. Anne-Marie Schimmel's *Gabriel's Wing* uses his Urdu as a source, but her book is confined to a study of his religious thought.

The best general study of Iqbal that I know of is Aziz Ahmad's *Iqbal: Nai Tashkil* (1950)—which may be roughly translated *Iqbal: A New Presentation*—a book of 594 pages in the edition that I have. Aziz Ahmad could access all relevant sources in both Urdu and English. In the second half of the book, he explores the socialist elements in Iqbal's thought, but the canvas of the first half is much broader. It illuminates, in a way that no other writing that I know of does, the tradition which produced Iqbal, to which he made his own contribution, modifying it as he did so. During the last decade or so of Aziz Ahmad's life, I repeatedly urged him to cover the same ground in English, and a few years before his tragic illness overtook him, he had agreed to do so and to come to London for that purpose. Now, alas, someone else will have to take up this task.

13

Hindi and Urdu, Languages and Scripts

1996

Over a lifetime of teaching Urdu to English speakers in the United Kingdom, I have constantly needed to explain to those new to the languages the connections between them, historical and current. All this is common knowledge to people in the sub-continent but it is still a subject that attracts academic attention. In recent years there have been two full-length books dealing with the emergence of modern Hindi and modern Urdu, Amrit Rai's, *A House Divided: The origin and development of Hindi/Hindavi,* and Christopher King's *One Language, Two Scripts*—a title that David Lelyveld, reviewing King's book in *The Annual of Urdu Studies,* is correct to call an 'unfortunate over-simplification'.

It is remarkable how much traditional mythology about these issues is still being peddled, often accompanied by a sort of continuing historical sense of grievance. Present-day users, whether of Hindi or of Urdu, aren't to blame for whatever people long dead did, and the sustained recital of resentments on either side serves no useful purpose, to say the least of it. The sensible thing to do is to come to terms with the present situation, and the first step towards this, obviously, is to describe correctly what the present situation is.

Hindi, Urdu, and the 'Link' Language

This is how I introduce the origins of the languages to my students:

Both Urdu and Hindi derive from a dialect known as *khari boli,* the speech of the people of the western part of the Indian state of UP and the country around Delhi. The *khari boli* speech has, in one form or another, for centuries been the common language, alongside the separate regional

A Life in Urdu. Edited and with a Foreword by Marion Molteno, Oxford University Press. © Oxford University Press India 2023. DOI: 10.1093/oso/9789391050948.003.0013

160 A LIFE IN URDU

languages and dialects, of an area extending far beyond its homeland over most of the north of the sub-continent and down into the central plateau. It came into existence, and reached maturity, during the five centuries from about 1200 to 1700, when Muslims from the North-West invaded, settled, and established dynasties which in their heyday dominated all the north and centre of the country. People in this area have called this common language Urdu or Hindi according to the script in which the literate among them write it.

Though one cannot find an acceptable name for this 'link' language, the reality of its existence and of its usefulness is shown by its use as the medium of the mass-circulation of Indian films, which are seen, enjoyed, and understood all over India and in areas of South Asian settlement elsewhere in the world. It is the language long employed by the BBC in its programmes for South Asian immigrants in the United Kingdom, although some would feel that the BBC tends towards the Urdu side of centre.

Spoken and Written Forms

One way to gauge the extent of overlap between Hindi and Urdu is to look at the vocabulary used in Snell and Weightman's *Teach Yourself Hindi*, and check how much of it would also be considered to be Urdu. On the first two pages of their Hindi-English vocabulary, there are a total of 73 entries (counting such entries as *akela*, *akele*, and *akelapan* [alone, loneliness] as a single entry). Of these, 54 can equally well be called Urdu. Another 18 are Hindi, and not Urdu, but one finds elsewhere in the vocabulary synonyms for some of them, which are as current in Urdu as they are in Hindi. For example, *adhik* on p. 252 is matched by *zyada* on p. 270 [many] and *akas* on p. 253 by *asman* on p. 255 [sky]. Other words vary only in pronunciation, but either would immediately be intelligible to speakers of either language, such as *intazar/intizar* [wait] and *amerika/ amrika*. Substantial random sampling of other pages suggests that a complete analysis of the whole vocabulary would yield similar results.

But the range of language which could equally well be called Urdu or Hindi has never extended much beyond routine conversations of everyday life, and in the conversation of educated people and in literature, the divergence between the two is, and long has been, considerable.

HINDI AND URDU, LANGUAGES AND SCRIPTS   161

Though the grammar and a certain basic vocabulary are virtually identical, Hindi literature is overwhelmingly the work of Hindu writers, depicting the life of Hindus, and drawing heavily for its literary vocabulary from Sanskrit. And Urdu literature is predominantly (though not entirely) the work of Muslim writers, depicting the life of the Muslims of India and Pakistan, and draws upon Persian (and through Persian on Arabic) for its literary vocabulary. It is true that both Hindi and Urdu speakers would use identical words to say 'How far is the station from here?' And it is equally true that they would not use the same words to say 'The eighteenth century was a period of social, economic and political decline'. The Urdu is '*atharavin sadi samaji, iqtisadi aur siyasi zaval ka daur thi*', while the Hindi equivalent is '*atharavin sadi samajik, arthik, aur rajnitik girav ki sadi thi*'. It would be possible for the Hindi version to be even further removed from the Urdu: my colleague Rupert Snell tells me that in Hindi, one could say '*shatabdi*' instead of '*sadi*' and '*tatha*' instead of '*aur*'; and instead of the second '*sadi*' (which simply repeats the word for 'century'), one could say '*samay*' (which means simply 'time').

This is far from being a 'one language, two scripts' situation. Urdu speakers would not understand the Hindi version, and vice versa, and to find a version that could equally well be called Urdu and Hindi would be quite impossible. For all practical purposes, therefore, Urdu and Hindi are two separate languages and should be described as such.

The Development of Modern Literary Hindi

It seems to me that what I have written so far is indisputable. But there is, of course, more to the question than this, and there are aspects of what I am about to say that will be more controversial.

There is no doubt that modern literary Hindi came into existence as the result of a widespread feeling amongst Hindus that Urdu was the product of centuries of Muslim domination and that Hindu self-respect demanded that 'Muslim' words should be expelled from their *khari boli* base and replaced by words of pure Indian origin. (The first part of this assessment was entirely warranted, and the second part entirely *un*warranted. Words that come into general use in a language become part of that language and cease to be foreign, no matter where they have come from and why.) This feeling, inevitably, was stronger among the educated than the uneducated. Obviously, it was the educated who wrote the Hindi books and newspapers, employing in them the kind of language that met the new self-imposed standards, and a literary Hindi thus came into existence which differs fairly substantially from the spoken Hindi of the great mass of less highly educated people who have Hindi as their mother tongue.

R.S. McGregor, in his *Outline of Hindi Grammar*, described modern Hindi generally accurately when he said, in effect, that there were words which you may speak but not write (many of them common to Hindi and Urdu) and others which you may write but not speak. To which one should add that the gap between colloquial and literary naturally tends to narrow in the case of speakers who have had a Hindi-medium education.

In this sense, modern Hindi was, so to speak, invented—a statement to which I should at once add that 'invented' should not be regarded as a nasty word. All living languages experience a process of 'invention' all the time, in which not only are new words for new concepts coined but new words even for concepts for which perfectly adequate words already exist. (This latter process is much beloved by modern academia.) What one has to see is whether these new words become generally current, and if they do, it is pointless to raise objections to them. The new element in modern Hindi was perhaps an exceptionally large one, but that is neither here nor there. It took root with millions of people, and from that point onwards to deny it the status of a fully fledged language was absurd. I do not know enough to date its achievement of this status, but it is certain that this was the position by the outbreak of the First World War in 1914.

Premchand, Urdu and Hindi

Here it becomes relevant to say something about Premchand. He was fluent in both Urdu and Hindi, wrote in both, and is regarded as a great writer in both. Having used Urdu in the first period of his writing, at about this time, he decided that he should, without abandoning Urdu, start also to write in Hindi. The fact that he took this decision is in itself conclusive proof that Hindi was now a living, flourishing language. And if at this point anyone jumps in to say, 'Oh, but Premchand's Hindi is simply

HINDI AND URDU, LANGUAGES AND SCRIPTS 163

Urdu in Devanagari script', let me say at once, 'No, it isn't'. Premchand's Urdu is standard literary Urdu, and his Hindi is standard literary Hindi.

It is ironic that Premchand himself should have contributed to the myth that his Hindi is simply Urdu in Devanagari script, and conversely that his Urdu is simply Hindi in Urdu script. There is an easily discernible historical background to this. In the early part of the twentieth century, many leaders of the independence movement—Gandhi and Nehru among them—saw that a major task before them was to attempt to achieve Hindu–Muslim unity, and believed that language could be a powerful factor in this. The policy they advocated was to extend the common area between Hindi and Urdu, to make this the basis of a national language—which they called 'Hindustani'—and to recognize both the Urdu and Devanagari scripts as acceptable forms in which to write it.

In 1939, Premchand wrote an essay in Hindi expressing this view—and wrote it in a Hindi which in no way exemplifies the language it is advocating! It is about as remote as it could be from 'Hindustani'. I give below a sample paragraph in English translation. I have put in italics words that, in the original Hindi, would probably not be understood by most Urdu speakers:

> Everyone is agreed on the point that to make a *state firm* and *strong* it is very *necessary* that the country should have *cultural unity, and* the *language and script* of any state is a *special part* of this cultural unity. Miss Khalida Adib Khanam said in one of her speeches that the unity of the Turkish *nation* and state had come about *because* of the Turkish language alone. And it is an *undoubted* fact that without a national language the *existence* of a state cannot even be *imagined.* Until India has a language it cannot lay claim to *statehood.*

In addition, there are totally unnecessary departures from the common Hindi–Urdu stock of words which would be entirely acceptable even in written Hindi (and believe it or not, they include his Hindi equivalent of English 'and').

Let us for the moment put aside this remarkable contrast between Premchand's theories and his practice. The true relationship between his Hindi and his Urdu has not, to my knowledge, been adequately investigated in any published work; and I guess that the primary reason for

164   A LIFE IN URDU

this is that most of those who have written about his language have been fluent readers either of Hindi or of Urdu, but not of both. However, nearly twenty years ago, Alison Barnsby (now Safadi), a student of mine at SOAS who graduated with first-class honours in Urdu with Hindi as her subsidiary subject, produced a valuable study in her dissertation, which in my opinion, would be well worth publishing. She made a detailed study of both the Hindi and the Urdu versions of ten of Premchand's short stories, representative of the whole period from 1910 to 1936. It provides conclusive proof of the truth of my earlier assertion that Premchand's Urdu was standard literary Urdu and his Hindi standard literary Hindi, and that, by and large, he made no attempt to write in the 'Hindustani' he advocated. It is, I imagine, possible that the Hindi and Urdu versions of the stories are not all Premchand's own work, but even if that were the case it seems, to say the least of it, unlikely that either version would have been published without his approval. Barnsby's study quotes numerous examples of sentences that could equally well be described as Hindi or Urdu but which are *not* used in both versions.

Premchand's example is clearly one of the greatest interest, but its main importance is that it proves that Hindi and Urdu already were, by around 1915, two separate literary languages and should long ago have been classified as such.

Insha's and Ghalib's Experiments

There are nevertheless some persistent misconceptions about all this. One example relates to a work by Insha—c. 1756–1817, a contemporary of Mir—called *Rani Ketki ki Kahani,* sometimes referred to as a pioneering work of Hindi literature. This somewhat extraordinary idea is the product of hindsight and has nothing to do with the actual genesis of the book. In fact, Insha was a versatile linguist who composed poetry in Urdu, Persian, Arabic, and occasionally Turkish and Punjabi, and he wrote *Rani Ketki ki Kahani* as a *tour de force*, to demonstrate that he could do so without using any words of Persian or Arabic origin, and for no other reason. A similar motive prompted Ghalib when writing *Dastambu* in 1857. It is a journal of his experience of life in Delhi in the momentous days during the occupation of Delhi by the rebel sepoys in May, and its recapture by the British in September, and there is no reason to doubt that his reasons for writing it were what he said they were—to produce a work of 'pure' Persian free of all Arabic-derived words and by engaging in this difficult task to keep his mind off his troubles. If one can imagine a movement among modern Iranians to 'purify' Persian by expelling all words that came into it from Arabic, one might find them discovering Ghalib's *Dastambu* as a pioneering work of pure Persian. There is no suggestion either with Insha or Ghalib that the 'pure' languages they were challenging themselves to use in this one instance were or should become standard languages.

'Sanskritized' and 'Persianized' Language

Those who attack the use of excessively Sanskritized Hindi, and who advocate that the common stock of Hindi and Urdu vocabulary should be used as far as possible in the literary versions of both languages, sometimes demonstrate their fairness by attacking with equal vigour an alleged form of Urdu so highly Persianized and Arabicized as to be the counterpart of the most highly Sanskritized form of Hindi. They generally add that a form of this kind is especially evident in Pakistan. This would be a convenient argument if it had any basis in fact, but it hasn't. Urdu, as written both in India and Pakistan, is no more Persianized/Arabicized today than it ever was. Its Persianization, if one wants to use that term, was already accomplished when modern Hindi came into existence, and there is virtually no further scope for it. There has never been, is not now, and never can be any effective 'Muslim' movement to 'Muslimise' Urdu in the way that the creators of modern Hindi 'Indianised' their language. To use the terminology of many of the advocates of Hindi, Urdu is a language with a large 'foreign', 'Muslim' element imposed upon its 'purely Indian' base, and the most 'Muslim' of Urdu speakers can't get away from the fact that Urdu is a partly 'Indian' and partly 'foreign' language. Hindi, on the other hand, can be to a great extent 'purely Indian' through and through. (I have used quotation marks to indicate that though I understand what those who use these terms mean by them, I do not accept them as valid descriptions of the phenomena they purport to describe. 'Foreign' and 'Muslim' are considerable oversimplifications, and even

166 A LIFE IN URDU

the most Sanskritized Hindi cannot be accurately described as 'purely Indian'.)

A good many other totally unsound propositions are bandied about in these controversies and could be examined. But the basic questions are those which I have tried to discuss here, and I hope (though well aware that I am not entitled to expect!) that the picture I have drawn will be widely recognized as being, in all essentials, accurate.

* * *

Urdu in India since Independence

I read recently with great interest an account by the distinguished Urdu scholar Shamsur Rahman Faruqi on what has happened to Urdu in India since 1947. Such experience as I have had in my year-long stays in India in 1949–1950, 1958, and 1964–1965, and in shorter stays in the period since then, supports the picture he presents. But I should like to add something to that picture.

For anyone not familiar with the situation, let me briefly summarize. While Urdu literature has always been primarily the literature of Muslims in South Asia, there were prominent writers in the pre-independence period and after who were Hindu—for example, Premchand, Krishan Chander, Nehru—and Sikh—like Rajinder Singh Bedi—who chose to write in Urdu. It had been widely taught in government schools in areas where native speakers of both Hindi and Urdu have for centuries lived alongside each other. Since 1947 the government has shown apathy and worse towards the teaching of Urdu, and the transmission of competence in Urdu to each new generation has been gravely undermined.

In what is regarded as the heartland of Urdu—UP, Bihar, and neighbouring states—it became clear in the early years of Independence that state governments were intent on destroying the influence of Urdu. This was achieved by an absurd interpretation of the 'three language formula' devised by the Government of India at Independence. This recommended that in every state, three languages should be taught in the schools: (1) the language of the state (which would normally be the mother tongue of the majority of its inhabitants); (2) another modern Indian language (Hindi would often be chosen where the first language was not Hindi); and (3) one other language. A good deal of elasticity was envisaged in the implementation of this formula. In UP and many of the states where Hindi was the majority language, Urdu was the second most widely used mother tongue. In these areas, Urdu could, and should, have been chosen as one of the three languages. The UP government, and I understand, the governments of the other states of the Hindi-Urdu-speaking area, decided instead to declare Sanskrit a modern language, and the teaching of Urdu in the schools was discontinued.

Nehru, who spoke Urdu well, was opposed to the policies of the UP government, but the centre was not in any position to dictate the course that the state governments should follow. From Indira Gandhi's time onward, the national government has had its own reasons for doing something to support Urdu—political considerations which did not have much to do with sympathy for Urdu. A series of committee was set up, the Gujral Committee in 1972, followed by another 1979, and again in 1990, which found that 95 per cent of the recommendations made in the Gujral Committee Report had not been adopted. Some changes did happen as a result of these central government actions. The state government of Bihar, and shortly afterwards that of UP, did at least recognize (on paper) Urdu as an official language of their respective states.

The impression one gets is that positive results have been minimal. An article by Som Anand (in the Bradford based journal, *Ravi*, January 1992) says: 'An example of the way in which Urdu is deliberately being finished in UP is this: About twenty years ago the centre advised the UP government that seven thousand Urdu teachers should be appointed for the primary schools... The education department of the state took on these teachers but no time was allotted to them for the teaching of Urdu and they were told that any child who wished to read Urdu must read it outside school hours. The teachers who had been taken on to teach Urdu were ordered to teach other subjects'.

The lack of good teaching at the primary school level has had far-reaching consequences at higher levels in the education system, where an appreciation of literature could be fostered. Shamsur Rahman Faruqi, in an interview in *The Nation* (8 July 1994), said that teachers at the university level had started a retrograde strategy to save their jobs. They convinced

168　A LIFE IN URDU

university authorities that since enrolment in Urdu was dwindling seriously, it was necessary for the life of Urdu departments in universities that even those students who did not read Urdu at any level whatsoever, or inferior students, should be granted admission if they wished to study Urdu as a subject in BA or MA. This resulted in the intake of incompetent candidates as Urdu students. These incompetent people, having obtained their degrees, joined the Urdu departments as teachers. 'Then followed the illiterate line of students taught by these illiterate teachers. It seems that now this phenomenon of generations of illiterates after illiterates will never come to an end'.

The Next Generation of Readers?

It is obvious that this has grave implications for the future of Urdu literature. For a language and literature to thrive, it is not enough for it to remain a spoken language in homes where it is a mother tongue: each new generation needs to gain sufficient competence in reading and writing that they will be able to appreciate, and contribute to, its literature.

Waheed ud Din, in an article called 'Indian Press and the Muslims' in *The Nation,* Lahore (9 July 1993) says, 'The reality is that problems and opportunities are always there in the world. The correct approach is to find out the opportunities lurking among the problems and urge the people to utilize them while overlooking the problems'.

So what are the opportunities? What can individual Urdu speakers, or small voluntary organizations formed by them, do to support the maintenance of the language? One small but obvious thing is to ensure that their own children learn to read and write Urdu. If the schools are not providing this teaching, any parents literate in Urdu can provide it. Over the past decades, I have encountered many Urdu speakers who love its literature and whose children were also interested in it, who had nevertheless not ensured that their children could read and write it. Many of these young people enjoyed Urdu poetry; they would go to mushairas and most of them could understand what was being said, but they had no independent way of reading it. I remember seeing a young relative of the late Habibur Rahman writing down in Devanagari script Urdu verses that appealed to her. Ismat Chughtai told me that her daughter could not

HINDI AND URDU, LANGUAGES AND SCRIPTS   169

read and write Urdu. Why didn't these well-educated parents make sure that their children could read and write Urdu?

Beyond the family, those who have a command of Urdu could start teaching it in their own neighbourhoods. In countries like Britain with many immigrant communities, the educational system does not provide for teaching of what some people call their heritage languages, parents have themselves set up classes, hired rooms, and given some instruction to their children. There is no reason in my opinion why Urdu speakers in India shouldn't do the same. When I first made this point, in an article in the *Economic and Political Weekly* (January 1999), Syed Shahabuddin took exception to it on the grounds that Urdu speakers in India are not an 'immigrant community'. Of course they are not, and it would never have entered my head to suggest that they are. I am merely drawing a parallel between the problems of language maintenance faced in the two situations, and giving an example of measures that the former have taken to address this problem. Nor do I accept Shahabuddin's assertion that the Urdu community is too poor to undertake this. Of course, many sections are, but there are also many resources within the Urdu-speaking community which could be dedicated to this, if there were a sense of collective responsibility to try and solve the problem.

Given all the limitations of the current situation, there is one major factor that could help to foster a continued interest in Urdu literature. Despite the efforts of the Hindi chauvinists, the lingua franca—the 'link language' of everyday communication—continues to be, as it was before Independence, one which is just as much Hindi as it is Urdu. The immensely popular Hindi films could equally accurately be called Urdu films. The Gujral Committee in paragraph 140 of its summary of conclusions, rightly says: 'The major contribution of films is that they have not allowed any barriers to grow between Urdu and Hindi'. These two factors alone indicate that spoken Urdu is still a language widely understood by millions of Indians, many of whom are not Muslims.

Interest in Urdu literature (especially its poetry) remains widespread among large numbers of people who do not know the Urdu script and have only a partial understanding of the literary language. All this means there is a large potential readership for Urdu works written in Devanagari script, and also for Urdu works introduced through English.

Urdu Literature and Devanagari Script

A lot of nonsense has been talked about the Devanagari script and Urdu, so I should first make clear my own views about it. Any language community has the right to use whatever script it likes for its language. There is no doubt that Urdu speakers overwhelmingly favour the script in which it has been traditionally written. Arguments of linguistic efficiency are totally irrelevant here. One can easily prove on linguistic grounds that Devanagari more adequately represents the sounds of Urdu than its traditional Arabic-based script does; and one can equally easily prove that the Roman script based on the international phonetic alphabet, which was devised by J.R. Firth about sixty years ago could do so even more accurately and *much* more economically than Devanagari. But such arguments are pointless. The script a language uses will, and should, be that which the users of the language choose, and Urdu speakers are no more willing to change this script than the English are willing to discard traditional English spellings for the much more sensible American ones (e.g. *plow* instead of *plough*). It is quite pointless to tell people to do what one is quite certain they will not do.

However, this does not mean that the use of Devanagari for writing Urdu need be of no interest to the Urdu-speaking community. On the contrary, it should be of the utmost interest. First, in relation to schools. All organizations which work for the advancement of Urdu—government-sponsored and voluntary—need to face up to the fact that there are now many Urdu speakers who do not know the Urdu script, or who may have learnt it at a basic level but may not have an effective enough command to read with ease. Where this applies even to teachers of Urdu, no learning will take place. An obvious way to cut through the problems would be to produce Urdu teaching materials also in the Devanagari script. With parallel texts in both scripts, teachers and pupils could initially use the more familiar Devanagari script while becoming gradually accustomed to the Urdu script. I have used a similar method in my own teaching in SOAS. My course books for English speakers use a transcription of Urdu sounds in the familiar English alphabet (with small modifications for sounds that do not occur in English) while gradually introducing the Urdu script. It has proved entirely effective.

HINDI AND URDU, LANGUAGES AND SCRIPTS   171

What about Urdu literature? Given that among those who understand spoken Urdu, there are many who cannot read the script, the obvious way forward is to make works of Urdu literature available in a script they can read. Many millions of users of Devanagari script are admirers of Urdu writing and would read it if it were made available to them in their script. In my opinion, it would be entirely within the remit of the government-funded organizations to produce texts of important and popular Urdu authors in the Devanagari script. This would also give access to the literature to a wider audience. Hindi speakers offer the next most favourable audience for Urdu literature after that of Urdu speakers themselves. Of course, there are *some* in the Hindi-speaking community who are vociferous opponents of Urdu, but it would be a great mistake to think that all Hindi speakers share their attitude. There have always been people among them who have worked sincerely and seriously in widening access to what Urdu literature has to offer.

This is demonstrated by the number of publications of Urdu works already issued by Hindi publishers in the Devanagari script. In the early 1950s, there was a multi-volume publication called *Sher o Sukhan,* a comprehensive selection of Urdu poetry presented in the Devanagari script with, at the bottom of the page, explanations in Hindi of the meanings of Urdu words which the editors thought their readers would not otherwise understand. Similarly in 1965, I encountered a periodical published in Allahabad called *Urdu Sahitya* (Urdu Literature), edited by Balwant Singh, presenting contemporary writing in Urdu in the Devanagari script, with explanations of difficult words. Ali Sardar Jafari took an admirable initiative many years ago in producing Devanagari editions of Ghalib and Mir. Ismat Chughtai told me that in her later years, she could always find a publisher for her stories in Devanagari before any Urdu-script version was published. In 1995 when OUP in Delhi published *An Anthology of Urdu Verse* edited by my colleague in SOAS, David Matthews—a bilingual text, with the Urdu text on the left-hand page and the English translation on the right-hand page—the publishers themselves suggested that the Urdu text be presented in the Devanagari script. In February 1997, I visited a big Hindi bookshop in New Delhi and found twenty selections from popular Urdu poets, published by Hindi publishers, very moderately priced and in a format that presented the verse in the Urdu script on

172 A LIFE IN URDU

the left-hand page and in Devanagari script on the page facing it, with a gloss giving the meanings of Urdu words with which Hindi readers would not be familiar. In the same shop, I saw two different editions of the *Divan e Ghalib* in Devanagari. I have seen a multi-volume collection of all of Manto's works in Devanagari script, beautifully produced—much more beautifully than any of the Urdu versions of his writings that I have seen—and was delighted to learn that this has already been reprinted more than once. Mohammad Umar Memon of the University of Wisconsin, US, tells me that almost all of Manto's works are now available in Devanagari. All of this is evidence that there is a bigger audience for Urdu literature if it's in the Devanagari script than if it is presented only in the Urdu script.

Adoption of Devanagari was also one of the recommendations of the Gujral Committee Report: 'There is a strong case for publishing Urdu books in Devanagari script... The *diwans* of Urdu poets and the anthologies of Urdu poetry in Devanagari script have sold in thousands. In our opinion, the experiment should be extended to cover fiction and humour also'. Subsequent government committees repeated this recommendation. In a stimulating article in *Akhbar i Nau* (9–15 February 1990), Rahi Masum Raza said that unless the classics of Urdu literature were published in the Devanagari script, they would cease to exist for future generations. I consider this forecast an entirely plausible one. He was also of the opinion (and here I differ from him) that Urdu speakers should discard their traditional script and adopt Devanagari instead. There should be no compulsion to adopt the Devanagari script, but equally, there should be no opposition to those who choose to do so, and in any case, every support should be given to publication of Urdu works in Devanagari as well as in Urdu-script editions.

There are some among the champions of Urdu who resent the publication of Urdu classics in Devanagari. One such person wrote to me a year or two ago saying that to publish Ghalib's verse in Devanagari was 'an insult to Ghalib'. Many appear simply unaware that this is going on, or if they are aware of it, they take an attitude more or less of indifference—and they certainly should not. In an article called 'Future Prospects of Urdu in India', in *Mainstream Annual* (1992) Ather Farouqui commits himself to the quite untenable opinion that: 'If at any future point of time Urdu were to come to be written in the Devanagari script, the distinction between Urdu and Hindi will virtually disappear'. This is certainly not the case. Far from it. Urdu in Devanagari will still be Urdu and Hindi will still be Hindi. But making as much Urdu literature as possible available in Devanagari would do something to hinder the efforts of Hindi chauvinists to expel from contemporary Hindi what they falsely call 'un-Indian' elements.

A broad view of these issues is essential. The defence of the rights of Muslims and the promotion of Urdu are not the concern of Muslims alone. These things are the concern of all those who uphold the declared ideals of independent India, and Urdu speakers need to reach out to all of them and work in harmony with them for these common ideals.

Urdu Literature in English Translation

There is another, and increasingly important, group of potential readers of Urdu literature—those who can only approach it through the medium of English.

When the books I wrote in collaboration with Khurshidul Islam, *Three Mughal Poets*, and *Ghalib, Life and Letters,* were published in 1968 and 1969, we assumed that the audience for these books would be primarily amongst people in Britain, North America, Australia, and so on. It has become increasingly obvious in recent years that the readership for these books is far wider than that, and particularly in South Asia itself—demonstrated by the fact that Oxford University Press, Delhi, has kept both books in print.

In those parts of India where Hindi is not in widespread use, English is a preferred second language. This applies across much of South India, but even in the Hindi-Urdu speaking areas, several generations of children from better-off families have had their education through English medium, which is now their de facto primary language. They may have learnt Hindi or Urdu as a subject and be able to read it at a basic level, but they are usually more comfortable using English, and much more likely to read for work and pleasure in English than in the language of their background. And the same applies anywhere outside India and Pakistan, where South Asians have settled, where for the second and

174   A LIFE IN URDU

third generations, English is undoubtedly their primary language, and they may not even have basic literacy in the family's heritage language.

For all these people, the only access to Urdu literature will be through English translation. The most encouraging trend of recent years is the increase in good translations, and the increasing willingness of publishers to produce them. Let us hope it continues.

14

How Not to Write the History of Urdu Literature

1987

When I was a student in 1946–1949, the only histories of Urdu literature then available in English were Ram Babu Saksena's (1927) and T. Grahame Bailey's (1932). I read both with mounting amazement and indignation—amazement because it passed my understanding how people who had such a poor opinion of Urdu literature could want to write a history of it, and indignation because a student who as yet could not read Urdu with facility would obviously turn to these books in the first instance and find, as I did, that anything more likely to *discourage* the study of Urdu literature would be difficult to imagine.

Then in Pakistan in 1965, I was told of the publication of a new, full-scale history of Urdu literature, written in English by Muhammad Sadiq and published by Oxford University Press. I looked forward with some excitement to reading it, hoping that it would be very different. When I read it, my hopes turned to disappointment and anger. I began to ask myself, more strenuously than before: Why do these people write like this? Why can't they see all the things that are so glaringly wrong with what they write? And I promised myself that I would one day write an article on how *not* to write the history of Urdu literature, or at any rate, how not to write it for English-speaking readers.

A Life in Urdu. Edited and with a Foreword by Marion Molteno, Oxford University Press. © Oxford University Press India 2023. DOI: 10.1093/oso/9789391050948.003.0014

176   A LIFE IN URDU

The Nature of Urdu Poetry

The first striking aspect is how they describe Urdu poetry, and particularly the ghazal, which most lovers of Urdu literature, including me, regard as perhaps its greatest achievement.

Saksena introduces his reader to Urdu poetry (pp. 23–31) by telling us that 'old Urdu poetry [was] an imitation of Persian poetry' and that

> its range is very limited for it sank into the ruts of old battered Persian themes and adorned itself with the rags of the cast off imagery of Persian poetry having absolutely no relation to India, the country of its birth ... This greedy absorption and servile imitation invests Urdu poetry with a sense of unreality and often is the cause of its debasement.

He then describes 'The defects of such an imitation', with paragraph headings:

> It made Urdu poetry seem unnatural.
> It made Urdu poetry rhetorical.
> It made Urdu poetry conventional.
> It made Urdu poetry mechanical, artificial and sensual.
> It made Urdu poetry unnatural. [Yes, once again—RR].

This last paragraph is worth quoting almost in full:

> Not only did imitation make poetry conventional, rhetorical, artificial and sensual but it made it what is worse, unnatural ... the vitiated and perverse poetry of the Persian celebrating the love of a man for a boy of tender years was copied without excuse or justification. The boy is regarded as a mistress and his [beauty is] ... celebrated with gusto in a sensual manner revolting to the mind.

He goes on to review the main forms of poetry, mostly in the same derogatory way, and then in a final half-page, to the reader's astonishment, informs him that

HOW NOT TO WRITE THE HISTORY OF URDU LITERATURE 177

Urdu poetry, however, with all its limitations and at its best is sublimely emotional and makes a powerful appeal to sentiment. It is very sweet and subtle and is pre-eminent in its special sphere.

Grahame Bailey's overall tone is much the same. He complains that the ghazal 'is characterized by ... monotonous sameness of subject, the theme of love ...' He tells us that Mir and his contemporaries 'had nothing new to say', that in the period of Mushafi and Insha 'there was no real advance', and that this 'monotonous theme' characterizes the ghazal to this day (pp. 41–42).

Sadiq tells us that the ghazal 'stands very low in the hierarchy of literary forms' (p. 20). He doesn't tell us what this hierarchy is, or what other forms stand where in it, but at any rate, the 'very low' is clear enough.

Comparisons with Western Literature

A common feature of all three books is the constant pointing of contrasts between Urdu literature and English—always to the detriment of Urdu. These contrasts are both general and particular. Saksena writes (p.29):

'Nature, so fruitful a theme for poets of West, had not much inspiration for Urdu bards. There are no Briants [Who's he? I've never heard of him—RR], no Whittiers, no Thompsons in Urdu. There is no rapturous adoration of nature like Wordsworth.

And (p. 30):

The *Masnavis* ... are said [By whom?—RR] to supply the place of epic and drama but fall very short of the requirements of those two great forms of literature ... a mere knowledge of the essentials of drama would disclose that *Masnavi* do not even mean [*sic*] an approach to it.

Similarly, Grahame Bailey tells us (pp. 101–102):

Epics can hardly be said to exist ... There is no dramatic poetry ...

178   A LIFE IN URDU

If the Urdu writers of today would make a study of Shakespeare, Milton, Tennyson and Browning, they might create a whole new world for their readers.

In Sadiq, this contrast is repeated ad nauseam. Practically every writer is compared and contrasted with European writers. Here is a typical example, from the satirical poet Akbar Illahabadi (pp. 403–404):

Akbar has not the geniality of Dickens or Fielding. He stands between the two extremes—not an Aristophanes, or a Cervantes, or a Rabelais, much less a Dickens or a Meredith, but a cross between Thackeray and Swift.

The words tell us nothing relevant except his opinion that Akbar is lacking in geniality, for Dr Sadiq does not tell us what his 'two extremes' are, or what qualities are in his view, exemplified by the authors in his impressive list, or what he thinks 'a cross' between the last two produces.

This constant parading of Western parallels and (more often) contrasts (invariably to the detriment of Urdu) is not merely annoying; it suggests at every step the relevance of comparisons that are in fact not relevant at all. It is as though one were to write a history of the nineteenth-century English novel proclaiming on every page that Dickens cannot compare with Tolstoy or Gaskell with Dostoevsky. Of course, they cannot, but what rational critic *does* compare them? Orwell has aptly remarked that to ask if you prefer Dickens to Tolstoy is like asking whether you prefer a sausage to a rose—'their purposes barely intersect'.

Look at the passage more closely and see exactly what Sadiq is telling us. First, he is telling us that he has read all these authors, or at any rate sufficient of their works to form a judgement of their characteristic features. I don't doubt that he has, though the reader only has his word for it. But what has this to do with Akbar Ilahabadi?

Secondly, he is telling us, in effect, that we too, like him and all other truly educated people, have read these works, know the major qualities of all these writers, and so, of course, don't need to have them spelt out. Well, perhaps we do, or perhaps we don't. I belong to Sadiq's generation, and grew up aspiring to read those works of literature that our generation was taught to value most. Even so, I don't score anything like full

HOW NOT TO WRITE THE HISTORY OF URDU LITERATURE 179

marks on Sadiq's list. Of the authors, he refers to I have read one play of Aristophanes (*The Frogs*—in Greek, fifty years ago, at school), Cervantes' *Don Quixote* (but not his other works), Rabelais' *Gargantua and Pantagruel,* nine of Dickens's fifteen novels, nothing at all of Meredith, one novel of Thackeray (*Vanity Fair*), and Swift's *Gulliver's Travels, A Modest Proposal* and a few shorter pieces of his verse and prose. It seems probable that younger readers, whose reading has been different from ours (and not necessarily worse than ours), would probably score even poorer marks. And the chances are that we are expected to feel ashamed of our deficiencies or, at any rate, awestruck by Sadiq's immense range. Well, we may be or we may not be. Personally, I'm not. Nobody has read everything they'd like to have read, because everyone has a lot to do in life besides reading books, and there just isn't time to do all you'd like to do, let alone read all you'd like to read. So *everyone* has gaps in their reading, and while that may be a cause of mild regret, it is certainly no cause for shame. And anyway, the judgements that Sadiq, or I, or anyone else may have made of these writers may be interesting, but again, what have they to do with Akbar Ilahabadi? I am reasonably competent to make judgements about, say, two-thirds of the works that Sadiq lists for comparison, and I can't see much point in comparing any of them with any of the others, let alone with Akbar. There is, as far as I can see, no name in the list except Swift, to whom reference is in any way relevant. And that reference too is totally unnecessary. What needed to be said about Akbar could perfectly well have been said (and would far better have been said) without reference to any other author whatsoever.

And this is not all. Within two pages (pp. 308–310 in the first edition, pp. 396–397 in the second edition), we are told of Akbar that he is 'like the Tractarians in England', that 'What S.A. Brooke says of Matthew Arnold is true of Akbar also', that 'his strictures... remind one of Carlyle' and that 'This reminds me of what Trollope writes of Thackeray'. Readers may be impressed, but they are more likely to feel disappointed, and even irritated, and to wish that they could have an account of Akbar by someone whose heart was not in so many other places at the same time.

If you're going to write about Akbar, study *Akbar,* and tell people what they want to know about him, assuming in them only an intelligent, sensitive interest in literature and a desire to know about a worthwhile writer that they don't yet know about. In all probability, you won't need to refer

180   A LIFE IN URDU

to any other writer at all. If you do, let it be a writer whose works you can reasonably expect your reader to have read, and let your reference be one that is both intelligible in itself and really helpful to the understanding of Akbar.

Saksena, albeit in a more limited way, suffers from the same childish desire to show off. He writes of Farhad, the legendary figure who appears in Urdu poetry, that 'he dug through a second Athos' (pp. 23–24). All that it was relevant to say was that he dug through a mountain. Why 'a second Athos'? The only reason can be that he wanted to show that he knew something about ancient Greece. But what student of Urdu literature needs to know that? It is ironical that one who considers it a grave defect in Urdu that all its literary references are to Persian legend, and that this makes it un-Indian (as if one were to condemn *Paradise Lost* as un-English because all of its references are to Hebrew, Greek, and Roman legend), thinks it quite alright to use metaphors which assume a knowledge of Greek and Latin references—to talk about 'Athos' when all he needed to say was 'a mountain' and talk of 'Venus and Bacchus' (p. 28) when what he means is simply 'love and wine'.

All three writers share the assumption, which they seem to think a self-evident fact, that the only literature which really deserves the name of literature is that which educated English readers of their and my generation have traditionally prized—that is, English literature, plus those classics of ancient Greece and Rome and of the European middle ages and renaissance long available to English readers in English translation. Well, everyone is entitled to his own point of view, but this particular point of view is one that disqualifies you from writing a worthwhile history of Urdu literature. People want to know what Urdu literature has to offer them, not to be told three times on every page what it *doesn't* offer them. How it compares or doesn't compare with English (or any other) literature is totally irrelevant.

Totally irrelevant—but since writers of Urdu literature regularly make the comparison let me digress to say a few words about it. The literature that Saksena, Sadiq and Co value so highly is, they tell us, far richer both in quantity and in quality than Urdu literature is. On the whole, *of course* it is, and the reasons are obvious. English, in approximately its present form, has been the language of major works of poetry and prose literature since the sixteenth century; Urdu, in approximately its present form, has

HOW NOT TO WRITE THE HISTORY OF URDU LITERATURE 181

been the language of such literature in poetry since the early eighteenth century and in prose for little more than a hundred years. People who have English as their mother tongue and speak roughly the same language as that of English literature number hundreds of millions; people who have Urdu as their mother tongue and read it easily are nowhere near as numerous. Speakers of English are mostly literate. Speakers of Urdu are mostly not. Speakers of English can, for the most part, afford to buy books, at any rate, occasionally. Speakers of Urdu mostly can't—not even books on cheap paper, badly calligraphed, and badly bound. In the English-speaking world, popular fiction writers can make a comfortable living by writing. Their Urdu counterparts will commonly be published in editions of at the most 1500 copies, and making a living by writing and thus being able to devote their whole time to it, is out of the question. So of course English literature is richer and more abundant. And what relevance does this have for the would-be historian of Urdu literature? None at all. Absolutely none. His job is to tell us what Urdu literature has contributed, and still contributes, to the world's stock of worthwhile writing.

How Do They Describe the *Marsiya*?

Their treatment of one genre in particular illustrates clearly what is wrong—the *marsiya*, a long poem on one or other episode in the tragedy of Karbala, which culminated in the martyrdom of Husain. Saksena here gives us a pleasant surprise: he abandons his prevailing tone of censure and tells us that the Urdu *marsiyas* are 'excellent' (p. 30). Not so Grahame Bailey, however. He writes (p. 61):

> They are essentially religious ... under Anis and Dabir the marsiya became practically a form of epic having however this limitation that it must always revolve round the death of Hasan, Husain and the members of their family. Subject to this limitation, which is a very serious one, marsiyas take in Urdu the place that epic poetry occupies in western lands ... They suffer of course from their narrowness; every character is either friend or enemy, altogether good or entirely evil, and the only emotions are those which would be brought out by such a tragedy as that of Karbala.

182 A LIFE IN URDU

He graciously concludes: 'Yet with all that, there is nothing so admirable in Urdu poetry as the marsiya'.

And now Sadiq (p. 40):

The *marsiyas* are not organic wholes. They are like strings of beads, the poet exhausting all his strength on a single episode at a time without treating the subject as a whole. They suffer, besides, from a conscious tendency to overdo the pathetic. Most of them are marred by cheap sentimental effects and seldom, if ever, rise to the austere heights of tragic sentiments.

In a chapter of twenty-five pages, praise is mixed with blame, echoing all of Grahame Bailey's criticisms and adding some of his own. He considers 'excessive tearfulness' to be inconsistent with 'manliness, fortitude and endurance' (p. 212). He says he has 'a long list of grievances against Anis, both in regard to his style and sentiment' (p. 213). This list includes 'the use of colloquialisms, cheap endearments and sob-stuff' (p. 213) and of 'debased erotic imagery' (p. 216).

Let us take these adverse criticisms one by one:

'The *marsiya* isn't really an epic'. Quite true. But who says that it ought to have been? Urdu has no epic like those of Homer and Virgil and Milton. So what? So nothing. Classical Greek and Latin and English have no *marsiya*. So what? So nothing. Grahame Bailey and Co would think you mad if you criticized the epic for not being a *marsiya* and they would be right. It is no less mad to criticize the *marsiya* for not being an epic. An epic is an epic and a *marsiya* is a *marsiya* and no literature is under any obligation to have every genre that every other literature has.

'The *marsiyas* don't tell a connected, coherent story'. Quite true. But who says they should? And how come that people who find this 'limitation' ... 'a very serious one' appear to find exactly the same feature in the European epic quite unexceptionable? Neither the *Iliad* nor the *Odyssey* nor the *Aeneid* nor *Paradise Lost* tell a connected, coherent story of the kind that Grahame Bailey seems to think the *marsiya* should tell. They tell parts of a story. They don't need to tell it in full because their audience knows the full story already. And so does the audience of the *marsiya*.

HOW NOT TO WRITE THE HISTORY OF URDU LITERATURE 183

Marsiyas 'suffer … from their narrowness; every character is either … altogether good or entirely evil'. So? Isn't the same feature evident in the greater part of *Paradise Lost?*

As for the 'tearfulness' versus 'manliness' theme—Sadiq is treating modern Western convention as a universal, eternal one. Dorothy Sayers made an apt response to this kind of narrow attitude in the introduction to her translation of the French medieval epic, *The Song of Roland*. She wrote of the portrayal of Charlemagne:

> I think we must not reckon it weakness in him that he is overcome by grief for Roland's death, that he faints upon the body and has to be raised by the barons and supported by them while he utters his lament. There are fashions in sensibility as in everything else. The idea that a strong man should react to great personal and national calamities by a slight compression of the lips and by silently throwing his cigarette into the fireplace is of very recent origin. By the standards of feudal epic, Charlemagne's behaviour is perfectly correct. Fainting, weeping and lamenting is what the situation calls for.

With regard to Sadiq's other 'grievances' all that can be said is that he is entitled to his own taste and his own opinion, but that neither I nor most of those who value Urdu literature would agree with him. Anis's use of colloquialisms is in no way inappropriate; his endearments are *not* 'cheap'; and his use of erotic imagery is not 'debased'. (One suspects that to Saksena, Grahame Bailey, and Sadiq, sentiment which is 'erotic' is by definition also 'debased'—just as homosexual love, rightly accepted as legitimate in, for example, both ancient Greece and Shakespeare's sonnets is, to Saksena, 'revolting to the mind'.)

English readers don't want, and don't need, to be told all this stuff. They need to know what the *marsiya* is, who were the poets who wrote it, what impelled them to write, who they wrote for, how it was conveyed to its audience, and in what context and on what occasion. But this information is either missing or is supplied with vague and/or disparaging remarks. Grahame Bailey tells us that it is 'a religious poem'. Sadiq, rightly and properly, gives us an outline of the story of the Karbala tragedy. He further tells us that the reason why the *marsiya* is in the form it is 'is not clear' (p. 209) and that 'probably' this 'was dictated by the requirements of

184   A LIFE IN URDU

the mourning assemblies' (p. 209). On the contrary, it is entirely clear, and there is no 'probably' about it. What he suggests is not 'probably' but quite certainly (and, one might add, obviously) the case.

The *marsiya* can be read, or listened to, at any time, but it is intended above all to be recited in that month of the year when Husain's martyrdom took place and to give expression to the grief and the sense of tragedy that all Muslims, and especially Shia Muslims, feel when that anniversary comes around. This emotional atmosphere is all-pervading. The audience knows every detail of the Karbala story and can respond at once to every detail of every episode that the poem presents. Not only the intense emotional tone of the poem, but its very form is determined by this situation. Look at any of Anis's *marsiyas* and you can almost *see* it being recited. It is composed in six-line stanzas, and the rhyme scheme is AAAABB CCCCDD and so on throughout the poem. The first four lines, often in the gorgeous language which people all over the world think appropriate to such solemn occasions, build up to a climax, like great clouds massing in the sky, and the last two, often in simple language which makes an immediate, forceful impact, are like the torrential rain which falls as the clouds burst. There is naturally a pause before the next stanza is presented, which gives time for the tears and cries of grief of the audience to subside.

Disparaging critics often belittle the *marsiya* as a poem composed 'merely' to make you weep. Why on earth should that be considered a defect? Isn't the tragedy of Karbala one to which any sensitive person would react in this way? I am not a Shia, not a Muslim, and not even a believer in any religion. I became an atheist at the age of fifteen and have continued to be one over all the years I have lived since then. But I am moved by the spectacle of *any* people, of any religion or none who will endure suffering and death before they will betray the principles by which they live. So the *marsiya* moves me too, and will move any person of strong feeling and firm conviction who is open to receive what it has to give him, and doesn't let irrelevant display of his profound understanding of English literature get in the way. Those who go in for such comparisons and object to the extravagant grief of the *marsiya* reciter and his hearers, might reflect on the expressions of extravagant grief of the characters, reciters, and listeners in Homer (who belongs to the European tradition and so is, quite rightly, admired by Sadiq and Co). Read in the Book XVIII of the *Iliad* how Achilles responds to the news of the death of Patroclus, and

HOW NOT TO WRITE THE HISTORY OF URDU LITERATURE   185

read in Plato's *Ion* the account of the extravagant emotions with which the rhapsodes (professional reciters) recited Homer's poems to an equally emotional audience.

Guidelines for Would-Be Historians

It is time to conclude with some remarks on how to write in English a history of Urdu literature.

The starting point—don't embark upon it unless you genuinely feel that Urdu literature has something substantial to give the world and you want to help people understand what that something is. If you don't think much of Urdu literature, please don't go to the trouble of writing a history of it. You are under no obligation to do so, and it would be much better for all concerned if you spared yourself the labour and your readers' disappointment.

If you are confident that you can write a good history, there are still things that you need to think about. First, since you are writing in English, make the most of your medium: realize how many millions of people in how many different countries you can reach and, as far as you can, write for them all, bearing in mind that it will be through your book that most of them will be making the acquaintance of Urdu literature for the first time. Assume that they *want* to know—not that they already do know—something of the subject. If you are an academic, you may have fallen prey to the absurd, but, alas, very widespread idea that you need to display to a (you hope) admiring audience how extremely learned and original you are. Actually, you don't need to and shouldn't want to do that even in writing for an academic audience, and you must certainly not do it in a work of this kind. Tell your readers what they need and want to know—and only that.

Second, 'literature' covers a vast range of writing. Don't try to cover it all. Give major coverage to major writers, writers who produce the kind of literature that makes a writer really great, the kind of literature that has the power to *change* you, enlarging both your capacity to enjoy life and your ability to understand more fully yourself, and other men and women, and the world around you. By all means, include lesser writers too, but let the space you give to writers be proportionate to their greatness.

186   A LIFE IN URDU

Third, realize that Urdu literature is the product of a particular society and of a history of which most of your readers will know very little. So set the literature in its social and historical perspective. Tell them what they need to know of these things if they are to understand and appreciate it—and, for example, don't be coy about love. Your readers need to know that the love which Urdu poetry celebrates is, in the eyes of the society in which it was written, illicit love. Otherwise, they'll think Urdu love poetry very odd stuff—which, of course, it isn't.

I must add a tailpiece to say that the publication in 1985 of *Urdu Literature*, by D. J. Matthews, C. Shackle, and Shahrukh Husain, marked the appearance at long last of a short account of Urdu literature in English, written, by and large, as it should be written. Its one major defect, in my view, is that it does not perform adequately my third guideline above— for example, it continues the tradition of coyness on the subject of love. For all that, it is a vast improvement on its predecessors, and a forerunner, I hope, of still better followers to come.

Afterword: Ralph Russell—As Others Saw Him

Chris Freeman

I first met Ralph in 1939 when we were students, and he remained a steadfast friend for the rest of his life. For some years in the 1950s, we and our young families shared a house. My children remember him as someone full of love—*happy* love, my daughter said. One of his characteristics that made him an exceptional and wonderful person was that he remained true to the ideals of his youth throughout his life, and lived by those ideals. This did not make him a dogmatic ideologist because he kept his sense of humour even about his own beliefs. He always sang as he did household chores, the original songs, and several parodies, many of which he made up himself. There was hardly a hymn or a national anthem that he did not parody. When he was making the supper, he often sang parodies of the Russian partisan songs—I remember one where, instead of 'Chapaiev was swimming, red blood in his wake', he would sing 'Chapaiev was swimming, lovely gravy in his wake'. The gravy which he made for supper was always very good too.

Ursula Rothen Dubs

In the early 1950s, I came from Switzerland to study Urdu at SOAS. At first, I was the only student doing a full Urdu degree, so I had lessons alone with Ralph. I was reading my way slowly, so slowly, through the prescribed texts when Ralph said, 'At this speed you will never get through them all, so let's sit together and I'll read them out to you'—which he proceeded to do throughout the four years. And how Ralph enjoyed himself! How he laughed at Khoji's misdeeds! How he enjoyed Nazir's market scenes!—so much so that instead of looking at the text, I watched Ralph's face as he read. How he suffered with the unfortunate lovers! How he

188 AFTERWORD

filled the bare little winter room with the garden greenery and the mauve clouds of the rainy season! How he felt with the lovers, the indifference of their various beloveds and at the imaginative doings of the revolving heavens! Ralph did teach, yes—unforgettable his way of getting through all those drawn-out relative sentences, but even more, he *lived* Urdu literature and made a student feel the innermost emotions of the writers and poets. My life has been enriched ever since. The feelings of mankind are the same the world over; poets of different cultures just find different words for expressing them. Thank you, Ralph, for making me realize this.

Ashraf Faruki

As a young kid in 1960, I vividly remember Ralph Russell coming to our house in Delhi. My father, Professor Khwaja Ahmad Faruqi, was head of the department of Urdu at Delhi University and they were great friends. I was mesmerized by his eloquent conversation in chaste Urdu. He spoke the language with a perfect accent and fluency. The book which my father wrote, *Mir Taqi Mir: Hayat aur Shairi,* became the topic of many discussions at our house.

Khalid Hasan Qadiri

I was Russell Sahib's colleague for many years, but before that I was his student, for he supervised my PhD. My father was a well-known Urdu scholar but I had taken a hatred to school, so I had left university at the time of Partition and gone to Pakistan. In 1960, I came to London for a job in the BBC, and the desire to study came back, so I went to SOAS to see if I could register for a part-time MA. After questioning me for a short while Russell Sahib said I should do a PhD instead. At my first suggestion of a topic, he said he couldn't supervise me on that because he knew nothing about it. To me, that was a shock—an *ustad*, admitting to knowing nothing about a topic! When he found I was interested in Hasrat Mohani, he suggested I make that my topic. At first, I was anxious that I would have to write things Russell Sahib would approve of, and I had

AFTERWORD 189

no idea how to please someone who was a communist and an atheist. But instead, he would challenge me on things I had written—'Do you believe that?' To me, it was a novel principle that I shouldn't write things unless I personally felt them to be true, and they were what *I* wanted to say. A few times, he invited me to his home so we could spend the day working together on my draft. It was in Harlow, some way out of London. He said, 'Since you'll be here the whole day you'll need to say your prayers, so just make yourself comfortable and use whatever spaces you need'. Then he himself would remind me when it was time. So touching. Just imagine, an atheist going to that trouble to make sure a practising Muslim could be completely at ease.

Terry Byers

In 1962, I came to SOAS as a young Research Fellow in the newly established Department of Economic and Political Studies. Ralph had been teaching there already for twelve years and was soon to be appointed a Reader, but we quickly became friends and remained so till his death. Despite his outstanding scholarly credentials, he was never made a professor. That was wholly political, because he was a communist. It was the norm in British universities at the time, and a disgrace. SOAS was in fact the most reactionary university institution in Britain—for instance, the only one in which the teachers' union did not have official recognition. Ralph's concern was to bring it on a par with other universities, in its employment practices and its working culture. He fought long and hard to achieve that. I and a few others joined him in that effort, but he was the driving force and the organizing genius. He knew SOAS inside out and was determined to see it transformed—a formidable undertaking, given the ingrained attitudes of deference among the vast majority of the staff. Whatever changes took place for the better up to the time of his retirement were largely due to his efforts. He was a brilliant organizer—articulate to a marked degree, and indomitable. A truly remarkable man—fiercely honest and a loyal friend.

190 AFTERWORD

Ibadet Brelvi

For six years from 1962, I was a lecturer in the South Asian Studies Department in SOAS, and I had the chance to observe him very closely. We worked together in the same room, drank coffee together, and ate our midday meal together. In his character, there is something of the ascetic. He is an extremely simple-living man, who lives like a dervish, oblivious of material needs. He is unconcerned about appearances and doesn't bother about his own comfort. He hardly knows the meaning of a desire for wealth or status. He doesn't think of getting a car for himself—he goes everywhere by bus, train, and tube, explaining that he prefers it because he can read on the journey. He eats in the student canteen, standing in line with everyone else, not in the staff one, which has formal tables and waitresses. He delights in joking and playing with words and is never serious for long, but there is never any question of wasting time or sitting around not doing much, and no such thing as 'leisure' in his lifestyle—it's his work itself that is his recreation. He does this work absolutely oblivious of any need for praise, or any idea of material gain or fame. Working on his subject is, for him, nothing less than an act of dedication. To him, work is what life is about, and life is founded on work.

When he is in Lahore, he stays with us, and the times he spends in my home are filled with life. He is completely at ease and informal. He spends time with the children, tells funny stories, is joking and laughing, and because of his presence, the whole house is lively and happy. At the same time, he is an exceptionally serious and sincere student of all things to do with Pakistani and Indian ways of life—social, religious, the way people speak, the way they behave. He goes to endless trouble, travelling towns and countryside, to make himself familiar with everything about our way of life. And there's no doubt that he knows more about these things than many people who live here.

Russell Jones

I joined the staff of SOAS in 1967 as a lecturer in Indonesian. My first impression of Ralph was when I saw him familiarly putting his arm around an Indian colleague and joking, which was not what most (white) SOAS

AFTERWORD 191

teachers did. He was clearly utterly at home with the language, which facilitated such self-confidence and familiarity. SOAS staff were very hierarchical, and it was everyone's (or almost everyone's) concern to toe the line. It was so refreshing to see someone being utterly straightforward and expressing independent views. For this reason, no doubt, although he was miles above many professors in SOAS, he never became a professor, and he would have been well aware he had to pay a price for his individuality and honesty.

Richard Harris

I started studying Urdu under Ralph in 1969. My interest was in the cultural and political impact on the United Kingdom of migrants from the subcontinent. I had studied French and German in my last years at school and was very surprised by Ralph's different approach to the process of learning a language. I was expecting a year of grammar books and classical texts—what I got seemed at first like an even more old-fashioned approach—he made me learn by heart a number of short passages, and recite them, not once but dozens of times. But he had hit upon a fundamental truth of language learning. With the exception of those who have been blessed with the aural equivalent of a photographic memory, the patterns of any language can really only be internalized by endless repetition. By the end of the second term, I could recite many hours of useful Urdu, all short sentences and all with some daily application or relevance to the background culture. Now, whenever anyone comments politely on my flawed Urdu, I always say to them that it was 'ustad sahib ki mahnat'— the hard work of my teacher.

Jill Matthews

I met Ralph Russell in 1972 when I should have been studying for an MA in South Asian Studies in SOAS. I had chosen it because I taught in London schools and wanted to know more about the cultures of my pupils, but most of the tutors were not in the least interested in this. So I thought, well at least I could learn a South Asian language—*that* would

192 AFTERWORD

be useful. I found Ralph down a corridor with a door wide open. He liked my reasons for coming to him and welcomed me into his Urdu class. I don't remember any form filling—just a brilliant teacher, a dedicated class, and loads of laughs. When I moved to Lancashire in the late 1970s, I needed Ralph's help again—my teaching colleagues too wanted to learn Urdu. Ralph said, 'Teach them all you know, then I'll come up'. So in 1979, he arrived in my living room and inspired a band of local teachers. As the group enlarged, we asked the Lancashire Education Service for a venue and time off from work to study Urdu intensively—and that's how the courses in Chorley College began. We were devoted to his teachings because in learning the language, we better understood the culture. 'Them' versus 'us' went out the window along with stereotypes and sanctimonious platitudes. We came away from those courses exhilarated because we had been so real and alive.

Alison Barnsby/Safadi

I almost didn't get into SOAS. From the age of about twelve—I cannot explain why—I was immensely interested in everything to do with India and Pakistan and Urdu in particular, but my parents were completely opposed to my plans to study Urdu. Despite that, I did apply—this was 1974—and was invited for an interview. Ralph wasn't there that day but a short time afterwards he phoned me at home to talk about my application. I was very surprised that someone in such an elevated position in a university should bother to phone a prospective student. Perhaps this was the first indication that he was not like other university teachers. I went to see him and explained that my parents were not exactly thrilled at the idea of me studying Urdu, to say the least. He offered to ring my father, which he did. I do not know what was said, but, according to Ralph, it was a very civilized conversation and my parents did eventually give in.

Of all the teachers I have ever had, Ralph had the biggest impact on my life, and continued to influence it long after he ceased being my teacher. His style of teaching was very different, both from that, I had experienced at school and from most of his colleagues at SOAS. The course we used was excellent, the one he had written, called *Essential Urdu*. We worked very hard, but the lessons were informal, relaxed, and full of fun and laughter. As a person, he was frank and open and encouraged his students to be the same. His views were often unorthodox and at times controversial—something that did not endear him to the SOAS establishment. This did not bother him at all, rather it amused him and his account of various incidents often reduced us to fits of laughter.

My parents' objections to me studying Urdu were mainly due to the worry that I would not subsequently get a good job. As a parent of grown-up children, I now sympathize more with this than I did at the time. However, they need not have worried—Ralph had that covered too! By spearheading the campaign for the teaching of Urdu in British state schools, and getting it established as a modern language, he also provided me with a career! I have earned my living teaching Urdu for nearly twenty years. Without his dedication, I, and many others, would not have had such an interesting and rewarding career.

CM Naim

Anyone who came in contact with Ralph Russell always remembered him as a remarkable man. He not only knew Urdu so well, but insisted on using it—you either used English or talked in Urdu with him—no mixing of the two, certainly not the way most of us do. Then there was his knowledge of Urdu literature. He had read much and digested it better than most. Talking about some literary topic, he could surprise you by referring to something that you of course knew but had not occurred to you as relevant. But those who got to know him slightly better also found him remarkable on other accounts. For me, one reason was his intolerance for humbug. He spoke frankly and firmly but never arrogantly. I never heard him make fun of someone just for the heck of it, while he always showed readiness to laugh with you at some foible of his own. Simultaneously, he was a principled man, and always ready to take a position, if he thought it was right, against popular acceptance. His 'progressivism' was that of a true subaltern and not of the coffee-house type that prevailed in Urdu circles for decades.

194 AFTERWORD

Daniela Bredi

In 1975, when I arrived in Britain on a scholarship from Italy, I knocked at the door of Ralph's room in SOAS. There was a smiling, white-haired man sitting at a table near the window in a room full of books and papers. I had come to ask if he would accept me as an occasional student in his Urdu classes. We had a talk and immediately liked each other. I knew very little Urdu at that time, but attending his classes, I was infected by his enthusiasm and obvious pleasure at teaching. He was a fantastic teacher, able to make learning easy for his pupils and keen to establish human relationships with them. I told him that I would like not only to learn Urdu but to do some research about Pakistani peasants. He teased me, wondering how an Italian girl who had never seen a Pakistani peasant might understand something about it. But despite that, he helped me—he introduced me to people who were in touch with Punjabi people of peasant background living in England, and later made possible my first experience of Pakistan. In October 1976, when I arrived at Islamabad airport, Ralph was there to receive me. Reassured by his company, I set out for Kanyal village with him, and after his departure, spent more time there. Everywhere we went in Pakistan, everybody seemed to know and appreciate him, and not only for his books and his scholarship. At ease with everybody, from the editor of the magazine *Viewpoint* to the rickshaw-vala, he had the gift to make people talk. They felt that his was not curiosity but a genuine interest in their lives.

Sughra Choudhry Khan

I have known Ralph since 1977 when I was studying for a degree in South Asian studies, specializing in Urdu. Learning Urdu was a 'returning to roots' experience for me—I am a British-born Pakistani of Kashmiri origin—and my discussions with Ralph allowed me to take what I needed from my both my cultures, and to adapt or reject things that I questioned. I admired his immense knowledge of Urdu and Urdu literature, and his cool ability to appreciate it as if from within and yet be able to stand outside and criticize with reason. For me, he was the kind of father that I never had—one who appreciated the questions that I asked of life and

AFTERWORD   195

human behaviour, and believed in my ability to do whatever I wished to do. I could talk to him about anything that I wished, all the difficulties in my personal life and in the various jobs that I held. When I went to him, solving a problem always seemed so clear and logical, and yet a few minutes after leaving him that wonderful clarity shared with him would all disappear in a sea of emotions! He has always had more confidence in me than I have in myself and has been a pillar of strength in my life.

Barbara Metcalf

He was truly unlike anyone else, not only in his cultivation of Urdu but in his relentlessly honest personality and his extraordinary commitment to what he believed in. He was so generous in what he did. His help to me—a foreigner with zero skills in Urdu when we met—his selfless kindness, was really a landmark in my life.

Alison Shaw

In 1979, I started graduate studies in Social Anthropology at Oxford and needed to learn to speak Urdu to do my research. Urdu was not taught there, either at the university or elsewhere in the city, so I contacted SOAS and got to speak to Ralph. His response was immediately positive and decisive: 'I have a ten-day intensive course starting on Monday', he said, 'Get yourself down to London and I'll cut through the red tape'! Being on this course was a revelation and an inspiration. With great energy and enthusiasm, Ralph got each of us talking Urdu right from the start. We learnt to say our names, what we do, where we live, and so on. We were also encouraged to ask each other these questions, which gave us lots of speaking practice and enabled us to initiate conversations as well as to reply. Ralph's method was radically different from the teaching I was used to. Rather than passively writing down what the lecturer said, each of us was actively involved in learning to talk, mostly without the help of any English translation. Over ten days, he taught us what we needed to know to be able to talk with Urdu speakers on everyday topics. At the same time, he provided a systematic introduction to Urdu grammar. Years

196 AFTERWORD

later, inspired by his teaching, I went on to use his teaching materials to run courses in Oxford.

Star Molteno

I met Ralph in 1982 when I was seven years old and he was 64, so to me, he was already an 'old man'. He used to make me laugh by taking his false teeth out and looking really old and silly. Having lost my own grandfathers when I was a baby, he filled a gap in my life and was important to me as a grandfather figure. I also viewed him as an 'elder' in an old-fashioned community sense—someone who has lived a long time and thought about life and has a clear view on things. Yet through all the different roles, the main thread of our relationship was that of loving friendship. This cut across age, life differences, and everything.

One quality he had in abundance was generosity. He was not one to give gifts at conventional moments, but if he became aware of a need for something, he would delight in being able to help meet that need. His generosity also spread into how he went about things in daily life. One of my grievances as a child was having to do the washing up. When Ralph was there, he would offer to do this chore, willingly and with joy—even singing as he did so. I took much inspiration from this attitude and it has helped me enormously in life.

He had a special capacity for talking one to one. Sitting down to talk with him, we would cover all aspects of my life with interest and seriousness. He had a very rational approach to emotions which was refreshing, though in times when my own life was somewhat confusing for me, I remember having to gear myself up for talking to him, being ready to justify my choices.

I have explored several different spiritual approaches to life and Ralph was always interested to share this journey, even though his firmly rooted communist beliefs didn't waver. Despite our superficial differences in philosophy, we've always shared a common belief in the human potential for goodness and the power of love.

AFTERWORD 197

Jill Catlow

Ralph's Urdu courses in Chorley, from 1982 to about 1986, became a way of life for scores of us. It was obvious that Ralph was genuinely interested in every one of his students, which made us all feel very special indeed. Most of us were teachers, and the courses were for usually for a week, residential, several times a year. We would go back afterwards and immediately be able to try out what we had learned with the children we taught, their parents, local shopkeepers, taxi drivers, and Urdu-speaking colleagues. I loved the way our lessons were interspersed with insights into Urdu speakers' culture and way of life, both here in the United Kingdom and in Pakistan. Ralph's stories were sometimes very funny, like about the All Asia Engineering Company, which was a small bicycle repair shop run by one of his friends; sometimes empathetic, such as stories about well-qualified people living in this country who were unable to get suitable employment due to discriminatory policies. Sometimes the insights were linked to the language structures we were learning—I particularly remember realizing how things that we express actively in English are often expressed passively in Urdu—lateness, marriage, pregnancy, and broken pencils are all things that just happen to us. Knowledge 'comes' to us, or perhaps in some cases, doesn't! I pondered on whether this reflected or indeed promoted a fatalistic way of viewing life's twists and turns—if Allah wills it or Inshallah! The experience I gained of being a language learner still rates as the most powerful professional development I have ever undertaken. The struggles to get our tongues around sounds that we don't use in English sensitized me to the difficulties many of the children I taught were experiencing.

Mohammed Umar Memon

In 1989, Ralph had moved into an apartment in Theatre Street, and he invited me to stay at his place anytime I visited London—as he did to many Urdu-wallahs. 'It will be no trouble', he said, 'you will do your work and I will do mine, and we will talk when I have time'. I had been to London many times, yet Ralph met me at Heathrow. I was not only pleasantly surprised but also quite embarrassed. What with my decades of living in

198   AFTERWORD

the West I still retained something of the Easterner—and he was a good twenty years my senior. The kind gesture left a deep impression on me. Another time I was flying in and out of Gatwick—his Theatre Street *Sarae* was only a couple of blocks from Clapham Junction Station with access to trains for Gatwick. On the day of my departure, as we were ready to leave, Ralph picked up one of my bags and slung it over his back like a knapsack (the veritable image of a South Asian railway-station coolie) and said, 'Let's go'. Try as hard as I could, I was not able to convince him to set the bag down. He insisted, I unwillingly relented, and we set off for the station.

He did not try to hide the fact that he had not read much of my work and what little he had read disenchanted him. He disagreed with many of my judgements about literature, and would tell me so, bluntly. But to my constant surprise, none of that made any difference. What drew me to him was the feeling that I could be myself in his presence. His disarming innocence, his forthrightness, his total honesty, and frankness about himself and the world at large left no room for pretensions or masks. I came to look upon my visits to the *Sarae Ralf* as something of a necessity, which prompted me to visit as often as I could, indeed so often and so regularly that I left a pair of slippers and a towel at his place so I would not have to lug them along every time. In the serenity pervading his small living room—which he regularly used for taking naps, not on the couch but on the thinly carpeted floor—the feeling of being close to him, even when we just sat together, each immersed in his own work, was such that debates on subjects we disagreed on seemed pointless, without any existential gravity or weight. There, in that haven of repose, only the comfort of togetherness seemed real, the sole meaning of life. I always came away feeling strangely light and renewed.

Dipak Kripilani

On a late November afternoon in 1991, I discovered *Three Mughal Poets*. Growing up in Bombay, I had always been fascinated by the lyrics of Hindi film songs, which I learnt had often been written by Urdu poets, and that had led to a desire to read Urdu poetry directly. The thing that struck me about *Three Mughal Poets* was the ability of the authors to reconstruct and bring alive the lives of Mir, Sauda, and Mir Dard and the times they lived in. It was both fascinating and engrossing. Then came *Ghalib: Life and Letters*, the most detailed account I have come across of the poet's life and the social and political milieu of those times. Only a personal diary could have gotten closer.

Three Mughal Poets whetted my appetite for the main course—*The Pursuit of Urdu Literature*—two years later. The treatment of the subject was unlike anything I had come across before, and was presented in an easy-to-understand, chatty style. It combined the knowledge of an expert with the tone of a guide and the familiarity of a favourite uncle who took you as a child to the ice-cream vendor or the cricket ground.

John Bray

From about 1991, for more than a decade until I left the country, I was a regular attendee at a weekly conversation class Ralph held in his home. Even now, wherever I am, I feel a certain twitchiness on Wednesday evenings ('Surely I ought to be in Theatre Street tonight?'). Those evenings were very special, and we all realized that we were privileged to sit at Ralph's feet, or at least at his sofa. I can't claim to have been a brilliant student, but at least my Urdu skills didn't decline, and I have been able to put them to good use in India. Those evenings brought us much more than an improved knowledge of Urdu grammar, or indeed of the many varieties of beer available at the local off-licence (our contribution, since he insisted on not charging for the class.) We also benefited from selected excerpts from his own history, and from his views on life, universities, and everything. The two qualities that always struck me most were, first, a warm interest in people, and secondly his personal and intellectual honesty. His honesty of course led to an impatience with humbug of all descriptions, and his repertoire included many stories of his subversive encounters with higher authority.

M Asaduddin

I was acquainted with Ralph's works long before I met him. One essay that I liked immensely was 'How not to write the history of Urdu literature'

200 AFTERWORD

that seemed to encapsulate what is wrong with Urdu literary historiography. In those days, I used to review books regularly, and among them were two or three by Ralph Russell himself. In 1995, when he was coming to Delhi, he let me know that he would like to see me; this was through his friend, Sajjad Sahib, a fellow communist with whom he stayed in Delhi, spurning invitations from more celebrated hosts. When we met, I was totally blown over by his forthright and candid approach, his fierce honesty, his passionate search for truth, and his distaste for cliché and shibboleth of all kinds. I was also taken by his lack of pomposity and his ability to laugh at himself. To know him was to engage with him—he didn't allow you to remain lazy or indifferent. He would disagree without being disagreeable and had the ability to carry on a rigorous debate without personal animosity or rancour.

Helen Goodway

I discovered *The Pursuit of Urdu Literature* in my local library at a stage when I knew very little about Urdu literature—and I deprived other readers of access to it for quite a while by renewing it seventeen times! It has been of profound importance to me. It is subtitled *A Select History* but, whatever else I read on the subject, it is this work that provides the framework of knowledge on which to rest everything else. Later I was co-editing an Urdu/English journal, *Tabeed,* and I made an unannounced approach to Ralph. His response to my enquiries was immediately generous, and encouraging in all aspects of my journey. Part of the beauty of *The Pursuit of Urdu Literature* is the limpid clarity of its language. The quality of directness, that lies at the heart of his linguistic powers, matches, I think, his character as an honest human being.

Frances Pritchett

Ralph Russell and I are old friends, and the ongoing debate with each other about the poetry we both love seems to be a lifetime affair. Well, there are many worse ways to spend a lifetime. I have long been grateful to him for his excellent knowledge of the language and literature, for his

AFTERWORD 201

great scholarly integrity—and even for his heartfelt commitment to what I find to be a very unsuitable critical methodology. He provokes me to think carefully, in order to sort out areas of agreement and disagreement; our arguments help me to clarify my own ideas. I always end up admiring him, and admiring the solid achievement of his work … A lifelong foe of academic pretentiousness and unnecessary jargon, he insists that scholarly writing should be kept as open as possible to all interested and intelligent readers; and since he has always practiced what he preaches, his lucid, straightforward books have influenced me from the beginning.

Asad Abbas

He mentioned a book of folk stories that I had never heard of and which he cited as an example of popular culture. I was about to visit Pakistan and asked him where I could buy a copy. He said I could find it in any bookstall in a railway station. To me, it was a perfect example of how he took an interest in whatever surrounded him and was open to any experience. I had always simply assumed that books sold in a station would be of no interest to me.

Rahima

[note to Ralph after an event in 2007 celebrating his life and work; name in Hindi script]

I came across your work only last year and am amongst the many, yes many, younger generation of inspired students. You have unleashed a new understanding and appreciation of Urdu ghazals for me. So thank you.

Sheila Rosenberg

I didn't meet him until he was 90. I was editing a book of memoirs of a friend, and I asked if I could visit to get advice about how to go about it. He was so warm, welcoming, and knowledgeable. In those few hours, he taught me a lot, but he was also interested in my project. He invited me

202 AFTERWORD

to call again in a month's time. But three weeks later he died, and I am writing this now instead. I shall always value that afternoon visit.

Lorraine Lawrence

Things I will always remember about him:

- His curiosity, sometimes infuriating, but always genuine, about just about everything.
- His ability to make you feel completely welcome when you came to visit or stay with him; endless but unobtrusive hospitality; the knack to let you get on with your life while he got on with his, interspersed with delightful times of chat and meals.
- His acceptance of difference—I am a Catholic, he a communist, but we always talked, never fought or hurt each other about the differences. He often found positive things to say about a faith that he certainly must have great difficulties with (since I do myself!)

David Page

He was absolutely unjudgemental, and extraordinarily encouraging. He made one feel completely at ease with one's inadequacies. He wasn't just an excellent teacher—he was also the hub of so many friendships. He had a hugely positive influence, everything done with such good humour and lightness of touch. I miss the man himself, with his wonderful generosity, his extraordinary example as a scholar, and his capacity to encourage even wayward Urdu students like myself—but also the companionship of those evenings and the friendships with others that he helped to deepen.

Shamsur Rahman Farouqi

The greatest thing about him was his forthrightness, his lucidity of thought, and his contempt for can't and jargon, be it literary or political. He was easily the best Urdu scholar in the West and he knew more Urdu literature than many native speaker professor types. His essay about how not to write a history of Urdu literature is just one example of how his teachings and ideas can benefit native Urdu readers and writers.

CM Naim

His contributions to Urdu are many and lasting. He was a superb translator, as in his exquisite translation of Aziz Ahmad's novel, *Aisi Bulandi, Aisi Pasti*. Of his joint work with Khurshidul Islam, *Three Mughal Poets* still remains the best introductory book to put in the hands of any student interested in Urdu poetry. Scholars may differ with some of their conclusions but the overall usefulness and excellence of the book cannot be denied. And their *Ghalib: Life and Letters* will last a long time—a biography of Ghalib using Hali's book on Ghalib and Ghalib's own letters, woven together with excellent commentary. It's a beautifully conceived book, and can be read for pleasure and instruction alike. In terms of real influence and effectiveness, the prime place goes to Ralph's Urdu pedagogical books and his years of teaching Urdu to hundreds of non-academic men and women in England, people who then used the knowledge in their professional work with the South Asian community in the United Kingdom. He was the first, and perhaps the last, Urdu academic to think of undertaking that very important work.

Francis Robinson

He was a remarkable scholar but an even more remarkable human being. His powerful sense of the brotherhood of humankind and his service to humankind in his own life is an example that has influenced my life, as I am sure it has influenced those of many others. My memories are of unstinting intellectual and personal generosity, combined with a great sense of fun. He was the great expounder of Urdu love poetry in English. This was evidently done by a man who understood the forms this 'madness' might take; and when it came to verse, he knew, as Mir said, that 'poetry is a task for men whose hearts have been seared by the fire of love and pierced by the wounds of grief'. He was such a memorable presenter of

204 AFTERWORD

Urdu literature because it was his delight to engage with the humanity of the Urdu writer and enable us to share it.

Khalid Hasan Qadiri

It is not possible to adequately describe his good qualities. The truth is that we did not properly recognize him, did not understand his stature. We did not value him as we should have, did not accord him his rightful honour. Guided always by his own high standards, he dedicated himself to the service to Urdu language, Urdu literature, and Urdu criticism, providing an example that cannot be matched anywhere.

M Asaddudin

Urdu literature has gained immensely from his perspective of an outsider not born to the language.

Nasreen Rehman

I find it difficult to accept that a person as warm, generous, and vital as Ralph is no more. He was a rare human being, who did not fit into any mould.

Books by Ralph Russell

The Autobiography of Ralph Russell, edited by Marion Molteno
   Part 1: Findings Keepings—Life, Communism and Everything, 1918–1946
   Part 2: Losses Gains 1945–1958
   (Three Essays Collective, Gurgaon, 2010)

A Thousand Yearnings: A Book of Urdu Poetry and Prose
   Translated and introduced by Ralph Russell; edited & with a foreword by Marion Molteno (Speaking Tiger Books, 2017)
   A good starting point to get an idea of some of the genres and periods of Urdu literature, with substantial translated examples for each. Includes a short selection of Twentieth Century Short Stories; examples of Popular Literature; an explanation of the ghazal—Love Poetry; and samples of Nineteenth Century Prose.
   [Earlier editions were entitled *Hidden in the Lute: An Anthology of Two Centuries of Urdu Literature* (Carcanet, 1995); and *An Anthology of Urdu Literature.*]

The Famous Ghalib: The Sound of My Moving Pen
   Ghazals selected and explained by Ralph Russell; revised edition: Marion Molteno
   (Roli Books, Delhi, 2015).
   Ralph's detailed introduction to understanding Ghalib's ghazals. [This is the definitive version, including material he had published as separate essays in an earlier edition.] All the points made are brought alive by examples from Ghalib's verse. Followed by over 200 translated verses, with parallel text in the original Urdu, Devanagari script, and romanized Urdu.

Three Mughal Poets: Mir, Sauda, Mir Hasan, by Ralph Russell & Khurshidul Islam

206 BOOKS BY RALPH RUSSELL

(Oxford University Press, Delhi, 1991)
A beautifully explained introduction to eighteenth century classical poetry, including three chapters on the love poetry of Mir, built around extracts from his *masnavis* (long story poems) and *ghazals*. The ghazal verses quoted are all given in Urdu and English translation together.

Ghalib: Life and Letters, by Ralph Russell & Khurshidul Islam
(Oxford University Press, Delhi, 1994)
Ghalib's life told primarily through his own words. An exceptional biography, detailed, engaging, and easy to read.
Both the above are classics—first published in 1968 and 1969, respectively, and still popular.

The Oxford India Ghalib: Life, Letters and Ghazals, edited by Ralph Russell
(Oxford University Press, Delhi, 2003)
A compendium volume, including *Ghalib, Life & Letters;* the full collection of Ralph's translations from Ghalib's ghazals, but without the original Urdu text; and articles about Ghalib's poetry which are also separately published by OUP in *Ghalib: The Poet & His Age.*

The Pursuit of Urdu Literature: A Select History
(Zed Books, UK, and Oxford University Press, Delhi, 1992).
A companion volume to *A Thousand Yearnings*—describes some major movements in Urdu literature, illustrated with brief translated extracts. (As the title makes clear, it does not attempt to be comprehensive.) Now out of print, but you might get a copy in a library.

Editor's Note

Selection

I was guided by Ralph Russell's often expressed intention to communicate with anyone who might be interested in the subject.

- I omitted five chapters from *How Not to Write the History of Urdu Literature* which would be of interest only to Urdu scholars (see list below).
- Half the chapters in this new volume are edited versions of those in *How Not to . . .* —the new Chapters 3, 4, 9, 11, 12, 13, 14.
- The other half are drawn from across the range of his published work, selecting extracts that are likely to have a broad appeal.

Articles from *How Not to . . .* which I have not included are:

- A review of Aijaz Ahmad's *Ghazals of Ghalib: Versions from the Urdu*
- 'The Urdu Ghazal: A Rejoinder to Frances W Pritchett and William L Hanaway'
- 'Strands of Muslim Identity in South Asia'
- 'Maududi and Islamic Obscurantism'
- 'Urdu in Independent India: History & Prospects' (a few sections of this have been included in chapter 13, 'Hindi & Urdu, Languages & Scripts')

Of the personal accounts in *How Not to . . .* I omitted 'A Day in Jhelum, Pakistan', and 'Meeting a Pir's Disciple', as there are now substantial new chapters on related themes. Extracts from 'A Day in a Pakistani Village' have been included in Chapter 3, 'Experiencing Village Life'.

Editing within Chapters

Where there was writing on a particular theme in several different publications, I have combined them and rearranged material to form a single connected text. Full details for each chapter are given in *Sources and References.*

Over the forty years of writing from which these articles have been drawn, Ralph's style naturally changed. Some of the earlier writing was wordier, with complex sentences which flowed as easily from his pen as the rhetoric of the nineteenth-century essayists he had read as a boy. In his last decades, he was himself editing material he had written much earlier, and he was consistently appreciative of changes I suggested which resulted in his points being made more concisely. Any textual editing I have done has been with this in mind, being careful not to compromise his characteristic vigour.

In essays first published in academic journals, diacritics were used to indicate an accurate transcription of sounds. In later publications aimed at non-scholarly readers, Ralph used a much simpler transcription, which I have done here. I have avoided footnotes. *Sources and References* gives details where needed.

Acknowledgements

Many people who have been inspired by Ralph's writing, teaching, and life, have encouraged me in the work of bringing out new editions of his work. My particular thanks to all those—academic colleagues, former students, friends—whose comments are included in the *Afterword.* Also those who have helped with publication or publicizing the new editions: Asad Zaidi, Renuka Chatterjee, Kartikeya Jain, Priya Kapoor, Neelam Narula, Rakhshanda Jalil, Saif Mahmood, Kanishka Gupta, Gillian Wright, Nadir Cheema, Rana Safvi, Susan Murray, Muzaffar Ali Shamiri, the late Kasim Dalvi, and Ralph's family members, Ian, Sarah, and Alice Russell. Several people read a draft of this book and gave me helpful responses: my thanks to Kami Kidwai, Tayyaba Jiwani, Nicky Road, Angela Piddock, and Umber Khairi.

EDITOR'S NOTE   209

I make due acknowledgement to the following, where material included in this book was first published—all details are in *Sources and References*.

Journals: *Indian Literature*, Sahitya Akademi (1959), *Asia Major* (1966), *Asian Review* (1969), *Mahfil* (1969), *South Asian Review* (1972), *Annual of Urdu Studies* (1987, 1996, 2002, 2009), *Bulletin of the School of Oriental & African Studies* (1988), *Jang*, London (1989), *Indo-British Review* (1992), *Indian Review of Books* (1995), *Economic and Political Weekly* (1999), *The Hindu* (2002).

Publishers: New Age Publishers (1964), Allen & Unwin (1970 and 1971), Vikas (1977), School of Oriental & African Studies (1978, 1986), Manohar (1983), Oxford University Press, Delhi (1992, 2003), Carcanet (1995), Three Essays Collective (2010), Zubaan (2010).

Sources and References

Ralph's books are referred to here in abbreviated form; publisher details are given in *Books by Ralph Russell*.

Chapter 1. Learning Urdu in Wartime India [1942–1945]
Abridged from *Findings Keepings,* chs 9–13

Chapter 2. Early Encounters with Urdu Literature [1946–1950]
Abridged from *Losses Gains,* chs 8, 14, 18, 21, 22. Some sections had been earlier published in 'Urdu and I', in *The Annual of Urdu Studies* 11 (1996)

Chapter 3. Experiencing Village Life [1950 and 1976]
Abridged from *Losses Gains,* ch 20
'Islam in a Pakistan Village: Some Impressions', first published in Robert Jackson, ed. *Perspectives on World Religions* (SOAS, London, 1978); and subsequently in *How Not To . . .*

Chapter 4. An Infidel among Believers [1999]
This combines edited extracts from three essays in *How Not To . . .*
- 'An Infidel Among Believers'
- 'Salman Rushdie, Islam and Multiculturalism', first published in instalments in the English section of the London Urdu language daily, *Jang,* 12–16 Aug 1989; subsequently in *Yad-nama, In Memoria di Alesandro Bausani,* Vol. X (University of Rome, 'La Sapienza',1991).
- 'Interfaith Dialogue, Tolerance & Intolerance', first published in *Indo-British Review, A Journal of History,* Vol XX (1), 1992.
References:
- Nazir Ahmad's article about God's creation of Adam is summarized at length and with substantial quotation in *The Pursuit of Urdu Literature,* pp. 119–120. The original in Urdu is reprinted in Iftikhar Ahmad Siddiqi, *Nazir Ahma* (Majlis i Taraqqi e Adab, Lahore, 1971), pp. 444–446. The Urdu original of the words quoted here is on p. 444.

212 SOURCES AND REFERENCES

- Akbar Ilahabadi: for the verse quoted, see *The Pursuit of Urdu Literature*, p. 144.

Chapter 5. An Eighteenth-Century Satirist [1959]
Edited from an article of the same name, first published in *Indian Literature*, Vol. 2:1 (1959); and subsequently incorporated in *Three Mughal Poets*, ch. 2, from which I have included one further brief translation.

Chapter 6. Rusva and Premchand: Stories of Courtesans [1970 and 2003]
Combines edited extracts from:
- On Rusva: 'The Development of the Modern Novel in Urdu', in *The Novel in India: Its Birth and Development*, ed. T.W. Clark (Allen & Unwin, London, 1970), later included in *The Pursuit of Urdu Literature*, ch 6.
- On Premchand: *The Pursuit of Urdu Literature*, ch 12.
- Foreword to *Courtesan's Quarter*, translated by Amina Azfar (Oxford University Press, Delhi, 2003).
- *A Thousand Yearnings*, introductions to extracts from Rusva and Premchand.
- *Losses Gains*, chs 19 and 23.

References:
- Robert Scholes and Robert Kellogg, *The Nature of Narrative* (Oxford University Press, London, 1968).

Chapter 7. Popular Literature [1973]
Combines edited extracts from:
- A talk to the Pakistan Society, London (1973).
- 'The Development of the Modern Novel in Urdu', in *The Novel in India: Its Birth and Development*, ed TW Clark (Allen & Unwin, London, 1970).
- *A Thousand Yearnings*, section on Popular Literature.

References:
- The section on the *dastan* draws on information in Raz Yazdani, 'Urdu dastanon par kam ka tajziya aur tabsira', in *Ajkal*, Delhi, July 1960.

SOURCES AND REFERENCES   213

- The details Ralph gives on the length of the *Dastan i Amir Hamza* suggest he may have been referring to the 1855 edition by Ghalib Lakhnavi (Matba e Hakim Sahib, Calcutta), one of the earlier printed versions in Urdu.

Translations of *Dastan i Amir Hamza* published after this article was written:

- Musharraf Ali Farooqi, *The Adventures of Amir Hamza* (Random House, Modern Library Classic, New York, 2007) is an unabridged translation of the 1871 Naval Kishore edition by Abdullah Bilgrami.
- Frances Pritchett, *The Romance Tradition in Urdu: Adventures from the Dastan of Amir Hamzah* (Columbia University Press, New York, 1991) gives translated excerpts from a shorter 1969 version.

Chapter 8. Remarkable Women—Two Memoirs [2002–2006]

Edited extracts from:

- Translator's Note to Begam Anis Qidvai, *Children,* an extract from *Azadi ke chaon men,* in *The Annual of Urdu Studies* 17, 2002. The Urdu edition was published by Qaumi Ekta Trust, 1974. The full English translation, by Ayesha Kidwai, was published as *In Freedom's Shade* (Penguin, India, 2011).
- Introduction to Shaukat Kaifi, *Kaifi and I: A Memoir,* translated by Nasreen Rahman (Zubaan, Delhi, 2010). I have used the Introduction as Ralph wrote it, dated November 2006, which differs slightly from the one in the published translation. The page references he gives are to the original Urdu edition, published by Star Publications, Delhi, 2006.

Chapter 9. Urdu Poetry Versus the Fundamentalists [2001]

Combines edited extracts from:

- 'The Islam of Urdu Poetry', dated 20 October 2001, published in slightly abridged form in *The Hindu* online edition, 7 April 2002.
- 'The Concept of Islam in Urdu Poetry', in *How Not To . . .*

Verses quoted can be found (with Urdu originals) in the following (see Bibliography):

- Mir: *Three Mughal Poets*
- Ghalib: *The Famous Ghalib*
- Akbar Ilahabadi: *The Pursuit of Urdu Literature*

214 SOURCES AND REFERENCES

- 'Drink wine, and burn the Quran …' is quoted in Rusva's *Umrao Jan Ada,* as being by Hafiz. Ralph said in the *Jang* article: 'I looked for it in his *divan* but could not find it, and have still not been able to discover who wrote it. (A Pakistani friend tells me it is Khaqani's.) But people in Iran are well acquainted with it. I asked my Iranian colleague at SOAS whose verse it was, and had got no further than 'Drink wine…' when he at once completed the rest. But he too did not know whose verse it was.'

Chapter 10. On Translating Ghalib [1969]

Abridged from a lecture presented at the Ghalib centenary celebrations in Delhi in 1969; 1st published in *Mahfil* 5(4) (East Lansing, 1969), and later in *The Oxford India Ghalib* and *The Seeing Eye.* I have included also an extract from the Introduction to *Ghalib: Life and Letters.*

Note on the date: Ralph was translating Ghalib's ghazals from 1958 for the next forty years, but the description of his working principles was formulated for the article in 1969.

Chapter 11. Leadership in the Progressive Writers' Movement, 1935–1947 [1977]

First published in B.N. Pandey, ed, *Leadership in South Asia* (Vikas, Delhi, 1977); and later in *How Not To …*; given here with minor edits.

References:

- Manifesto of the Indian Progressive Writers Association, London, 1935; printed in *New Left Review,* Vol. 2, 1936–1937. This was adopted, with minor modifications, at the first PWA conference, Lucknow, April 1936. A second conference in Calcutta, December 1938, made further minor amendments. This 1938 text is given in *New Indian Literature* 1:116–117.
- Sajjad Zahir, *Raushnai* (Maktaba Urdu, Lahore, November 1956).
- Sajjad Zahir, 'Reminiscences', translated by Kahlique Naqvi, *Indian Literature* 2 (Communist Party of India, 1952).
- Premchand, 'Mahajani Civilisation', translated by Ravi Bakaya, in *Indian Literature* 1 (1952).
- Ali Sardar Jafari, *Taraqqi Pasand Adab*, Vol. 1 (Anujuman i Taraqqi i Urdu [Hind], 1951).
- Krishan Chander, *The Seven Faces of London*, translated by L Hayt Bouman (Paradise Publications, Delhi, n.d.).

SOURCES AND REFERENCES 215

- Krishan Chander, ed, *Nae Zaviye* (Maktaba Urdu, Lahore, Vol. 1, 1939, Vol. 2, 1944).

The notes in the original give an overview of sources on the PWA, which would be useful to historians but have not been included here.

Chapter 12. Aziz Ahmad and Urdu Sources on South Asian History [1983]

Combines edited extracts from:

- *Aziz Ahmad, South Asia, Islam and Urdu,* in Milton Israel, and NK Wagle, eds, *Islamic Society and Culture, Essays in Honour of Professor Aziz Ahmad* (Manohar, Delhi, 1983); and later in *How Not To . . .*
- Preface to Aziz Ahmad, *The Shore and the Wave,* translated by Ralph Russell (Allen and Unwin, London, 1971).
- Review in *Asian Review,* Vol .1 (4), July 1968, of Aziz Ahmad, *Islamic Modernism in India and Pakistan 1857–1964* (Oxford University Press for Chatham House, London, 1967).
- 'Strands of Muslim Identity in South Asia', first published in South Asian Review, Vol. 6 (1), 1972, and later in *How Not To . . .*

References:

- Abdul Halim Sharar, *Lucknow: The Last Phase of an Oriental Culture,* translated by ES Harcourt and Fakhir Hussain (Paul Elek, London, 1975).
- Lieut. GFI Graham, *The Life and Work of Syed Ahmed Khan* (first edition, Blackwood and Sons, Edinburgh,1885; second revised edition, Hodder and Southgton, London, 1909. Reprinted with a new introduction by Zaituna Y. Umer, Oxford University Press, Karachi, 1974).
- Aziz Ahmad, *An Intellectual History of Islam in India* (Edinburgh University Press, Edinburgh, 1969), pp. 112–116.
- Aziz Ahmad, *Islamic Modernism in India and Pakistan, 1857–1964* (Oxford University Press, 1967).
- Wilfrid Cantwell Smith, *Modern Islam in India: A Social Analysis* (Victor Gollancz, London, and Minerva Bookshop, Lahore, 1943).
- Mohammed Iqbal, *The Secrets of the Self,* translated by RA Nicholson (1st published Macmillan, London, 1920; revised edition, Sh Muhammad Ashraf, Lahore, 1940), p. xxx.
- Mohammed Iqbal, *Javid Nama,* translated by AJ Arberry (Allen and Unwin, London, 1996), p. 11.

216   SOURCES AND REFERENCES

- Anne-Marie Schimmel, *Gabriels' Wing* (Leiden, 1963).
- Altaf Husain Hali, *Hayat-i-Javed: A Biographical Account of Sir Sayyid*, translated by Khalid Hasan Qadiri and David J Matthews (first published 1979; republished Rupa, 1995).

Chapter 13. Hindi and Urdu, Languages and Scripts [1971–1996]

Combines edited extracts from:

- Introductions to Ralph's language teaching books, *Essential Urdu: A Course for Learners in Britain* (published by the author for students at SOAS, London, 1971) and *A New Course in Urdu and Spoken Hindi* (School of Oriental and African Studies, London, 1986).
- 'Some Notes on Hindi and Urdu', in *The Annual of Urdu Studies* 11 (1996); and later in *How Not To ...*
- 'The Sad Decline', *Indian Review of Books*, Vol. 5 (1), September 1995. Other versions on the same theme are: 'Urdu in Independent India: History and Prospects', in *How Not To ...* ; and 'Urdu in India since Independence', in *Economic and Political Weekly*, 2–9 January 1999.

References:

- Christopher King, *One Language, Two Scripts* (Oxford University Press, Bombay, 1994); the review by David Lelyeveld appeared in *The Annual of Urdu Studies* 10 (1995).
- Amrit Rai, *A House Divided: The Origin and Development of Hindi/ Hindavi* (Oxford University Press, Delhi, 1984).
- R Snell and S Weightman, *Teach Yourself Hindi* (Hodder and Stoughton, London, 1989).
- RS McGregor, *Outline of Hindi Grammar* (Clarendon Press, Oxford, 1972).
- Premchand's essay is in: *Urdu, Hindi aur Hindustani, Kuch Vicar* [Some Thoughts] (Sarasvai Press, Allahabad, 1965; first published in 1939), pp. 101–113. The words quoted here in translation are on p. 101.

Chapter 14. How Not to Write the History of Urdu Literature [1987]

Edited version of the article first published in *The Annual of Urdu Studies*, 6 (1987), and later in *How Not To ...* This drew on earlier reviews of Muhammad Sadiq's *A History of Urdu Literature* (Oxford University Press, Delhi, 1964 and 1985):

SOURCES AND REFERENCES   217

- A review of the first edition, in *Asia Major*, XII/New Series (1966).
- A review of the second edition, written in 1985 and subsequently published in the *Bulletin of the School of Oriental and African Studies*, and published in Vol. 51 (1) (1988).

The histories discussed, all titled *A History of Urdu Literature*, are by:

- Muhammad Sadiq (Oxford University Press, Delhi, 1964 and 1984).
- Ram Babu Saksena (Ram Narain Lal, Allahabad, 1927).
- T Grahame Bailey (YMCA Press, Calcutta, 1932).
- DJ Matthews, C. Shackle, and Shahrukh Husain (Urdu Markaz, London, 1985).

Other References:

Dorothy Sayers, tr, *The Song of Roland* (Penguin, London, 1957), p. 15.

Afterword: Ralph Russell—As Others Saw Him

Contributions are taken from:

'Remembering Ralph Russell': in *The Annual of Urdu Studies*, 24 (2009):

- Francis Robinson, 'What Ralph Russell Meant and Means to Me'.
- Alison Shaw, 'Ralph Russell and Teaching Urdu to English-Speaking Adults in the Community'.
- Ibadet Barelvi, 'On Ralph Russell', translated by Marion Molteno from *Gazlan e Rana* (Idara e Adab o Tanqid, Lahore, 1990).
- Alison Safedi, 'Ralph Russell: Teacher of Urdu'.
- Daniela Bredi, 'Ralph Russell as I Knew Him'.
- Muhammed Umar Memon, 'Remembrance'.
- Marion Molteno, 'The Theatre Street Years' (includes contributions from Khalid Hasan Qadiri, Lorraine Lawrence, Barbara Metcalf, Nasreen Rehman).

'On Ralph Russell's Reading of the Urdu Ghazal', Frances Pritchett, *The Annual of Urdu Studies*, 1996, and *Nets of Awareness*, Acknowledgements

'Subaltern Urduwala,' CM Naim (15 September 2008)

'A Celebration of the Life and Scholarship of Ralph Russell' (SOAS, London, 28 June 2007):

Presentations by Ursula Rothen Dubs, Richard Harris, Sughran Choudhry Khan, Daniela Bredi, Rahima

Contributions at a memorial event for Ralph Russell, London, September 2008:

Terry Byers, Francis Robinson, Chris Freeman, Star Molteno

218 SOURCES AND REFERENCES

Interviews and correspondence with the editor:

Khalid Hasan Qadiri, Jill Matthews, Jill Catlow, John Bray, David Page, Russell Jones, Dipak Kripilani, Asad Abbas, Sheila Rosenberg

Condolence messages:

Ashraf Faruki, Helen Goodway, Shamsur Rahman Farouqi, M Asaduddin, Khalid Hasan Qadiri

Index

For the benefit of digital users, indexed terms that span two pages (e.g., 52–53) may, on occasion, appear on only one of those pages.

Abbas, Asad, 201
Abbotabad, 4, 6–7, 8, 9, 10
Ab e Hayat (The Water of Life, Azad), 25
Achilles, 184–85
Adab i Latif, 34
Adam, 62, 95
Adazi ki chaon men (Qidvai), 97–100
Aeneid, 182
Afghans, 73
Afzar, Amina, 90
Agra, 39, 115–16
Ahmad, Akbar S., 109–10
Ahmad, Amina, 84
Ahmad, Aziz, 150–58, 203
Ahmad, Nazir, 20, 28, 29, 30, 62, 154–55, 187–88
Aisha, 67
Aisi Bulandi, 150–52, 203
Aisi Pasti, 150–52, 203
Akbar (Mughal Emperor), 92, 94
Akbar and Birbal stories, 94
Akbar, Muhammad, 6–7, 9, 10
Akhbar i Nau, 172
Akram, 47, 48, 50–51, 52, 53, 55–57, 58–59
Mrs Alexander, 60
Alexander the Great, 13, 95
Al-Ghazali, 108–9
Al Huquq o Al Farāaz, 155
Ali, Ahmed, 147–48
Aligarh, 33–35, 41–42, 62, 154–55
Aligarh Muslim University, 15, 23, 30–31
Alim, Abdul, 38, 140, 141, 144–45
Ali, Sabaz, 9
Allah, 61–62, 108, 197

Allahabad, 9, 10, 130, 135, 138
Allahabad Conference in 1938, 139
All Asia Engineering Company, 197
All India Congress Committee, 132–33
All-India Kisan Sabha (Peasant League), 16
All-India PWA Conference, 140, 144–45
America, 104
Americans, 86–87, 132–33, 170
Amin, Idi, 68–69
Amman, Mir, 25
Amritsar, 142
Amritsar MAO College, 142
Anand, Mulk Raj, 130, 140, 141, 147–48
Anand, Som, 167
Andheri, 36
Andhra Pradesh, 12, 101–2, 142, 148–49
Anis, 27, 38–39, 181, 182, 183, 184
Anjuman i Taraqqī i Urdū (Society for the Advancement of Urdu), 37, 138
The Annual of Urdu Studies (King), 159
Ansari, Akhtar, 32–33
Ansari, Mufti Raza, 62
An Anthology of Urdu Verse (Matthews), 171–72
Arabian Nights, 25
Arabic, 20, 29, 43–44, 92, 94, 107, 116, 160–61, 164–66, 170
Arabs, 75, 116
Arberry, 157–58
Aristophanes, 178–79
Arnold, Matthew, 179
Asaduddin, M., 199–200, 204
Asha, 88
Ashraf, K.M., 137, 142
Asian, 115

220 INDEX

Aslam, Muhammad, 53–54, 57
Assam, 13
Athens, 80
Athos, 180
Atish, 26–27
Australia, 173
Autobiography of an Unknown Indian
(Choudhuri), 151
The Autobiography of Ralph Russell
(Molteno), 205
Avadh (Oudh), 154
Avara, 38
Ayyar, Amar (Amar the Artful), 93
Azad, Abul Kalam, 12, 155
Azad, Muhammad Husain, 25
Azmi, Kaif, 100, 143, 148
Azmi, Khalil ur Rahman, 33
Azmi, Shabana, 100

Baba-e-Urdu (Grand Old Man of Urdu,
Haq), 37
Bagh o Bahar (The Garden and the
Spring, Amman), 25
Bailey, T. Grahame, 38–39, 175, 177,
181, 182, 183–84
Banaras, 143
Bandagi Becharegi, 37
Bangalore, 12
Bangladesh, 49, 68–69
Barelvi, Ibadet, 46
Barnsby, Alison, 163–64, 192–93
Battle of Stalingrad, 142–43
Bazaar e Husn (Premchand), 80, 84–90
BBC, 146, 160, 188–89
Bedi, Rajinder Singh, 145–46, 166
Begam, Jamila, 98–99
Bekhud, 23–24
Bengal, 140, 142
Bengali, 137–38, 140
Bhagalpur, 16–17
Bible, 28–29, 105–6
Bihar, 16–17, 133–34, 142, 166–67
Bihishti Zewar (Thanavi), 95, 155
Bijnori, Abdur Rahman, 112–13
Bilgrami, Hamid Hasan, 23, 26, 27–
28, 30–31
Birbal, 94

Bocaccio, 44
Bombay, 4–5, 36, 102–3, 130, 141–43
Bombay-vali, 7–8
Book of Common Prayer, 28–29
Book of Guidance, 108
Bose, Subhas Chandra, 140
Bradford, 167
Brahmin, 89, 106
Bray, John, 199
Bredi, Daniela, 194
Brelvi, Ibadat, 38, 190
Briants, 177
Britain, 22, 31, 46, 47, 48, 68, 134–35,
169, 173, 189, 194
British, 3, 6–7, 8–9, 10, 12, 13–14, 15, 21,
26–27, 28, 36, 43–44, 48, 60–61, 64,
65, 132–34, 141–42, 150–52, 153–
54, 189, 193
British Communist Party, 38
British Library, 155
British Raj, 41–42, 45
Britons, 64
Brooke, S.A., 179
Browne, Sam, 9
Browning, 178
Burma, 10–11, 12–18
Burton, Richard, 116
Burton-on-Trent, 46
Butalia, Urvashi, 97
Byers, Terry, 189

Calcutta, 22–23, 25, 139, 140
Cambridge, 130
Canada, 150
Canadian, 156–57
Catholic, 63, 202
Catlow, Jill, 197
Cervantes, 93, 178–79
Chander, Krishan, 36, 144–46, 166
Chand, Tara, 132
Chapaiev, 187
Charlemagne, 183
Chatterji, Bankim Chandra, 151
Chesterton, G.K, 87
China, 132–33
Chingiz ['Jengis'] Khan, 75
Chorley College, 191–92, 197

INDEX 221

Choudhuri, Nirad C., 151
Christianity, 52–53, 63
Christians, 58, 60–61, 63, 68, 92, 98–99, 105–7, 108, 109, 110
Christie, Agatha, 91
Chughtai, Ismat, 38, 145–46, 168–69, 171–72
Civil Lines, 135
Clapham Junction Station, 197–98
Communist Party, 34–35, 60, 132–33, 141–42, 144–45
Communist Party of India, 20, 38
Compulsions, 37
Congress, 8–9, 12, 45–46, 132–33, 141–42
Connaught Circus, 36
Courtesan's Quarter, 90
Coventry, 55

Dabir, 181
Dard, Mir, 198–99
Dastambu (Ghalib), 113, 164–65
Dastan-e-Tarikh-e-Urdu (Qadiri), 39
Dastan i Amir Hamza (Lakhnavi), 96
Day of Judgement, 28
Decameron (Bocaccio), 44
Deccan, 30, 38
Defoe, 32–33
Dehra Dun, 23
Delhi, 10, 11, 12, 15–16, 28, 30–31, 32–33, 36, 38, 73, 78, 81–82, 84, 95–96, 97–98, 142, 144–45, 159–60, 164–65, 171–72, 173, 188, 199–200
Delhi University, 38
Denmark Street, 130
Department of Economic and Political Studies, 189
Devanagari script, 162–63, 168–69, 170–73
Dhool Karnain, 95
Dickens, 178–79
Dimapur, 13, 16–18
Divan e Ghalib (Ghalib), 171–72
Don Quixote (Cervantes), 93, 178–79
Doon School, 23
Dostoevsky, 178
Dubs, Ursula Rothen, 187–88

Eastern India, 17
East Pakistan, 68–69
Economic and Political Weekly, 169
Egypt, 92
Ek Adabi Dairi (A Literary Diary), 32–33
Elliot, Henry, 154
Encyclopaedists, 138
England, 4–5, 15–16, 133–34, 141, 179, 194, 203
English, 3, 15, 23–24, 28–29, 32–33, 35, 43–44, 73, 86–87, 91, 113, 117, 119, 122, 123–24, 137–38, 140, 147–48, 151, 159, 170, 173–74, 180–81, 183–84, 185
Essential Urdu, 192–93
Europe, 52–53, 91–92, 93
European, 8, 9, 19–20, 35, 92, 95, 178, 180, 182, 184–85
European Renaissance, 35

Faiz, Faiz Ahmad, 23, 37, 100, 142, 146
Faiz, Faiz Muhammad, 23
Faizi, 92
Falklands, 65
The Famous Ghalib: The Sound of My Moving Pen (Russell and Molteno), 205
Faridabad, 142, 148–49, 180
Faridabadi, Sayyid Mutallabi, 148–49
Farkhundanagar, 151–52
Farouqui, Ather, 172–73
Faruki, Ashraf, 188
Faruqi, Khwaja Ahmad, 38, 188
Faruqi, Shamsur Rahman, 166, 167–68, 202–3
Fasana e Azad (The Tale of Azad, Sarshar), 24, 25
Fielding, 178
Firangi Mahal, 62
First World War, 23–24, 162
Firth, J.R., 170
The Flow and Ebb of the tide of Islam, 27
Fort William College, 25
Foundations of Leninism, 20
France, 138
Franco, 63

222　INDEX

In Freedom's Shade (Kidwai), 100
Freeman, Chris, 187
French, 183, 191
Freud, 136
The Frogs (Aristophanes), 178–79
Frontier Province, 8
Future Prospects of Urdu in
　India, 172–73

Gabriel's Wing (Schimmel), 157–58
Gandhi, 12, 85, 132–33, 163
Gandhi, Indira, 167
Gandhian, 132–33, 136, 137
Gaodan (The Gift of a Cow,
　Premchand), 33, 89
Gargantua and Pantagruel
　(Rabelais), 178–79
Gaskell, 178
Gatwick, 197–98
General Confession, 28–29
Germans, 12, 51, 191
Germany, 132–33
Ghalib, 23, 26, 32, 108, 111–25, 164–65,
　171–72, 203
Ghalib: Life and Letters, 114–16, 173,
　198–99, 203, 206
Ghalib: The Poet & His Age, 206
Ghaus, 75
Ghosh, Jyoti, 130
The Golden Ass (Apuleius), 115–16
Goodway, Helen, 200
Gorakhpuri, Firaq, 38, 138
Government of India, 99, 141–
　42, 166–67
Government of India Act of 1935, 16
Governor of Bihar, 31
Graham, 154–55
Grand Old Man of Urdu (Haq), 37
Graves, Robert, 115–16
Greece, 77–78, 180, 183
Greek, 3–4, 19–20, 21, 22, 75, 180, 182
Gujarati, 140, 141–42
Gujral Committee, 167, 169
Gujral Committee Report, 167, 172
Gujrat, 47
Gulliver's Travels, A Modest Proposal
　(Swift), 178–79

Gupta, Maithili Sharan, 139
Gupta, Promod Sen, 130
Gurez, 150–51
Guzashta Lakhnau (Sharar), 154

Hafiz, 16–17, 18, 58, 105–6
Haidar, Kamal ud Din, 154
Hali, Altaf Husain, 26–27, 38–39, 108,
　112–13, 114, 115, 117–18, 154–
　55, 203
Halqa-e-Ahbab-e-Zauq, 37
Hamari Shairi (Our Poetry,
　Rizvi), 38–39
Hamza, Amir, 92, 93
Haq, Abdul, 23–24, 36, 37, 138
Haqqi, Shanul Haq, 28
Hardy, 155–56
Harley, A.H., 22–23, 26, 27–28,
　30, 83–84
Harlow, 188–89
Harris, Richard, 191
Harrow, 132–33
Hasan, 181
Hasan, Shabibul, 32
Havelian, 9
Hayat i Javed (Hali), 154–55
Hazara District, 4
Hebrew, 180
Himalayas, 9, 133–34
Hindi, 22–23, 36, 84–85, 99–100, 136–
　37, 138, 139, 140, 141–42, 159–74,
　198–99, 201
Hindko, 6–7
Hindu Brahmin, 106
Hinduism, 61
Hindu Kayasths, 84–85
Hindu-Muslim riots, 33, 145–46
Hindus, 4–5, 8, 33, 42, 43–44, 51, 53–54,
　58, 60–61, 64, 76, 94, 97, 102–3,
　105–7, 108, 110, 148, 153–54, 160–
　62, 166
Hindustani, 132, 140, 163–64
Hindustani Academy, 132
Hir Ranjha, 49–50
Holy Law of Islam, 55, 58
Homer, 182, 184–85
Hori, 89

INDEX   223

A House Divided: The origin and development of Hindi/Hindavi (Rai), 159
Husain, 181, 184
Husain, Ihtisham, 23, 38–39
Husain, Mumtaz, 33
Husain, Shahrukh, 186
Husain, Zakir, 23, 30–31
Hyderabad, 30, 38, 50–51, 101–2, 133–34, 151–52

Iftikhar ud Din, Miyan, 135
Ikram, Shaikh Muhammad, 154
Ilahabadi, Akbar, 26–27, 62, 108, 178–80
Iliad, 182, 184–85
Imam Husain, 27
Independence, 141–42, 152, 153–54, 169
India, 3–18, 23–24, 30, 45–46, 49–50, 53–54, 57, 60–61, 85, 95–96, 100–1, 104, 111, 130–36, 138, 147–48, 151–52, 153, 160–61, 163, 166–68, 173–74, 192, 199
Indian, 3, 6–7, 8, 10–11, 13–14, 19–20, 41–42, 83–84, 86, 92, 111, 113, 119, 131, 132, 133–35, 137–38, 146, 147–48, 150–51, 153–54, 165–66, 169, 190
Indian Army, 3, 4, 26–27, 28
Indian Education Service, 22–23
Indian Muslims, 157–58
Indian National Congress, 31
Indian NCOs, 12
Indian People's Theatre Association, 142, 148–49
Indian Press and the Muslims, 168
India Persian, 111
Indonesian, 190–91
Indo-Roman, 132
An Infidel Among Believers, 109
Insha, 164–65, 177
Inshallah, 197
An Intellectual History of Islam in India (Ahmad), 155
Intiqam (Revenge), 146
Ion (Plato), 184–85
Iqbal: A New Presentation, 158

Iqbal, Mohammed, 27, 108, 136, 137–38, 157–58
Iqbal: Nai Tashkil (1950), 158
Iran, 68, 105
Iranian Muslims, 68–69
Iraqi Muslims, 68–69
Irish, 4–5
Irwin Hospital, 98–99
Islam, 27, 44, 52–55, 63, 66, 67, 68–69, 92, 93, 104, 106–7, 108–10, 155
Islam, Khurshidul, 34, 35, 41–42, 45–46, 113, 173, 203, 205, 206
Islamabad, 194
Islamic, 22–23, 42, 43–44, 57, 62, 64, 65, 66, 67, 93, 94, 95, 104, 105–7, 109, 111, 137–38, 143, 150, 155–57
Islamic Modernism in India and Pakistan, 1857–1964 (Ahmad), 156
Islam of Khomeini, 63
Italian, 194
Italy, 132–33, 151–52, 194

Jafari, Ali Sardar, 139, 171–72
Jahanabad, 78–79
Jahan, Rashid, 38
Jah, Muhammad Husain, 92
Jalianvala Bagh, 142, 148–49
Jama'at i Islami, 55
Jama'at i Mujahidin (Mehr), 154
Jama Masjid, 95
Jamia Millia Islamia (University of the Muslim Community), 31
Jang, 109–10
Japan, 132–33
Japanese, 3, 12, 23–24
Javid Nama, 157–58
Jesuit, 60, 62, 63
Jews, 67, 106–7
Jha, Amarnath, 132, 139
Jinnah, 8, 156–57
Jones, Russell, 190–91
Joshi, 141–42
Judd, A.R., 23–24, 26–28, 31
Jumna River, 11
Jurat, 23

Kaba, 105, 108

224 INDEX

Kabir, 105–6
Kafan (The Shroud, Premchand), 89–90
Kaifi, Shaukat, 100–3
Kakul, 4–10
Kali, 97
Kalu Bhangi, 36–37
Kannada, 140
Kanyal, 46, 47, 48, 50–51, 52, 53, 54, 56,
  58, 59, 194
Karachi, 15–16, 30, 37, 50–51
Karbala, 27, 38–39, 107, 181, 183–84
Kashmir, 84–85, 152–53
Kashmiri, 5–6, 194–95
Kashmiri Brahmins, 84–85
Kayasth, 84–85
Kellogg, Robert, 86–87
Kelly, Mary, 91
Kevin Barry, 4–5
Khan, Aurangzeb, 8–9
Khan, Halaku, 75, 76
Khan, Masud Husain, 33–34
Khan, Muhammad Nawaz, 14, 17
Khan, Sabaz Ali, 5–6
Khan, Sayyid Ahmad, 154–55
Khan, Sughra Choudhry, 194–95
Khanam, Khalida Adib, 163
Khizar, 95
Khoji, 187–88
Khomeini, 65, 66
Khvab-o-Khayal, 20
Kidwai, Anis, 100
Kidwai, Ayesha, 100
King, Christopher, 159
Kingsway Camp, 12
Kishanpalli, 151–52
Kishore, Newal, 92
Kripilani, Dipak, 198–99
Kurds, 68–69

Laden, Osama bin, 74, 104
Lahore, 30, 37, 46, 47, 135, 144, 168, 190
Lakhnavi, 38–39
Lakshmi Mansions, 37
Lancashire, 191–92
Lancashire Education Service, 191–92
Latin, 3–4, 19–20, 21, 104, 180, 182
Latin American Jesuits, 63

Lawrence, Lorraine, 202
Lelyveld, David, 159
Libya, 68–69
Licence, 37
London, 30, 33–34, 130–31, 146, 158,
  188–89, 191–92, 195–96, 197–98
Lucknow, 10, 30, 38–39, 62, 81–83, 92,
  100, 130, 135, 136, 139, 140

Madras Presidency, 12
Madrassis, 13, 17–18
Mahajani Civilisation, 137
Maharashtra, 143
Mahasin i Kalam i Ghalib (Beauties of the
  Verse of Ghalib, Bijnori), 112–13
Mainstream Annual (1992), 172–73
Majaz, 38
Malayalam, 140, 141–42
Maligaon, 143
Malihabadi, Josh, 38
Malik, Abdullah, 37
Manifesto of the Indian Progressive
  Writers' Association, 130–31
Manshera, 8
Manto, 37, 38, 171–72
Maratthi, 140, 141–43
Marx, 136
Marxism, 134
Marxist-Leninist, 20
Marxists, 39, 132–33, 134, 146
Masnavis, 177
Masuda, 45–46
Masum Bacca ('An Innocent Child'), 87
Matthews, David J, 84, 154–55, 171–
  72, 186
Matthews, Jill, 191–92
Maududi, 55–56
Maugham, Somerset, 32–33
Mauj i Kausar (Ikram), 154
Maulvi Munne, 42
Mavara, 146
McGregor, R.S., 162
Mecca, 107
Medina, 107
Mehr, Ghulam Rasul, 154
Memon, Mohammad Umar, 171–
  72, 197–98

INDEX 225

Meredith, 178–79
Metamorphoses of Apuleius, 115–16
Metcalf, Barbara, 195
Midnight's Children (Rushdie), 65
Mijwan, 102–3
Milestone Four, 17
Milton, 60, 178, 182
Mir, 25, 105, 106, 107, 171–72, 177, 198–99, 203–4
Mir Taqi Mir: Hayat aur Shairi, 188
Mohan, 44
Mohani, Hasrat, 138, 188–89
Moll Flanders (Defoe), 32–33
Molly, 41–42, 43
Molteno, Marion, 205
Molteno, Star, 196
Moneylender's Civilisation, 137
Mongol Hordes, 75
Moses, 95
Mufti, 99
Mughal, 49–50, 84–85
Mughal Empire, 73, 93, 154
Muhammad, 67, 109
Muhammad, Hadis, 16–18
Mujeeb, Muhammad, 113
Mullah Dopiaza (Birbal's rival), 94
Muqaddima e Sher o Shairi (Poetry and Poetics), 26–27
Muradabad, 41–42
Murree, 9
Musaddas, 27
Mushafi, 177
Muslim Abbasid Empire, 75
Muslim League, 141–42
Muslims, 8, 15, 20, 27, 31, 33, 42, 45, 52, 53–54, 57, 58, 61, 63, 65, 66, 67, 68–69, 94–95, 101–2, 105, 106–7, 108–9, 141–42, 148, 154, 155, 156–58, 161–62, 165–66, 173, 184

Nabi, Ghulam, 94
Nadvi, Abdul Hasan, 154
Nae Zaviye, 146
Nai Bivi (New Wife), 88
Naim, C.M., 193, 203
Nai Roshni, 96
Nanking Restaurant, 130

Naqsh-e-Faryadi (Faiz), 23
Nasuh, 20, 28
The Nation, 167–68
The Nature of Narrative (Scholes and Kellogg), 86–87
Nazm-e-Muntakhab (Selections of Poetry), 26–27
Nehru, 12, 130, 132–33, 139, 140, 141–42, 163, 166, 167
Newal Kishore Press, 92
New Indian Literature, 140
Nicholson, 157–58
Nietzsche, 136
Nizami, Kwaja Hasan, 23–24, 95–96
Nizam's Dominions of Hyderabad, 154
Nizam-ud-Din, 95–96
Norfolk, 23–24
North America, 173
Northern Indians, 14
North India, 91
North-West Frontier, 42
North-West Frontier Province, 4, 8
Numani, Shibli, 155

Odyssey, 182
One Language, Two Scripts (King), 159
Opus Dei, 63
Oudh, 136, 154
Outline of Hindi Grammar (McGregor), 162
Oxford, 130, 195–96
The Oxford India Ghalib: Life, Letters and Ghazals (Russell), 206
Oxford University Press (OUP), 21, 171–72, 173, 175, 206

Page, David, 202
Paharganj, 99
Pakistan, 8, 30, 36, 38, 47, 49, 50–51, 55, 61, 68–69, 91, 98–99, 104, 129–30, 153, 160–61, 165–66, 173–74, 175, 188–89, 192, 197
Pakistani Punjab, 46, 58
Pakistanis, 46, 49–50, 52, 53–55, 83–84, 113, 119, 190, 194–95
Pakistan Times, 135
Paradise, 95

226 INDEX

Paradise Lost, 180, 182, 183
Paris, 130, 133–34
Pathan, 14, 16
Patroclus, 184–85
Peoples' Party of Pakistan, 48–49
Pericles, 80
Persian, 15, 20–21, 29, 35, 58, 84–85, 92, 97–98, 104, 105, 109, 111–12, 113, 114, 115–16, 157–58, 160–61, 164–66, 176, 180
Persianization, 165–66
Petticoat Lane, 146
Pinocchio, 10
Plato, 184–85
Platts, John T, 21
Poet of Revolution, 138
Post Office, 48
Premchand, 33, 36, 80–90, 136–38, 139, 162–64, 166
Premchand Conference, 38
Pritchett, Frances, 200–1
Progressive Writers' Association (PWA), 36, 37, 38–39, 89–90, 100, 129–30, 133–34, 135, 136–38, 139, 140, 141–49
Progressive Writers' Conference, 144–45
Progressive Writers' Movement, 33, 129–49
Prophet, 38–39, 66, 67
Prostitute, 80
Punjab, 15, 47, 49, 133–34, 135, 137, 142, 148–49
Punjabi, 4–5, 6–7, 32–33, 48, 49–50, 51, 53–54, 109, 146, 164–65, 194
Punjabi Sufi, 49–50
Punjab Peasant Committee, 142
Punjab PWA, 142
Punjab University, 8
The Pursuit of the Urdu Ghazal, 26
The Pursuit of Urdu Literature: A Select History, 26, 199, 200, 206
Pushtu, 109
PWA. *See* Progressive Writers' Association (PWA)

Qadiri, Hamid Hasan, 39, 61–62

Qadiri, Khalid Hasan, 154–55, 188–89, 204
Qaisar ut Tavarikh (Haidar), 154
Qamar, Ahmad Husain, 92
Qasba, 47, 48
Qasmi, Ahmad Nadim, 37
Qassas ul Anbiya, 94
Qidvai, Anis, 97–100
Quit India, 12
Quran, 29, 43–44, 52, 67, 68, 94–95, 105

Rabelais, 77–78, 79, 178–79
Rabelaisian, 78
Radio Pakistan, 37
Rahima, 201
Rahman, Habibur, 168–69
Rahman, Nasreen, 103
Rahman, Nurur, 31
Rai, Amrit, 159
Ram, 108
Rampuri, Najm ul Ghani, 154
Ramzan (Ramadan), 52–53, 54
Ranadive, 100–1, 141–42
Rani Ketki ki Kahani, 164–65
Rao, Raja, 140
Rashida, 46, 47
Rashid, Abdur (Sir), 135
Rashid, N.M., 146
Raushnai (Zahir), 38, 129–30, 135, 139
Ravi, 66, 167
Rawalpindi, 9, 47
Raza, Rahi Masum, 172
Razmnama e Anis, 38–39
Rehman, Nasreen, 204
Reminiscences, 133–34
Rhubarb, Rhubarb!, 153–54
Rin-Tin-Tin, 7–8
Rizvi, Masud Hasan, 38–39
Robinson, Francis, 203–4
Rohilkand, 42
Rohilla Pathans, 42
Roman, 3, 170, 180
Rome, 180
Rosenberg, Sheila, 201–2
Rudaulavi, Chaudhry Muhammad Ali, 136

INDEX 227

Rufus, 4–5, 6–7, 8, 9, 10
Rushdie, Salman, 63, 65, 66–67
Rustam, 77
Rusva, Muhammad Hadi, 80–90

Sadi, 104
Sadiq, Muhammad, 175, 177, 178–79, 180–81, 182, 183–85
Safadi, 163–64, 192–93
Sahib, Alim, 38
Sahib, Khalil, 33
Sahib, Miyan, 135
Sahib, Rashid, 32–34
Sahib, Russell, 49–50
Sahib, Sajjad, 199–200
Sahib, Zakir, 30–31
Sahiba, Begam, 135
Sahitya Akademi (Academy of Letters), 147–48
Said, Edward, 41–42, 43–46, 104
Saif ul Muluk, 49–50, 53–54
St Augustine, 105–6
St Jerome, 155–56
Saksena, Ram Babu, 175, 176, 177, 180–81, 183
Salim, 56–57
Saman, 85–86
Sanskrit, 19–20, 21, 160–61, 165–67
Sanskritized Hindi, 165–66
Sarae Ralf, 198
Sarguzasht i Mujahidin (Mehr), 154
Sarshar, 24
Satanic Verses, 66, 67
Sathe, Anna Bhao, 142–43
Sauda, 23, 25, 73–74, 75, 76, 77–78, 79, 198–99
Saudi Arabia, 68–69
Sayers, Dorothy, 183
Sayyid Aḥmad Shahid (Mehr), 154
Schimmel, Anne-Marie, 157–58
Scholes, Robert, 86–87
School of Oriental and African Studies (SOAS), 19–30, 33, 38, 46, 61–62, 83–84, 150–51, 163–64, 170, 171–72, 187–93, 194, 195–96

Second World War, 23–24, 132–33, 141, 151–52
Secrets of the Self (Nicholson), 157–58
Seven Faces of London, 146
Shackle, C., 186
Shah, Bulhe, 49–50
Shah, Qabul, 6–8, 9, 10, 11, 12–13
Shahabuddin, Syed, 169
Shahid Sagar (Hussain Sagar), 151–52
Shahnawaz, Begam, 135
Shaikh Cilli, 94
Shakarganj, Farid ud Din, 42
Shakespeare, 8, 178, 183
Shame (Rushdie), 65
Sharar, Abdul Halīm, 154
Sharif, 50–51, 53–55, 57
Shaw, Alison, 195–96
Sheikh, Maqsood Elahi, 66
Sher o Sukhan, 171–72
Shia, 32, 184–85
Shia Muslims, 184
The Shore and the Wave, 150–51
Siddiqi, Rashid Ahmad, 31
Sikandar, 13, 95
Sikhs, 58, 60–61, 64, 97, 102–3, 106–7, 148, 166
Sindhi, 109
Singh, Balwant, 171–72
Sirat i Sayyid Aḥmad Shahid (Nadvi), 154
Smith, Wilfred Cantwell, 156–57
Snell, R., 160–61
SOAS. *See* School of Oriental and African Studies (SOAS)
Social Anthropology, 195–96
Society for the Advancement of Urdu (Anjuman i Taraqqī i Urdū), 37, 138
The Song of Roland, 183
South Asia, 30, 156–58, 166, 173
South Asian Islam, 155, 156
South Asians, 32, 37, 39–40, 61, 64–65, 97–98, 152–53, 155–56, 160, 173–74, 191–92, 194–95, 197–98, 203
South Asian Studies Department, 190, 191–92

228 INDEX

South India, 13, 173–74
Soviet Union, 132–33, 137
Spain, 63
Statesman, 139
Sufi, 50, 53, 64, 107, 108–10
Sufi Sahib, 53–54
Sufism, 104, 108–9
Sufi Tabassum, 113
Sullivan, 9, 10
Sunni, 58
Swift, 178–79
Switzerland, 187–88

Tabeed, 200
Tabindanagar (Secunderabad), 151–52
Tablighi, 108–9
Tagore, Rabindranath, 32–33, 136, 139, 140
Tale of Amir Hamza, 92–93
Tales of the Prophets, 94
Taliban, 104
Tamil, 140, 153–54
Taraqqi Pasand Adab (Progressive Literature), 139
Tarikh i Avadh (Rampuri), 154
Tasir, M.D., 130, 142
Taubat un Nasuh (The Repentance of Nasuh, Ahmad), 20, 29
Teach Yourself Hindi (Snell and Weightman), 160
Telegu, 140
Tennyson, 178
Tess of the Durbervilles, 155–56
Thackeray, 178–79
Thames, 22
Thanavi, Ashraf Ali, 95, 155
Thanavi, Shaukat, 37
Theatre Street *Sarae,* 197–98
Thompsons, 177
The Thousand and One Nights, 93, 94, 116
A Thousand Yearnings: A Book of Urdu Poetry and Prose (Russell and Molteno), 96, 205, 206
Three Mughal Poets: Mir, Sauda, Mir Hasan, 173, 198–99, 203, 205

Tilism-i-Hoshruba, 92
The Times, 132–33
Tolstoy, 178
Tory, 132–33
Tractarians, 179
Trikha, 48–50
Trinity, 132–33
Trollope, 179
Turkish, 163, 164–65
Turkish Muslims, 68–69
Twentieth Century Short Stories, 205

UK Urdu, 109–10
Umrao Jan, 81–82, 83
Umrao Jan Ada (Rusva), 80, 81–84
Umri, 41–44
United Kingdom, 159, 160, 191, 197, 203
University of Allahabad, 132
University of London, 19, 113
University of Wisconsin, 171–72
Upper Jhelum Canal, 47, 48
Urdu, 3–18, 19–40, 41, 43, 48, 61, 65, 80, 83–85, 92, 94, 96, 97–98, 99, 103, 104–10, 111, 112–13, 118, 122, 123, 136, 137–39, 140, 143, 148, 150–58, 159–74, 175–86, 191, 193–96, 197, 199–200, 202–4
Urdu Literature, 186
Urdu Sahitya, 171–72
Uttar Pradesh (UP), 33, 34–35, 41–42, 48, 89, 135, 136, 141–42, 143, 159–60, 166–67

Vanity Fair (Thackeray), 178–79
Vedas, 112–13
Venus and Bacchus, 180
Viewpoint, 194
Virgil, 182

Waheed ud Din, 168
Wahhabis, 154
Wali Ullah, Shah, 156–57
Walt Disney, 10
Weightman, S., 160
Western Europe, 104
West·Germany, 51

INDEX   229

Whittiers, 177
Wordsworth, 177
World War, 85
Writers' Conference, 144–45

Yadgar i Ghalib (Memoir of
    Ghalib), 112–13
Yad ki Rahguzar (Kaifi), 100–3

Yamaha, 47
Yorkshire, 13–14

Zahir, Sajjad, 38, 129–30, 132–34, 135,
    136, 137, 138, 139, 140, 142–43,
    144–45, 148–49
Zanbil, 93
Zia ul Haq, 55, 65